Britain at War with the Asante Nation 1823–1900

Britain at War with the Asante Nation 1823–1900

'The White Man's Grave'

Stephen Manning

Pen & Sword
MILITARY

An imprint of
Pen & Sword Books Ltd
Yorkshire - Philadelphia

First published in Great Britain in 2021 by
PEN & SWORD MILITARY
An imprint of
Pen & Sword Books Ltd
Yorkshire – Philadelphia

ISBN 9781526786029

Typeset in Chennai, India
by Lapiz Digital Services.

Printed and bound by CPI Group (UK) Ltd, Croydon, CR0 4YY

Pen & Sword Books Ltd incorporates the imprints of Pen & Sword
Archaeology, Atlas, Aviation, Battleground, Discovery, Family History, History, Maritime, Military, Naval, Politics, Social History, Transport, True Crime, Claymore Press, Frontline Books, Praetorian Press, Seaforth Publishing and White Owl

For a complete list of Pen & Sword titles please contact

PEN & SWORD BOOKS LTD
47 Church Street, Barnsley, South Yorkshire, S70 2AS, England
E-mail: enquiries@pen-and-sword.co.uk
Website: www.pen-and-sword.co.uk

Or

PEN AND SWORD BOOKS
1950 Lawrence Rd, Havertown, PA 19083, USA
E-mail: Uspen-and-sword@casematepublishers.com
Website: www.penandswordbooks.com

Contents

To Will Churcher – a true friend who has given me such help and encouragement whilst writing this book about a country he knows so well

Acknowledgements

I would like to thank the staff at the Templer Library of the National Army Museum for their help and assistance and also the librarians of the Old Library, Ghana Collection, The University of Exeter. A thanks to Becky Eacott for her proof-reading skills and help with the maps. To my guide in Ghana, Doudou Dolo, and our driver, Samson, a massive thanks for your patience and sense of fun. Finally, thanks to my publishers for recognising that a new revised history of the Anglo-Asante conflicts was long overdue.

Plates

British cannon held in Kumasi Military Museum
British troops and sailors lead an assault on the Asante centre during the Battle of Dodowa
The interior of Cape Coast Castle today
The battlements of Cape Coast Castle today
The bridge over the Prah River
Wolseley with some of his staff officers at the Prahsu camp
The artillery harness designed by Wolseley
Lieutenant Eyre, 90th Light Infantry
Blunderbuss weapons reportedly used by Asante commanders against the British
An Asante warrior carrying a replica 'Long Dane', 2019
Captain Percy Luxmoore RN
Major Reginald Sartorius VC
Asante warriors firing their 'Long Danes' at the advancing British
British soldiers advancing on the march to Kumasi
British troops under Asante attack
The *Asantehene*'s stone palace, demolished by Wolseley's men
British troops landing at Cape Coast Castle
The march to Kumasi during the 1895–6 campaign
King Prempeh I kisses the feet of Governor Maxwell in supplication
King Prempeh I on his way to exile in the Seychelles
Warriors with weapons typical of what the Asante troops would have used during the conflict in 1900
The Golden Stool
Governor Sir Frederic Hodgson
Kumasi Fort, soon after it was finished
A soldier of the West African Frontier Force
Troops of the Central African Regiment with Sikh non-commissioned officers
Troops of the West African Frontier Force armed with Snider rifles
Colonel James Willcocks, commander of the Kumasi Relief Force
Taking the final Asante stockade in the relief of Kumasi
A cross in remembrance of Captain George Marshall
The grave of Captain Maguire
Kumasi Fort, 2019
Kumasi Fort, home of the Ghana Military Museum

Maps

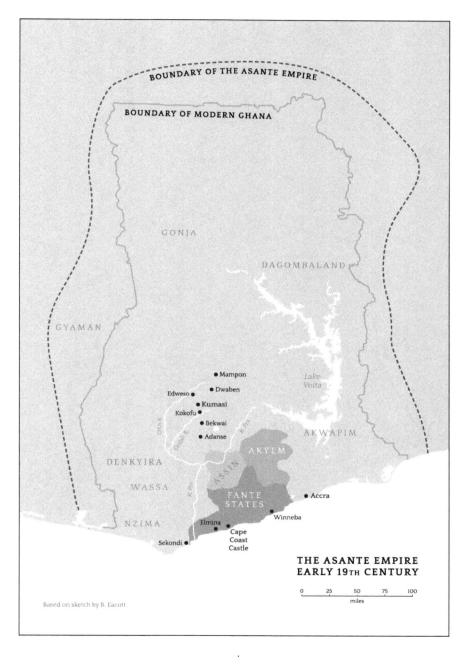

BOUNDARY OF THE ASANTE EMPIRE

BOUNDARY OF MODERN GHANA

GONJA

DAGOMBALAND

GYAMAN

Mampon
Dwaben
Edweso
Kumasi
Kokofu
Bekwai
Adanse

Lake
Volta

AKWAPIM

AKYEM

DENKYIRA

ASSIN

WASSA

Accra

NZIMA

FANTE
STATES

Elmina
Winneba

Sekondi

Cape
Coast
Castle

**THE ASANTE EMPIRE
EARLY 19TH CENTURY**

0   25   50   75   100
miles

Based on sketch by B. Eacott

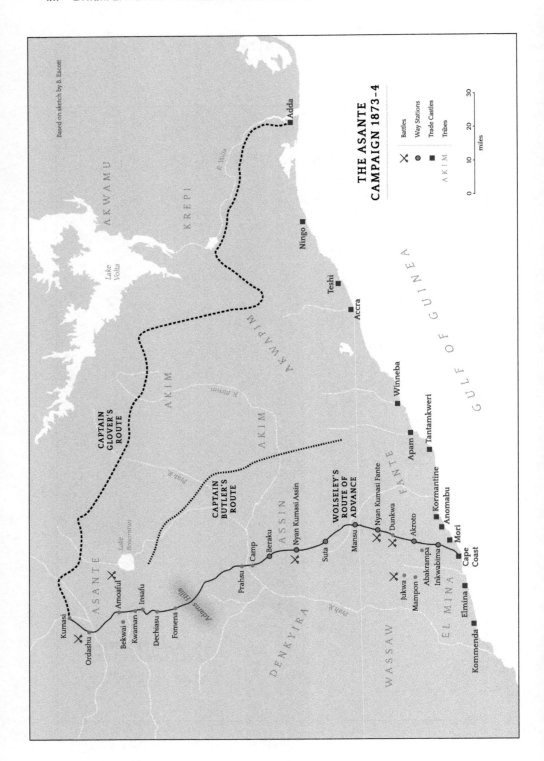

THE ASANTE
CAMPAIGN 1873–4

Based on sketch by B. Escott

✕		Battles
⬤		Way Stations
■		Trade Castles
A K I M		Tribes

0   10   20   30
miles

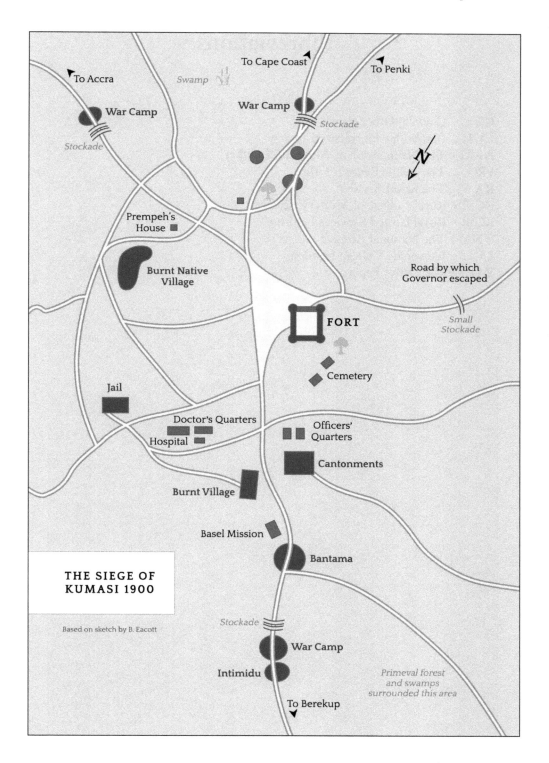

To Accra

To Cape Coast

To Penki

Swamp

War Camp

War Camp

Stockade

Stockade

N

Prempeh's House

Burnt Native Village

Road by which Governor escaped

Small Stockade

FORT

Cemetery

Jail

Doctor's Quarters

Officers' Quarters

Hospital

Cantonments

Burnt Village

Basel Mission

Bantama

THE SIEGE OF KUMASI 1900

Based on sketch by B. Eacott

Stockade

War Camp

Intimidu

Primeval forest and swamps surrounded this area

To Berekup

Abbreviations

CO   Colonial Office Papers
CUL   Cambridge University Library
NAM   The National Army Museum, London
PRO   The Public Records Office
RA   The Royal Archive
RCMS   Royal College of Military Science
RUSI   Royal United Services Institute
TNA   The National Archive
UCL   University College London
WO   War Office Papers

Introduction

The truly massive expansion in the British Empire throughout Victoria's long reign (1837–1901) saw British troops ('The Soldiers of the Queen') and naval personnel deployed across the world in such diverse countries as Russia, New Zealand, India, Canada, Egypt and South Africa, to name just a few. Such deployments were made to right a perceived wrong, to defeat a European foe, to stop a competing country securing spoils or simply to expand British prestige and power. On many such occasions British troops were placed in direct conflict with indigenous ethnic tribes or nations and the resulting military actions have become an important part of British colonial history, which some view with immense pride and others with shame or even disgust. Whatever personal views are held there is no doubting the immense bravery and fortitude of the British troops and equally these terms can be applied to their foes.

In most of the colonial wars of the Victorian age the British had a significant technology advantage in terms of weaponry over their enemies and this allowed them to achieve some crushing victories such as at the battles of Magdala (9 April 1868) and Omdurman (2 September 1898). Yet, there were occasions when despite this advantage the British were defeated, most famously at the Battle of Isandlwana (22 January 1879). When the British met defeat at the hands of an indigenous enemy such foes became respected and even achieved mythical status. This is certainly true of the British relationship with the Zulu nation, but it also applies to the Maoris of New Zealand, the Dervishes of Sudan and the Sikhs of Northern India. Less well known are the numerous conflicts that the British fought against the Asante nation in what is now modern-day Ghana in West Africa.

Whilst the Zulus did indeed inflict a crushing defeat upon the British at Isandlwana, a minor one at Intombi Drift (12 March 1879) and a more serious reversal as at the Battle of Hlobane (28 March 1879), the Asante nation was a thorn in the side of both British politicians and the military throughout the nineteenth century. Indeed, the casualties endured by the British in the various campaigns against the Asantes were comparable to those suffered during conflicts with the Zulus and the Dervishes. The Anglo-Zulu War lasted a mere seven months, although the unsatisfactory political settlement that was imposed by the British resulted in lesser conflicts which extended into the beginning of the twentieth century. By contrast, the Asante nation and the British were in both political and military conflict for over seventy years during the nineteenth century and three major wars resulted in which there were significant military

1

reversals for the British. This volume is split into three separate parts to reflect and illustrate these wars, each of which possessed fascinating moments and challenges which are captured in this work. Whether this is the death of the British Governor, Sir Charles McCarthy, at the Battle of Nsamankow (22 January 1824), Sir Garnet Wolseley's brilliant planned and orchestrated expedition of 1873–4, or the siege of the British fort at Kumasi in 1900, all offer a rich and engrossing history. Indeed, the 1900 siege tells a tale of bravery, fortitude and ineptitude that can stand alongside other more famous sieges of Victoria's reign, such as Ladysmith and Peking. One particularly fascinating aspect of these three major wars is how the unsatisfactory settlements reached at the conclusion of each were the lifeblood for further conflicts. There is also an Appendix which outlines the citations and a small biography of the six British troops that were awarded the Victoria Cross for gallantry in the 1873–4 expedition and 1900 Relief of Kumasi.

In addition, British troops and administrators had to endure the deadly climate and tropical diseases of West Africa which meant that the region acquired the unenviable name of 'The White Man's Grave'. A perhaps apocryphal story that appears in many histories of the Gold Coast is of an officer who has been posted there asking another who had just returned what kit he should take. The answer he received of 'take a coffin, that's all you will need' summed up the general fear and perception of the region. Many administrators, and their wives, as well as military personnel and missionaries fresh off the ship from Liverpool or Portsmouth were dead within weeks as a result of the harsh and unforgiving climate. For example, the Basel Missionary Society began their work on the Gold Coast in 1828 and of the four initial missionaries three were dead of disease within three weeks of their arrival.[1] Similarly, the first Methodist missionary, Joseph Dunwell, died within five months of arriving in 1835. The great and the good were not exempt from the horrors of the local climate and the British Governor, George Maclean, lost his wife, the then celebrated novelist and poet Elizabeth Landon, who died shortly after arriving in the Cape Coast in 1838.[2]

Although the military authorities were well aware of the dangers of the climate, scientific knowledge was lacking, particularly in the understanding of how diseases were transmitted and acquired. The climate also enhanced minor ailments so that a simple scratch could quickly become septic and life-threatening, whilst stomach upsets could develop into dysentery which was often fatal. There was also the threat from heat exhaustion in the humid tropical forests which could result in dehydration and death. It was this curse which makes British military success, particularly that achieved by Wolseley and his men, even more remarkable. That is not to say that even in Wolseley's campaign troops, and in particular officers, did not succumb to the harshness of the climate. Captain Henry Brackenbury, who was on Wolseley's Staff, and wrote the official history of the campaign, recorded the poignant death of Captain Huyshe:

On the morning of the 10th the first signs of illness showed themselves in him [Huyshe]; and the symptoms rapidly developed into dysentery, soon complicated by malaria fever. The combination of diseases was too powerful, and on the night of the 19th [January 1874] he passed away. And now the gallant spirit was at rest, and the body that had borne it was laid quietly in its last home under the huge forest-trees . . .[3]

Huyshe was just one of many who fell victim to the 'White Man's Grave' throughout Britain's military involvements against the Asante nation.

As with many of the campaigns of Victoria's reign, confusion abounded (and remains to a lesser extent now) surrounding the spelling of places and the names of individuals. At the time of many of the conflicts phonetic pronunciation would result in some interesting spellings and is was not uncommon for several different spellings of place names to appear in print even in the same newspaper or edition, and the Asante Wars were no exception to these inconsistencies. Asante is pronounced *Ashanti* which became the common contemporary English spelling. To avoid confusion in this work modern spellings of places and names have been used. Crucially, the phrase Asante has been used rather than Ashanti, unless the latter appears in a direct contemporary quote. This rule has also been applied to the Asante capital Kumasi, which is frequently seen as Coomassie in many nineteenth-century works. For the numerous Asante kings whose names appear in this work the current spellings as taken from the writings of modern Ghanaian historians have been adopted.

In late 2019 I was very fortunate to have found myself in the Asante capital for several days and was able to witness for myself Asante ceremonies and traditions that have changed little from when the British first recorded them in the nineteenth century. I was also able to spend time in Kumasi Fort which has not undergone any significant structural change from when it was under siege in 1900 and now houses an impressive military museum. Whilst this is not the first single-volume history of the Anglo-Asante Wars (that honour rests with Alan Lloyd's 1964 work *The Drums of Kumasi – The Story of the Ashanti Wars*), it does benefit from both modern research and contemporary reports and critically differs from Lloyd's book in that this work has been able to incorporate the thoughts of Ghanaian historians. It has also been divided into three separate parts, each of which focuses on historically defined periods of Anglo-Asante conflict. Unlike many of my previous works, such as *Evelyn Wood V.C Pillar of Empire* and *Bayonet to Barrage*, I have kept notes to a minimum to present what I hope is a thoroughly researched book which is not encumbered by academic style.

History, particularly military history, is written first and foremost by the victors: the historical portrayal of King Richard III of England (1452–84) until very recent times is a classic example of this. I am delighted to be able to address this, to some extent, in this work by illustrating the views of the vanquished and how modern-day Ghana is still very much influenced by the Anglo-Asante Wars of the nineteenth century. Not only have I been fortunate enough to have travelled extensively around Ghana to research this book, but I have been blessed in that the University of Exeter houses 'The Ghana Collection', the largest collection of works on the history of Ghana outside of the country. I hope you will agree with me that the story of conflict between the Asante nation and the British is a fascinating one and one that had a significant impact upon the two nations long after the conclusion of hostilities.

Dr Stephen Manning
University of Exeter, 2021

Part I

The Rise of the Asante Nation and the First Conflicts in the Anglo-Asante Wars

Early European Contact

European contact with the West Coast of Africa and the tribes that resided there dates to 1471 when the Portuguese first landed. By 1482 Governor Diogo d'Azambuja had negotiated with the local chief of the Edina territory, King Kwamena Ansah, to build the castle of São Jorge da Mina, located at the mouth of the Benya River.[1] This provided one of the few natural harbours on this otherwise open coastline. Initially this location was known as *A Mina*, or 'the mine' in Portuguese, but the name was eventually corrupted to become Elmina, although some believe it is a corruption of the Arabic for harbour, *mina*. Built ten years before Columbus set sail for the 'New World', it is the oldest European building in tropical Africa. The Portuguese church housed inside the castle is the first known Christian chapel in Africa, outside of Ethiopia.

It was from this castle and others that they built on this coast, such as São Antonia in 1515, close to the mouth of the Ankobra River and near the town of Axim, and São Sebastian in 1520–6, at the mouth of the Prah River in the town of Shama, that the Portuguese monopolised the trade of this area until the early seventeenth century. By the early 1600s, Elmina was a self-governing city-state, ruled by the Edina chief and elders and the Portuguese governor of Elmina Castle. There was little contact with the peoples of the interior but via the coastal tribes gold and ivory became important trade items in exchange for iron products, copper and brass ware and textiles. Gold was so abundant and readily mined that this stretch of coastline soon acquired the name the Gold Coast.

The Dutch began trading along the coast in the 1580s and built their first fort in 1612 at the town of Moree, and in 1624 the Dutch West Indian Company was established.[2] Competition between the Portuguese and the Dutch over trade, particularly the slave trade, was intense. This situation soon turned to conflict and in 1595 and 1625 the Dutch launched two unsuccessful attempts to seize Elmina. However, in 1637 the Dutch, utilising the hill overlooking the castle, where the smaller Fort St Jago now stands, managed to fire down into Elmina Castle and made the Portuguese defence untenable. The Dutch then used the castle as their own slave-trading base. By 1642 the Dutch had removed the Portuguese from the Gold Coast and Elmina entered its most prosperous period, with trade centred on gold and slaves. The Swedes, Danes, French, Brandenburgers and the English all soon established trading stations. Of these, most important were Christiansborg, which the Danes constructed near Accra in 1661, and Cape Coast Castle which the English seized from the Swedes in 1665. In 1672 the English founded the Royal African Company in direct competition with the Dutch and constructed James Fort in Accra. An indication of how important and intense the competition for the trade of this area became is that of the roughly 110 fortifications that Europeans erected on the coast of West Africa about 100 were located on the Gold Coast, of which some 30 can be identified today.[3]

By the middle of the seventeenth century gold and ivory had become of minor economic importance compared with the slave trade, and by the eighteenth century West African trade was almost completely focused on slavery. At the peak of this abominable trade some 80,000 souls were embarked each year for the plantations and mines of North and South America and the sugar cane fields of the West Indies. The coastal forts, particularly those of Elmina and Cape Coast, became central to the export of slaves, who may have spent up to three months in cramped, often unlit, unsanitary cellars before they passed through the 'Gate of No Return' and were herded onboard ships to sail the so-called 'Middle Passage' across the Atlantic; a journey which often resulted in a mortality rate of a third amongst the human cargo. Whilst the slaves were held in the coastal forts they were deliberately underfed so as to reduce their strength to resist their captors and those who did try to escape were literally left to starve to death. Such practices were common in first the Portuguese and then Dutch forts but the British, although having a good record as the leading abolitionist nation in the nineteenth century, also employed such measures in the seventeenth and eighteenth centuries.

Slaves were generally bought wholesale at the gates of the coastal forts from African slave traders or the coastal chiefs, who acted as middlemen whose profits came as much from the trade in human flesh as from the re-sale of trade goods such as weapons, textiles, metals and liquor. The source of supply lay beyond the coast zone, in the deep forests which the coastal people did not dare venture into and which were totally unknown to Europeans until the beginning of the nineteenth century. The strong martial states, such as the Oyo, Benin and the Asante, by military expansion and conquest, maintained a constant supply of fresh slaves to the coastal forts.

The Asante Nation

The people of Asante form part of an ethnic group known as the Akan, who speak the Twi language. Other Ghanaian tribes who belong to this ethnic group are the Fantes, the Bonos, the Akwamus, the Akyems, the Wassas, the Adansis, the Denkyira and the Assins. Historically the Akans are believed to have originated from an ancient Ghan Empire which existed in North Africa before migrating southwards and although this is the generally accepted view, some Ghanaian historians believe that the Akans migrated from the Nile region whilst oral traditions go further and claim that the Akans originated in Mesopotamia.

The Asante nation we know today, and that came into conflict with the British in the nineteenth century, is also known as Asanteman; a homogeneous society comprising twenty-four individual states, each with its own chief, serving one king, known as the *Asantehene* who resides in Kumasi, the capital of the Asante nation. The name Asante seems to have derived from a special red clay the people sent to the dominant tribe, the Denkyira, as a form of payment or tribute of allegiance. The Akans call clay 'Asan', therefore the Asantes were differentiated from others with the name 'Asan-tefo', or those who dig clay.[4]

The foundation of the Asante nation can be dated to the late seventeenth century with its rise as a military power under the leadership of its first king, Osei Tutu, and the inspiration of a priest, Okomfo Anokye. With the ambition of freeing the Asante people from the dominance and servitude of the paramount Denkyira tribe, and thereby forging a nation rather than simply a tribe, these two men realised the vital importance of both a religious and military system with which to bind a new nation together. As the historian R.S. Rattray has rather cynically written of Okomfo Anokye, 'with a true insight into the psychology of the people with whom he had to deal, he realised that the only way to unite independent and mutually jealous factions [within the Asante tribe] was by playing upon their superstitious beliefs'.[5] According to Asante tradition a wooden stool covered in gold was summoned from the sky by Anokye and this descended upon the lap of Osei Tutu, who was anointed as king. Anokye declared that the Golden Stool contained the spirits of the Asante ancestors and the strength and wellbeing of the new nation depended on its preservation. Every Asante, and heads of each of the twenty-four tribal states, had to show allegiance to the Golden Stool and its guardian the king, or *Asantehene*, the head of the Asante nation. The British lack of understanding regarding the paramount importance to the Asante nation of the Golden Stool was to be the central reason for the Anglo-Asante War of 1900.

To consolidate and reaffirm his position the king, Osei Tutu, quickly realised that the energy and resources of his new nation should be directed towards military conquest and this would begin, in 1701, with war waged against the Denkyira tribe. Although the Denkyira, under their king, Ntim Gyakari, initially achieved success against the Asante forces, Osei Tutu was able to draw the Denkyira into a trap and at the Battle of Feyiase the full military might of the Asante nation routed the Denkyira army. Ntim Gyakari was captured and beheaded on the battlefield. Having secured independence from Denkyira servitude, Osei Tutu now turned his focus on expanding his new nation.

By the end of the seventeenth century and into the eighteenth century slavery was at its height and it is no coincidence that the rise of the Asante nation occurred at the same time. Osei Tutu and then successive *Asantehene*, such as Opoku Ware (1720–50) and Osei Kwadwo (1764–77) directed forces against neighbouring tribal states. There was a seemingly never-ending series of wars. For example, the Sefwi, Bono and Gyaman states were added to the Asante nation during Opoku Ware's reign, whilst Osei Kwadwo defeated the Wassa and Banda peoples, annexing their lands. He also expanded the Asante nation northwards into Dagombaland to slow the southward spread of Islam into the region.

However, the thrust of Asante expansion was primarily southwards and was motivated largely by the desire to sell those captured in battle as slaves directly to European buyers on the coast. Even the passing of the Slave Trade Act in 1807 and then the Slavery Abolition Act of 1833 did not slow Asante expansion for there were always notorious traders and nations who would buy slaves. Furthermore, the Asante army was now dependent on firearms and gunpowder to maintain its supremacy and the various *Asantehene* and military leaders considered it imperative to have direct access to European suppliers of weapons, powder and ammunition who were based on the coast.

The Asante Army

The Asante army was not a regular force, although there did exist a small trained cadre stationed in Kumasi to protect the capital and the *Asantehene*. This formed the nucleus of any expeditionary force. However, in other respects the army was more akin to a feudal levy of the European Middle Ages in that most of the manpower was assembled at the outbreak of war from troops raised by the twenty-four tribal heads and later from tribes that had been annexed into the Asante Empire. At its maximum, the Asante army was said to have been up to 100,000-strong.[6] However, most armies were not as large as this; for example, around 40,000 warriors opposed the British in 1874. The fact that such a force could maintain its cohesiveness and discipline, especially as its ranks did include men taken from recently vanquished tribes, is miraculous and its success can be attributed to several factors.

The Asante military leaders quickly realised the important advantage that firearms gave them over their foes and the leadership generated a winning mentality and even a sense of superiority amongst their troops that they had a share in a glorious military tradition. This went even further in that the Asante nation, with each victory and conquest, rapidly gained amongst its people and from those of other tribes and nations, even European ones, a reputation as a self-governing, independent state that was wholly indigenous and not one that had evolved as a result of outside influences.

Once war was declared against another tribal state the decision to do so would be made by the *Asantehene*, his privy council, the chiefs of the twenty-four individual states that comprised the nation, and, as time went on, the chiefs of the newly acquired vassal states that had been brought into the Asante nation by conquest. However, the ultimate decision for war rested with the *Asantehene* and the success, or not, of the campaign would either increase or diminish the king's reputation and position. For example, in the case of the 1874 defeat at the hands of the British the king, Kofi Karikari, was deposed within seven months of the end of the war and some tribes such as the Banda, Gyaman and Sefwi, as well as several northern states, declared their independence. Although the military defeat was not the ultimate cause of Kofi Karikari's downfall (this was centred on his misuse of gold in the royal mausoleum), it certainly undermined his authority.

If war was declared, then the chiefs, who also served as the captains of the various states, would return to their lands and call their people to arms. Every male citizen was a soldier and all able-bodied men were expected to ready themselves for military service. However, a quota system existed so that only a proportion of men were called for action with the remainder left at home to provide security as well as, crucially, manpower to ensure that the farming systems continued, and future famines were avoided.

There was a large element of discipline, even subjugation, which was used to maintain the army's effectiveness. There were severe punishments, including death, for failure to report for duty, for desertion and cowardice. A military police force armed with whips and swords had to be used to encourage some into battle and those few that refused were despatched on the spot with an axe. Yet, overall the command structure centred on the king, his privy council and the army general staff was incredibly effective not only on the battlefield but also in bringing the army to readiness and for ensuring that logistically it was able to fight and achieve victories. Each army group took its own supplies of food and ordnance on campaign. Uniquely amongst African armies, the Asante boasted a corps of medical orderlies, the *Esumankwafo*, who accompanied the army into battle. This corps attended to wounded troops as well as removing the dead from the battlefield, for immense trouble was taken to conceal losses from the enemy.

A typical Asante battle column was said to have originated by observing ants on a march and comprised a body of scouts, an advance guard, the main body, in which the army commander was found and secured, left and right wings and a rear or home guard. Certainly, in wars with tribal states the battle could be effectively won if the opposing king or general was either killed or captured so the Asante army ensured that their battlefield commanders were well protected in the centre of the formation. The home guard was tasked either with staying in the capital Kumasi or returning immediately to the capital after a battlefield victory, or a rare defeat, to ensure that the security of the capital was maintained. The scouts would first engage with the enemy who would then be drawn in towards the main body. As this was happening the left and right wings would endeavour to surround the enemy for, although the principal aim was to defeat their foe, the secondary one was to capture as many as possible so as to sell them to the slavers on the coast. In addition, in a society in which fetishism and the worship of ancestors was important a number of the recently captured enemy were diverted to human sacrifice, a practice that continued right up to the late nineteenth century.

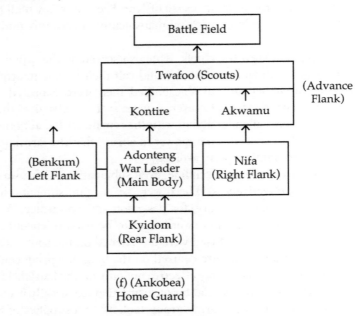

Taken from *A Handbook of Asante Culture* by Osei Kwadwo.

The Asante army was composed entirely of infantry for the inhospitable forest zone, and the presence of the tsetse fly there meant that horses and ponies would soon succumb. Most Asante troops were equipped with standard European trade muskets, which were poorly made with a limited range. On the West African coast such weapons had the common name of 'Long Danes', supposedly named as it was the Danes who first introduced them to the Gold Coast. This weapon was over 6ft in length and weighed nearly 20lb and a more unsuitable musket for forest warfare could not have been designed. In theory such guns had a range of 200yd but were rarely accurate beyond 30yd and although the enemy might be frightened by the explosive fire, it was unlikely to hurt them unless hit at very close range. Yet, the nature of the jungle fighting meant that if the enemy had not already fled at the sound of the approaching Asante army, then fire would often be at close proximity as the two protagonists were unable to see each other through the near-impenetrable forest. As the British observed in 1874, bush fighting was akin to fighting in twilight, as the lack of light penetrating the forest meant that soldiers were only able to see a few yards to their left or right.

Very few musketeers would have used wadding to compact the powder but would simply have poured down large amounts into the barrel, followed by any projectiles that were available, such as an assortment of lead slugs, of varying shapes and sizes, nails and even stones. When fired the 'bullets' would tend to fan out over a wide area and their velocity was much diminished. Yet, as the this was the only trade weapon available the Asante army made good use of it, although it is reasonable to believe that muskets were used for their pyrotechnic and psychological effect as much as their killing power.

European observers commented that, unlike other African tribes, the Asantes showed good dexterity with firearms. They understood the principal of sighting shots and the necessity of firing from the shoulder to improve accuracy, although in the dense undergrowth of the forest muskets were seldom aimed at specific targets. They could perform firearm drills and shoot from a number of positions, such as crouching and lying down.

The elite cadre and senior officers were occasionally armed with more suitable close-quarters pistols or blunderbusses and these weapons distinguished them from others on the battlefield, as did the carrying of swords, which frequently had wide and impracticable blades. All warriors would carry knives used for the removal of fallen foes' heads as trophies. The Asantes were masters of psychological warfare in the forest where the sound of drums and the shouting of troops as they advanced could be terrifying. The drumming would echo throughout the forest and could have the effect of magnifying the size of the army as well as its proximity. This combined with the loud noise and huge amounts of smoke generated by the 'Long Danes' frequently had the desired result of making their enemies flee to the rear and straight into the awaiting trap that had been closed by the advancing flanks of the Asantes. The firepower of the 'Long Danes' was often reduced by the lack of available ammunition and the poor quality of the gun powder which meant that the penetrative power of the fire was much reduced.

Ordinary clothing was worn into battle, which consisted of a large rectangular cloth which was wrapped around the loins and waist or thrown over the left shoulder. Some contemporary pictures depict tunics or smocks, covered with spiritual amulets sewn into the garment, which would have been worn by chiefs or more senior warriors. Head covering was not common, although head scarves and caps, decorated with shells and plumes, were occasionally worn by senior commanders. Leather ammunition pouches were carried across the chest, and for those troops who possessed muskets powder horns or gourds were similarly worn.

Despite the poor quality of their weapons the Asante army was a formidable force. The battlefield structure and command and the self-belief generated by constant victories against tribal foes made the Asante army a force to be feared. This army was to more than hold its own against European opponents. Indeed, from 1807 to 1900 the British fought numerous engagements against the Asantes and in several of these the Asantes were the clear victors thus becoming the only West African army to defeat the British in more than one battle.

Contact and Conflict with the British

It is usual for the Asante kings to reign until they die and then often for a blood-line relative, such as a nephew or brother, to be chosen by a series of council meetings of chiefs and other members of the royal family, to succeed as the new *Asantehene*. There have been exceptions to this rule with several kings being deposed. One of these, Nana Osei Kwame (1777–97), was reluctant to use war to expand and maintain the Asante nation and also dramatically reduced the number of human sacrifices. By doing so he lost the confidence of his chiefs and people. He was succeeded by his brother, Nana Opoku Fofie, who reigned for only two years before his death in 1799. During his brief reign the Gyaman tribe attacked Asante in an attempt to free themselves from Asante rule, and the fifteen-month war was brought to a bitter end, and a devastating Asante victory, in a battle on the banks of the River Tano. Opoku Fofie was succeeded by his younger brother, Nana Osei Tutu Kwame Asibe (1799–1824), and it was perhaps a reaction to the timidity of Osei Kwame's previous reign that the new *Asantehene* was soon in direct military conflict with the British.

From 1752 to 1821 the British presence on the Gold Coast was managed, staffed and controlled by the African Company of Merchants, who appointed a governor to oversee their interests and provide a limited military force. Overall management came from the African Committee, which was composed of nine members, three from each of the main ports that traded with the Gold Coast: London, Liverpool and Bristol. These individuals were elected by a general body of traders from these respective cities who, by paying an annual subscription of £2, were admitted to the company. However, the vast majority of funding came in the form of an annual grant that was approved by the British Parliament. This grant covered the cost of the London office of the company as well as nine trading posts, or forts, along the Gold Coast, the most important being

Cape Coast Castle. The African Committee had a responsibility to report to the Exchequer, the Admiralty and the Secretary at War.

Although the Asante nation had for many years wished to expand their direct influence, if not rule, over the coastal people, it would take a tribal dispute to act as catalyst for the Asante invasion of the Fante tribal coastal lands. A dispute arose between the two chiefs of Western Assin, Kwadwo Otibu and Kwaku Aputae, and the *Asantehene*. This disagreement centred on a ruling made by the Asante king that the two Assin chiefs had stolen gold and ornaments from the grave of a sub-chief of Eastern Assin. Osei Tutu Kwame ruled against the two chiefs and ordered compensation to be paid. Both men refused to acknowledge the *Asantehene*'s ruling and a state of war was declared. Osei Tutu Kwame himself led an army into Western Assin and his troops utterly defeated their opponents. The two offending chiefs then fled to Fantelands to seek sanctuary and to ask for protection.

Osei Tutu Kwame demanded that the Fante chiefs hand over the two fugitives but knowing that the two would very likely be tortured to death they refused and abused the king's messenger, thus accepting war against the Asante. In May 1806 Osei Tutu Kwame led the Asante army against the Fante, and despite the British openly supporting their Fante allies, the Asante's claimed a decisive victory at the Battle of Abora. This was just 4 miles from the town of Cape Coast, where the British commander, Colonel George Torrane, was defending the castle. With their immediate protectors defeated, Kwadwo Otibu and Kwaku Aputae turned to Torrance for their salvation and he allowed the two Assin chiefs to seek refuge in the Cape Coast Castle. The Asante advance guard, under of the King of Denkyira, now turned his forces east and headed 10 miles along the coast to the lesser British fort at Anomabu, where he knew many Fantes had fled. En route the Asante army surrounded the Dutch fort, Fort Amsterdam, at Kormantine, and the Dutch surrendered en mass.

Anomabu had a small garrison of just twenty-nine men, which included five officers of the African Company, White, Meredith, Swanzy, Smith and Barnes, with White in overall command. Behind the walls of the fort, White felt sure that he could defend his charge and inflict a defeat upon the Asante. Osei Tutu Kwame arrived at the head of the main Asante force and despite the numbers surrounding the fort, White was confident that his artillery could keep the enemy at bay and he thus refused the Asante's initial demand that he hand over twenty barrels of gunpowder and a hundred muskets as a preliminary gesture before surrender negotiations could begin. In return White threatened the king that he would discharge his cannon upon his army and scatter it. Many thousands of locals flocked to the fort for protection and although White let 2,000 souls inside, there remained several thousand huddled in large groups at the base of the walls or on the nearby beach.

On 15 June, the Asante force advanced upon the village of Anomabu. With no sign that his words had intimidated the Asante king, White unleashed a couple of artillery rounds into the besieging enemy forces. Rather than forcing a retreat, this act resulted in Asante bullets whistling across the fort and it was not long before many of the defenders began to fall. The Asante troops poured into the nearby village and encroached on the fort. This caused panic amongst the locals, many of whom attempted to escape by sea in canoes, but the Asantes advanced rapidly and a terrible slaughter began on the beach. White and his men did their best to check the carnage. A 24-pounder fired grapeshot into the pursuers and swept down dozens of Asante with every discharge and similarly a 3-pounder fixed near the fort's eastern gate claimed many Asante lives. Yet, neither artillery pieces deterred the frenzy of killing which came up to the very walls of the fort as the Asante warriors continued their butchery and dragged local women away with them to face another hideous fate.

White and his troops trained their rifles and artillery at the Asante for several hours but there was little they could do to stem the slaughter. Defenders continued to fall; White was wounded in both the mouth and left arm and command was transferred to Meredith. By dusk only eight men remained fit enough to offer resistance and all feared that the fort would be stormed, and no mercy would be shown by the attackers. Yet, as darkness fell the Asantes halted their assault. The garrison was unable to get any much-needed sleep for the Asante war drums and the fearful screams of their helpless victims filled the night.

The British awoke to a scene of utter slaughter. The bodies of some 8,000 locals and Fantes lay strewn along the beach and in the vicinity of the fort; many of them had been beheaded. In his 1893 work *A History of the Gold Coast*, Lieutenant Colonel Ellis recorded, 'heaps of dead encumbered the beach in every direction, or were washed hither and thither in the surf, and the sands were red with blood. For a mile along the shore to the east nothing was to be seen but flaming houses, or the black and charred ruins of those that had already been devoured by fire.'[7] In addition to the 2,000 locals cowering in the fort, a further 200 souls were clinging to rocks just a few hundred yards offshore. These were the only survivors of the local population.

Soon after dawn the Asante army again advanced coolly towards the fort and the defenders prepared to sell their lives dearly. Fortunately ammunition for both cannon and musket was plentiful, and the guns of the eastern defences delivered hailstorms of grapeshot into the attackers, claiming many victims. On the western side the walls were overlooked and soon the defenders had to abandon their artillery under fire from the Asante 'Long Danes'. Here the resistance rested with Meredith and Swanzy and these two officers gallantly defended the position with muskets alone. The Asante were so close and so packed together that the two British officers often claimed more than one victim as the musket balls would penetrate one warrior and pass through them to hit another. These two fired over 300 rounds between them to hold back the Asantes until their shoulders became so bruised by the recoil of their rifles, they could fire no more.

In the late afternoon, just as their grizzly fate seemed sealed, hope was offered to the defenders with the arrival of three officers and a dozen men from Cape Castle who managed to negotiate their way through the dangerous surf. These men carried orders from Colonel Torrance to show a flag of truce and begin a parley with Osei Tutu Kwame. In the discussions that followed, the king stated his case against the two Assin chiefs and insisted upon their surrender to him, as well as demanding an annual rent from the British to maintain their castles and forts along the coast, which they had previously paid to the Fantes. It was agreed that the truce should remain whilst this demand was put to Torrance. Faced with the imminent loss of Anomabu fort, as well as the men of the garrison, and potentially Cape Coast Castle too, Torrance acceded to Osei Tutu Kwame's demands. The Fante chiefs were indignant at the British breach of faith and the two Assin chiefs were warned that they were to be sacrificed. Whilst Kwaku Aputae was able to flee to obscurity, Kwadwo Otibu was seized by the British and, offering no resistance, he was despatched to the Asante camp. Osei Tutu Kwame ordered the chief to be slowly tortured to death and later his jawbone was affixed as a trophy to the king's death horn, a ceremonial horn played at royal funerals.

Alongside the surrender of Kwadwo Otibu, Torrance recognised the Asante title to the British castles and forts and their right of conquest over the Fante, although Torrance did gain the concession that Britain, whilst paying rent for the fortifications to the Asante, still maintained judicial authority over the towns under and around them. The British humiliation at the hands of the Asante was complete. Osei Tutu Kwame was later recorded as saying 'from the hour Torrance delivered up Otibu I took [the British] for my friends, because I saw their object was trade only and they did not care for the people'.[8] To celebrate his complete victory, the king, in October 1807, swam in the sea at Winneba and as a result he acquired the added name of 'Bonsu' which is the Twi name for whale. He now had the power of a whale in the eyes of his subjects as he had extended the Asante Empire to the coast and could claim a victory over both the Fante and the British.

Although Torrance had recognised that the Asante, through military conquest, now had a claim on the coastal lands, the Fantes thought otherwise and continued their resistance against the invaders. With his new title, the Asante king, Osei Bonsu, had returned in triumph with his army to Kumasi. In the absence of Asante warriors, the Fantes tried once again to assert their authority over the coastal people. Fante armies were sent against the chiefs of Accra and Elmina and although repulsed at Accra, they succeeded in blockading

Elmina and the Dutch in the castle there. Word was sent to Kumasi by the chief of Elmina informing Osei Bonsu of the Fante attempts to re-assert their claim on the coast and an Asante army, 29,000-strong, was despatched in 1811. Whilst the British and Dutch hid firmly behind the walls of their respective forts and remained pointedly neutral throughout the ensuring campaigns, the Fante tribes and the Asante manoeuvred up and down the coast, each army attempting to secure a tactical advantage over the other. There were several fierce clashes and one notable battle at Apam, but neither side could secure the complete victory they sought. With notable losses at Apam, and smallpox ripping through the Asante camp, the two generals, Opoku Frefre and Appia Dankwa, decided to retire to Kumasi.

It was not until 1814 that an Asante army once more headed south to eradicate the Fante threat to their newly acquired territory. Again, the Dutch and the British were spectators. The army was to stay on the coast, in both the vicinity of Accra and Cape Coast, seeking out the combined Fante armies for the next two years. Although there were no decisive engagements, the Asante did finally succeed in capturing the two leading Fante chiefs, Kwadwo Kum and Kwao Saforo, and whilst the latter was executed the former killed himself rather than face Asante retribution. Now leaderless, Fante resistance melted away and Osei Bonsu could categorically state that his empire now extended to the sea. The tribal lands of the Akyem, Akwapim and the Fantelands themselves were now placed under the rule of Asante governors.

Osei Bonsu was correct in his assessment that the British were focused only on trade. Yet, with the parliamentary victory of the abolitionists this trade, as far as the British viewed it, would no longer be based on slavery. Of course, one of the primary drivers of Asante military expansion was the need to secure supplies of slaves. Indeed, the African Company formally recognised as early as 1809 that the Asante nation could not be expected to 'acquiesce in the destruction of a trade [slavery] not inconsistent with their prejudices, their laws or their notions of morality and religion and by which alone they have been hitherto accustomed to acquire wealth . . .'.[9] This contradiction of aims would result in further conflict throughout the century and see the African Company losing its role as the main British presence along the Gold Coast. However, this was in the future and in 1817 the major British concern was the urgent need to come to some sort of arrangement with the Asante nation to secure Britain's immediate economic and political position.

The African Committee in London decided upon a direct course of action and ordered Governor John Hope Smith, who had replaced Colonel Torrance, to despatch a mission to the Asante capital of Kumasi to negotiate with the king for the establishment of a British Embassy at his court. Hope Smith selected four of the company's officers for the task. Thomas Bowditch, a clerk, was to write a detailed account of the mission and became the lead negotiator for the company. The officers set out from Cape Coast Castle on 22 April 1817, along with a retinue of carriers. The journey was to take them nearly a month before they arrived in Kumasi on 19 May. En route they passed through Fante towns and villages that had been devasted by the Asante army until they reached the jungle belt and the condition of the path slowed their progress. At the town of Fomena, the first in Asante proper, the group met the local chief, who expressed his delight that he was able to greet a white man before he died for he was awaiting execution having offended Osei Bonsu in some way. The chief was, according to Bowditch, philosophical about his circumstances and, seated on a cloth, displayed dignity rather than shame whilst he calmly awaited his fate. The chief's head duly arrived in Kumasi the day after the mission.

Kumasi grew from a tree-encircled crossroads of trading routes. Tree is *kum* in the local Twi language. The city itself was situated on a hill overlooking the Subin River and when Bowditch and his party pushed their way through the 5,000 warriors who had been sent by the king to greet their arrival they discovered a city of 27 major streets, the greatest of which was used for significant receptions and parades and was over 100m wide. There were named quarters, or *abrono*, and trades, such as goldsmiths or umbrella makers, occupied specific quarters. When the mission finally reached the palace, which was the largest building in the city, covering a total area of 5 acres, they were formally greeted by Osei Bonsu. Apart from being the royal residence, the palace also housed a forum in which the council of the nation would debate important matters. Bowditch wrote of the elaborately carved doors and windows and even the lavatories found in the palace and described the wealth he saw, in terms of gold ornaments and rich clothes. When his work was published in Britain it was met with scepticism for the reviewers could not comprehend that Africa could possess such a large and elaborate native city.

Bowditch and his colleagues remained in Kumasi for several months and although treated with respect, they were not given the freedom to explore the local area and at times they must have thought they were little more than prisoners. However, Osei Bonsu was keen to negotiate a treaty with the British and Bowditch was finally able to return to the coast with a treaty signed by the king. In it the king pledged himself to 'countenance, promote and encourage' trade between his subjects and Cape Coast Castle and allowed for a resident to remain in Kumasi. In return the officers in charge of the British forts would give 'every protection in their power' to such Asante people who might require it.[10] This feature of the treaty, point seven of ten, was quickly tested and the British were found wanting.

With the Asante army campaigning in the north against the Jaman tribe, the coastal people of Kommenda took the opportunity of turning upon a group of Asante visitors, who were beaten up and thrown out of town. When Osei Bonsu heard of this he sought redress from the governor, as set out in the treaty. However, Hope Smith pointedly refused to involve himself or the African Company of Merchants in the dispute, which enraged the king for he saw the British inactivity as a clear breach of faith. The London Committee was likewise angered and despatched Joseph Dupuis not to only smooth over the situation but also to journey to Kumasi as the first British Consul, much to the embarrassment and annoyance of Hope Smith.

Dupuis arrived at Cape Coast Castle in January 1819, but he was delayed in his attempts to journey on to Kumasi for he needed both to convince emissaries from Osei Bonsu, who had travelled to the coast, that he would be welcome at the Asante court, as well as overcome the strong ill-feeling and jealousy from Hope Smith who feared that his authority would be undermined by the new British Consul. Finally, after several months of negotiation, Dupuis was able to follow in the footsteps of Bowditch and on 23 March 1820 a new treaty was agreed between Dupuis and the king.

The new treaty superseded the one negotiated by Bowditch and although similar for the most part, it did formally recognise the Asante claim to Fante territory as well as smoothing over the issue of British protection for any Asantes on the coast. This point was reaffirmed and Osei Bonsu dropped a financial claim against the British for their earlier failure to involve themselves in the dispute with the Kommenda people. Dupuis returned in triumph to Cape Coast Castle, content in the knowledge that he had developed a good relationship with the king and the position of a resident British Consul now seemed secure. However, he was to be bitterly disappointed for Hope Smith refused to recognise or ratify a treaty to which he had not been party to. This resulted in a complete breakdown in relations between the two men and in disgust Dupuis sailed for England on 15 April 1820 stating, 'The King of Ashanti is so perfectly disposed to co-operate in all things for the mercantile interests of Great Britain that if the present opportunity is allowed to pass it may be the means of crushing at a single blow all future advancement towards commerce or the cultivation of this part of Africa.'[11]

Before he left, Dupuis assured Osei Bonsu that he would make personal representations to the British government to ensure that the treaty was ratified. However, he failed in his attempts for the government did not wish to recognise the Asante dominance over the Fante people nor pay any rent for the coastal forts. The king, though, was enraged that Hope Smith had refused to sign the treaty and, after waiting ten months for any word from London, Osei Bonsu forbade his people to trade with the British and thus all trade was diverted to the Dutch and Danish forts. He reflected that relations had not been the same since the passing of Colonel Torrance who he called a 'man of sense'.

Whilst not agreeing to recognise the Dupuis treaty, the British government finally decided to act against the African Company. For a number of years the abolitionists had grown increasingly impatient with the African Company for the slow pace with which its merchants had attempted to diversify the West African trade away from slavery, and indeed had even turned a blind eye to other nations who continued in this trade within their own territory. This combined with reports from Dupuis, as well as from Bowditch, which highlighted numerous examples of mismanagement and even corruption, led the government, in March 1822, to transfer all the African Company's possessions on the Gold Coast to the Crown. Britain and the Asante nation were now on a direct collision course for war.

Governor McCarthy: British Humiliation

The mechanisms and practicalities of the transfer saw the workings and assets of the African Company managed by the Governor of the Sierra Leone Colony, Sir Charles McCarthy. McCarthy was by background a military man of French/ Irish descent who had had a fascinating career serving many masters. In 1785, aged just 21, he joined the Irish Brigade of the French Royalist army and served in Germany. After the rise of Napoleon Bonaparte, he briefly joined the Dutch army as a volunteer and was wounded in action at the Battle of Louvain on 15 July 1794. Later in the year he returned to the Irish Brigade, which was now under British pay. He served in both the West Indies and Honduras and was wounded once again in 1798 when involved in an action with a French privateer. The Irish Brigade was officially disbanded in late 1798 and the following year McCarthy received a commission in the British army where he served in the 11th West Indies Regiment, the 52nd Regiment of Foot and in 1811 he achieved the rank of Lieutenant Colonel in the Royal African Corps.

In 1812, with Napoleon's defeat in Russia, the British acquired the colony of Senegal and Goree and McCarthy was appointed governor. When the territory was returned to France in the 1814 Treaty of Paris, McCarthy moved to become Governor of Sierra Leone. This colony had been established by the British in the late eighteenth century as a home for Black Loyalists fleeing North America after the American Revolutionary war. Resettled slaves from the West Indies, and those liberated from illegal slave ships, also found sanctuary there. McCarthy was the perfect man for the role of governor in such a colony for he was a fervent abolitionist, a friend and correspondent of William Wilberforce (1759–1833), the leader of the cause in the British Parliament, and he worked tirelessly alongside the Church Missionary Society to improve the welfare and conditions of former slaves now resident in Sierra Leone. From 1822 the Gold Coast was also under McCarthy's governorship and he remained totally committed to abolishing the slave trade. With such a principled man as governor, the British government and the Asante nation were only months away from disagreement and ultimately war.

Direct British control was to last a mere six years and was beset with difficulties from the start, which were so characteristic of Anglo-Asante relations throughout the remainder of the century. It was not just the governor's firm beliefs and personality that resulted in conflict but also misunderstandings arising from both the Bowditch and Dupuis treaties. These centred on confusion between the two parties over title and suzerainty to the coastal forts, staffed and run by the British, but also the role of the Fante people on the coast. Osei Bonsu clearly viewed the Fante as a vassal of his nation but expected the British, due to their de facto jurisdiction, to be responsible for, and police, Fante good behaviour. Within this problematic situation was added the fact that the Asante king was essentially feudal in nature and was prone to take offence at the smallest slight from one of his vassal tribes. It did not take long for a situation to arise in which the personalities of both McCarthy and the Asante king would collide.

McCarthy arrived on the Gold Coast on 27 March 1822 and immediately decided upon a quick tour along the coast to familiarise himself with his new charge and to further formulate ideas on how the Gold Coast should be governed as well as how to engage with the Asante nation. It did not take McCarthy long to realise that the Fante and coastal people were neighbours of the British and thus deserved the protection of the Crown. Also, the British were in physical command on the forts and were not going to be dictated to by another nation who claimed some right over them. In addition, his own strongly held views against slavery surely meant that he would never seriously negotiate with an inland nation that had been so instrumental in the continuation of that trade. Indeed, there is little doubt, from his subsequent actions, that McCarthy felt the power of the Asante nation had to be tamed. Thus, instead of trying to pacify and engage with Osei Bonsu by sending an embassy to Kumasi, McCarthy formed three companies of the Royal African Colonial Corps, composed of both white and black troops, as a standing force. A native militia was raised, and McCarthy met with coastal chiefs to impress upon them that their loyalty and future lay with the British. Feeling that he had made the coastal region more secure, by the middle of May 1822 McCarthy returned to Sierra Leone, leaving Major James Chisholm in command.

McCarthy had hardly left the colony when events happened that would lead to conflict. The trigger for the inevitable war began with a trivial argument between an Asante trader at the British fort at Anomabu and a mixed-race sergeant of the Royal African Colonial Corps stationed there. During a heated exchange, the trader verbally abused the governor and in turn the sergeant was disrespectful and damming of the *Asantehene*. News of the sergeant's words were quickly reported to Osei Bonsu and predictably he saw them as a personal affront to him and his nation which had to be punished by death. Orders were sent out for the sergeant's capture and he was duly kidnapped and carried 20 miles inland to the town of Dunkwa where he was clapped in chains, awaiting the king's orders. Yet, for nearly eight months Osei Bonsu patiently waited for a British response, perhaps hoping that his captive might be useful in restarting negotiations on the Dupuis treaty, but none came. So, in February 1823 the offending sergeant was beheaded, and his head sent to Kumasi.

In what he must have considered to be a warning of his strength and determination, Osei Bonsu sent a personal message to McCarthy that he would face a similar fate as the unfortunate sergeant. This was only seen by the governor as provocation, even though the king was still trying to press for secret negotiations via the Dutch at Elmina. Despite all his experience, McCarthy could not see the bigger picture that perhaps he should be considering a way out of direct confrontation for the good of trade and the future political relationship between the Asantes and Britain; he certainly did not possess the pragmatic approach of his predecessor, Torrance.

McCarthy quickly returned from Sierra Leone and ordered men of the Royal African Colonial Corps to Dunkwa to try and punish those responsible for the sergeant's execution. However, they were unsuccessful and returned to the coast empty-handed. An outraged McCarthy requested troops from Sierra Leone. He then called out the militia, alongside the Royal African Corps, and with support from the Fante, Denkyira, Wassa and Ga tribes, personally led his mixed force north towards the Prah River. In the meantime, hearing of McCarthy's mobilisation, Osei Bonsu ordered a large Asante force out from Kumasi to face the threat.

There is no doubt that McCarthy seriously under-estimated the military might and prowess of the Asante army. Despite warnings from his coastal allies, he seems to have been disdainful of what had become the best organised and successful military force in West Africa. McCarthy spent considerable time and energy in wooing and encouraging his native allies to join his force, perhaps at the expense of taking time to comprehend the extreme difficulties his expedition would face, and the threat posed by the Asante army. To the Fante, the actions shown by Colonel Torrance and what they perceive to be his betrayal were still very raw and McCarthy had repeatedly to reassure the Fante that he would never make peace with the Asante without consulting them and considering their interests. McCarthy was rewarded for his efforts when he was personally provided with a bodyguard of 200 Fante warriors who were tasked with always being by his side during the forthcoming expedition.

On 25 November 1823, McCarthy, appropriately attired in the cocked hat and tails of the governor, reviewed troops of the Royal African Colonial Corps and presented them with their colours. To the native soldiers he expressed his satisfaction with their good conduct and to the European soldiers he exhorted them to 'support the character and honour of their country, not by bravery alone, but by a strict adherence to justice and humanity'.[12] McCarthy clearly felt that he was leading a crusading army.

McCarthy received intelligence that the main Asante army was moving down to the coast via Wassa tribal lands in the west. Rather than keeping his own forces together he decided upon a rather elaborate three-pronged advance. Most of the militia and tribal warriors, commanded by Captain Blenkerne, were ordered on a looping march from the east to attack the enemy in the rear or flank. Captain Laing, with a large party of Fante warriors, was to march straight towards Kumasi as a diversionary move, with the hope that this would deflect some Asante troops away from the main army. McCarthy would personally lead the remainder of his force, which consisted of some 2,500 men and included the Royal Africans, including the regimental band, some troops of the 2nd West Indies Regiment and the remainder of the militia. Major Chisholm was nominated as second in command but there is no record of whether McCarthy consulted his officers or allies as to his plan of action, which seems in retrospect foolhardy in the extreme and clearly shows a lack of respect and understanding of the military prowess of the Asante army. One officer and a handful of men were left behind to guard Cape Coast Castle.

McCarthy led his own force to Dunkwa, where more tribal allies were recruited. For the next few days his new recruits and existing troops were engaged in hours of drill to prepare them for jungle fighting and bugle commands, although no thought was given as to how the solid formations used in open battle could be deployed in the thick undergrowth in which the force would be likely engaged. Whilst his allies expressed some qualms about why the governor should risk himself by being at the head of the force, McCarthy would not heed their warnings or delegate responsibility and his command headed for Wassa with the tall figure of the governor at the fore.

A long and tiring march was to follow in which McCarthy struggled to both maintain the cohesiveness of his force in the thick jungle terrain and to keep it sufficiently supplied. Major Ricketts had the unenviable task of ensuring supply lines were maintained, but native carriers were reluctant, and loads were frequently dumped along the wayside or pilfered. Men grew hungry and, as the rains made the limited jungle paths quagmires of mud, disgruntled. In addition, the torrents of rains, and the need to ford numerous streams and rivers, had soaked much of the gunpowder. Brandon, the ordnance storekeeper, was ordered back to Cape Coast Castle to seek fresh, dry powder and additional ammunition but neither he nor the governor knew when he might return.

In early January 1824, McCarthy received a plea from his Denkyira allies that the Asante army had entered their tribal lands and that help was required to deter their advance. The governor decided to answer their pleas and Major Chisolm, along with several hundred men, was despatched to their aid. McCarthy was again guilty of splitting his already weakened force. Despite reducing his own numbers, the governor ordered his men on and they, with difficulty, crossed the swollen Prah River into Wassa tribal lands. Within days the governor was greeted by a steady stream of Wassa and Denkyira warriors who were fleeing the advancing Asante army. Still undeterred, Sir Charles pressed on with his ever-dwindling force, determined to stop the Asantes with British lead. He did, however, take the precaution of recalling Chisholm, who, unfortunately was to receive the order too late.

By 22 January 1824, some of his native allies were becoming increasingly nervous as McCarthy led them closer towards Wassa territory. The governor was actually in conference trying to reassure them that the Asante army was still days away when scouts frantically entered the meeting to state that the main enemy force was ahead of them. McCarthy acted immediately and called his reduced force to form a firing line. With Chisholm's departure and an increasing number of desertions, McCarthy's main body was now in the region of 500 troops. In addition, his prized bodyguard had been positioned on the extreme left wing and nothing could persuade them to return to the centre to guard the governor. McCarthy's men were now about to face an onslaught from 10,000 disciplined and highly motivated Asante warriors.

By 2pm McCarthy had placed his men in a firing line along the southern banks of the Bonsa River, near the village of Bonsaso. As was their custom, the Asante army advanced towards them in a fan formation to surround their foe, the horns and drums of each distinctive chief filling the jungle air and spreading fear through the British and native ranks. At about half a mile from the northern riverbank the Asantes halted and their musicians continued their fearful sounds. McCarthy had no idea that he was facing over 10,000 warriors and furthermore he had been led to believe that the loyalty of many in the Asante army was questionable. In one of the most bizarre moments in British colonial history the prized band of the Royal Africans was pushed forward and told to play the British national anthem. McCarthy seems to have seriously felt that on hearing the anthem the Asantes would surrender in large numbers. On first rendition, the band did manage to silence the drums and horns, but as soon as the anthem had finished the warlike melody again filled the jungle, this time louder than before. This musical exchange was repeated, again and again, and each time the anthem was played McCarthy and his officers stood firmly to attention whilst his men looked on in bewilderment. Eventually the Asantes tired of this musical charade and the band were finally answered with an eruption of musket balls which ripped through the jungle foliage and tore into flesh. The Battle of Nsamankow had begun.

Men of McCarthy's command were soon falling, and the length of the firing line had to be reduced as more and more gaps appeared. The British and their allies returned fire at an invisible enemy not knowing if their own fire was effective. Just as both powder and ammunition were running low, and the fire from the British was slackening as a result, the civilian storesman, Brandon, returned from the coast with fresh supplies. On hearing battle, Brandon's porters had fled, and he alone struggled into camp with a few ammunition boxes that he could carry. McCarthy's sense of relief at seeing the storesman soon turned to anger for when the boxes were opened, they were found to contain biscuits and macaroni. The governor threated to hang Brandon from the nearest tree, but before this order could be carried out, an Asante slug suddenly slammed into Brandon's head, killing him instantly.

With troops running low on ordnance, the Asantes took their opportunity and charged the British firing line. As they splashed through the river a few warriors were felled and the men of the Royal Africans just had time to fix bayonets before the mass of the enemy descended upon them. Most were killed and then beheaded where they stood. A lieutenant of the militia, De Graft, rallied a few orderlies and manged to unleash a fire of musket balls from a small brass cannon into the charging mass of warriors before their position was over-whelmed. De Graft successfully fought his way out using his sword, but all the orderlies were butchered.

The battle now became one of individual struggles as men fought for their very survival. McCarthy, still wearing his governor's plumed hat, was last seen by Ricketts screaming for a bugler to sound the retreat, but he shouted in vain for the young lad had already been killed. Ricketts and De Graft fled into the jungle and spent the next three days scrambling, often on their bellies, through the undergrowth as they evaded Asante search parties. The exact fate of the governor is unclear. Some historians paint a picture of McCarthy, who had already been wounded three times, including a wound in his chest and an arm broken by a musket ball, standing back to back with two of his staff, a colonial engineer named Buckle and a young ensign named Wetherell, defiantly awaiting their fate. Others have recorded that rather than be captured and tortured, the governor placed his pistol to his chest and took his own life.

However, what occurred was recorded by one of the few survivors of the debacle, McCarthy's own colonial secretary, named Williams. He had stood by the governor throughout the battle but was felled by a musket ball in the thigh and passed out due to loss of blood. He awoke as a warrior was trying to severe his head. Fortunately for Williams he was recognised by an Asante chief to whom Williams had shown some kindness when he worked for the African Company and the warrior was restrained. Williams was taken in triumph to Kumasi where he remained a prisoner for several weeks. Through the offices of the Dutch governor at Elmina, Williams was finally released and was able to tell of the scene around him when he had regained consciousness. He stated that he saw the headless trunks of Buckle, Wetherell and McCarthy close to one another. McCarthy's head was taken as a trophy back to Kumasi where a cast of the skull was taken in pure gold and the skull itself became part of a skull fetish in the capital. Once a year at the Festival of Yams, the skull, wrapped in a white cloth, would be paraded through the streets of Kumasi.

Both Ricketts and De Graft evaded capture and certain death and were found collapsed by a jungle stream by scouts of Chisholm's returning force. It took Chisholm and his officers some time to recognise the men for they had suffered severally from cuts and bruises in their escape and were too exhausted to tell of their ordeal. Eventually the men were recovered sufficiently to inform Chisholm of the governor's likely fate and the defeat of his command. Chisholm had the foresight immediately to turn his command around and they headed post-haste back to Cape Coast Castle. In a strange mixing of fates, Osei Bonsu did not live to enjoy his victory. For whilst McCarthy was dying on the battlefield, the king passed away on the same day in his bed. He was succeeded as *Asantehene* by his brother, Osei Yaw Akoto, who, under the conditions of his accession, was bound to prosecute the war.

The defeat of McCarthy and his command at the Battle of Nsamanko was to be the high point of the Asante nation, both in terms of its prestige and power but also in its geographical spread. Yet, no one, including the new king, could have possibly foreseen this for after the death of the governor and Chisholm's flight back to the coast, the Asantes appeared to be unstoppable and certainly the paramount military force in West Africa. Osei Yaw Akoto clearly felt that he had some scores to settle against the tribes who had allied themselves with the British and he wasted no time in ordering his army on a campaign of revenge and retribution. In the meantime, Chisholm had safely returned to Cape Coast Castle and readied the castle and his men for the predicted Asante onslaught. Sailors and Marines from ships offshore reinforced Chisholm's new command and his men set about improving their store of ammunition by removing lead from roofs, gutters, pipes and any other lead item to make musket balls.

The Asante army marched rapidly towards the coast, sweeping all before it. The native allies were routed at Dompim and the Asante's advance upon Efutu was so fast that an allied force, including two British officers, was captured in the act of evacuating the town. The officers were sent as prisoners to Kumasi and although one died a year later of disease, the second, named Patrick Riley, remained a captive for four years. Fearing that the strategic town of Efutu would be used to concentrate Asante forces for an advance upon the coast, Chisholm resolved to try and retake the town. Sparing a few British troops from Cape Coast Castle, he led Wassa and Denkyira tribesmen in an attack on 21 May

1824. In a bitterly fought battle, the allies were victorious and by dusk the Asante army had been driven from the town with heavy losses. However, the allies had suffered too and were now not strong enough to maintain their position and just two days later the enemy re-occupied the town. Now, just as Chisholm had feared, Osei Yaw Akoto personally led a second Asante army to join his troops at Efutu and from here he sent a message of defiance to Cape Coast Castle warning of his impending attack.

On 21 June 1824, the king led his combined army to within 5 miles of the castle in what can be considered a reconnaissance in force. He returned on 7 July, but by then further reinforcements and ordnance had been secured from British ships and these extra troops and cannon deterred a full-scale attack upon the castle. The British were then fortunate in that another silent but deadly ally of dysentery and smallpox ravaged through the main Asante camp and hundreds succumbed. When Osei Yaw Akoto then received reports that the Danish governor was leading a force from Accra to outflank his own he decided to retreat to Kumasi. Dispirited and broken by disease, the Asante army stumbled into Kumasi in August 1824.

As the Asante army recovered and rebuilt itself, a new British governor, Major General Charles Turner, arrived in March 1825. News of McCarthy's death and defeat at the hands of a 'savage' army had shocked both the British government and public and Turner arrived with reinforcements and fresh ordnance with which to counter any further Asante threat. Soon after his arrival, on 2 April 1825, Turner issued a proclamation in which he laid down the British government's position on future relations:

> If the King of Ashanti will content himself with governing his own nation and his own people, and does not stop the trade of the interior with the coast, or attempt to oppress his neighbours, let him say so to me, and I will make a treaty with him on any of these terms, but I will not make peace with him on any other terms, nor until he gives up every claim to tribute or subjection from the surrounding nations.[13]

No response was received from Osei Yaw Akoto to Turner's proclamation and for the rest of the year the political situation was held in limbo. This lack of contact from the interior seems to have encouraged an element of disdain from the newly subdued coastal tribes which began openly to consider rebellion and breaking way from their Asante overlords. This was too much for Osei Yaw Akoto who in January 1826 led a large Asante army southward. Once again, the Asante troops left a trail of destruction in their wake. Settlements were burnt and plundered, and anyone who was unfortunate enough to be in their path was either enslaved or butchered. The coastal tribes, with advice and support from the British, avoided any major engagements with the Asante army for Osei Yaw Akoto had hoped to defeat each of the rebellious coastal tribes one by one. This game of 'cat and mouse' continued until the end of July when the Asante army finally decided to encamp just north of Accra, near the town of Dodowa. In this region the Ga tribe were to be found and the Asante king was particularly keen to teach them a lesson. Yet, there is an old Akan proverb which states: 'If you continue chasing a coward and don't stop, you at last meet his manliness.'[14] The tribes of the coast, the Gas, Fantes, Denkyiras, Akyems, Akwapims, Akwamus, supported by British troops, were now ready to spring a trap of their own.

The Battle of Dodowa and its Aftermath

Osei Yaw Akoto must have been overjoyed on the morning of Monday, 7 August 1826 when he saw the allied forces drawn up against him. That date was considered propitious in the Asante calendar, and this was regarded a good omen for likely success against the enemy as he had been hoping for a pitched battle against the unruly tribes for several months. Furthermore, his army had recently humbled the British so the king, his chiefs and his troops must have all been confident that the day would result in yet another crushing victory for the Asante nation. Yet, the king's confidence was misplaced for not only had the allies been carefully avoiding battle for months, but they had been deliberately leading the Asante enemy into a position in which they would have an advantage. The coastal chiefs knew from bitter experience that the Asantes were the masters of jungle warfare and, to their cost, the British now knew this too. So the allies had deliberately chosen a site for battle upon open ground on which the Asante's skilful use of drums and horns to unsettle their foes would be much reduced and their tactics of using the cover of the bush to approach unseen and to envelope their enemies in their traditional fan formation would be nullified. Yet, despite the allies having placed themselves in such an advantageous position, the forthcoming battle, known to Asantes as the Battle of Katamansu, would be a bloody close-run one.

The Asante forces were split into two divisions, one was commanded by the king himself, the other by Asante *Gyasehene*, or commander, Opoku Frefre. The king had brought the Golden Stool with him from Kumasi and both he and the stool were in the centre of the army, guarded by elite troops. The total number of Asante warriors was in the region of 10,000. Facing them on that fateful day was an allied army 11,000-strong, composed of British troops, as well as a Danish contingent from the castle at Christiansborg and a varied collection of coastal tribes. The allied firing line extended east to west for about 4 miles. Overall command was in the hands of Lieutenant Colonel Purdon with a staff consisting of officers from the Royal African Colonial Corps: Captains Hingston and Rogers and Lieutenant Calder.

Purdon deployed his forces with the militias of the Cape Coast, Anomabu, Accra and Christiansborg in the centre, with the Royal African Colonial Corps posted in the rear as a reserve to shore up and plug any holes in the line that the Asantes might exploit. The Akyems, commanded by their monarch Nana Afia Dokuaa, who was the only woman commander at the battle, were positioned on the right. The left was taken by warriors of the Denkyira and Akim tribes, with lesser numbers of other tribes in support of both flanks. So as to avoid friendly fire from the European troops, all the native warriors were distinguished by having strips of calico tied to the barrels of their muskets and large seashells hanging from their necks, both front and back. The beating of the king's drum heralded the start of the battle and at about 9.30am the Asantes attacked from right and left, trying to turn the allied flanks. In fierce fighting the native allies bravely held their ground and the initial Asante attacks were repulsed. The king had placed himself in the centre of the Asante line as he knew this was where the British and Danish troops were, and he wished to have the prestige of attacking them. Yet, the warriors of the Asante centre had advanced only a mere hundred metres or so when a crashing volley of musketry halted them in their tracks. Seeing that this had caused the Asantes to waver, Purdon ordered his centre to advance, firing as they moved. The Asante troops could not stem the allied push but stubbornly fought for every piece of ground as they steadily fell back. On the flanks the fighting had developed into a fierce hand-to-hand struggle in which the opponents wrestled and stabbed and cut at each other. No quarter was shown or expected. Wounded on both sides were killed where they fell, despatched with a club to the head or decapitated. The native troops took great pride in ripping out the hearts of the dead Asantes and despite the best efforts of European orderlies this carnage could not be stopped.

In the centre the advance of the militia was temporarily stalled when an Asante chief detonated a keg of gunpowder, blowing himself to pieces and injuring some European troops. Yet, the centre pressed on. Resistance stiffened as the allied troops got closer to their target of both the king and the Golden Stool. Indeed, had it not been for the sacrifice and bravery of a few Asante chiefs then the stool would have been captured. So important was the stand of these warriors that their names, Antwi Panin, Dwabenhene and Kwasi Boateng, have been recorded in Asante oral history. As the allies pushed forward some cohesion was lost as men stopped to claim spoils from fallen Asante warriors and the king took this lessening of pressure to unleash a reserve division at both the enemy's centre and the flanks. The Asante fire from their 'Long Danes' was claiming many lives and Purdon, realising that the battle hung in the balance, called up his reserve of the Royal Africans as well as the Congreve rockets, which had been recently received from Britain. It was these weapons that won the day for the allies. The noise and smoke as the missiles shot through the air and then the violent explosions as they landed caused consternation amongst the ranks of the Asante who had never seen such weapons. Indeed, they concluded that the British had a new great 'fetish' which allowed them to fight with actual thunder and lightning. Panic set in amongst the Asantes and they broke and fled in wild disorder and the allied victory was complete.

The Asantes lost all their camp baggage in the rout and the wounded king was just able to flee to safety with the Golden Stool. His second in command, Opoku Frefre, was later to kill himself because the disgrace of such a catastrophic loss was too much for him to bear. The battle had been so fierce that up to seventy *Abrempon*, or Asante chiefs, were killed. The king took the defeat very badly. He remained at Seuwa, 12 miles from Kumasi, for six months before he could bring his humiliated army back to the capital.

The Asante defeat at Dodowa had some very important and immediate effects, but it also influenced Anglo-Asante relations for decades to come. Perhaps the most significant and direct result of the battle was that the British and Danish claimed ownership, by right of conquest, of the land on which their forts and castles stood and thus the 'Notes' (legal contract) held by the Asantes over the battlements, and the rent to which they considered they were entitled, were nullified. This was a serious loss of income for the Asante treasury and would be a major area of dispute throughout the century.

Just two weeks after the battle a new governor, Sir Neil Campbell, arrived at Cape Coast Castle. He was keen to avoid the mistakes made by his predecessor, McCarthy, and made overtures to the Asante court for a peace treaty and a British envoy. However, he was frustrated in his attempts by the allied coastal tribes who insisted that it was for the Asantes, as the defeated nation, to make the first move. This they finally did the following year and requested that initial negotiations should take place at Yancommassie Assin, with the Chief of Adansi acting as an intermediary. This was not acceptable to the British who insisted that the Asante king send envoys to Cape Coast Castle. The firm British position resulted in months of haggling before, in October 1827, negotiations began. The British were initially surprised at how accommodating the Asante were. First, the king conceded that he had been in the first wrong in fighting the British and indicated that he would consider accepting some form of political submission in the future. At a second meeting preliminary peace terms were agreed. These included an indemnity payment of 4,000oz of gold, paid by the Asantes and held in Cape Coast Castle as a guarantor of future good and peaceful conduct. This gold would be forfeited if the Asante nation showed any aggression to either the British or they native allies. In addition, two members of the Asante royal family were to be sent to the Cape Coast and held as hostages and guarantors of good conduct by the Asante nation, and any white prisoners held in Kumasi should be released.

A British embassy was sent to Kumasi in February 1828 and two European prisoners, Patrick Riley and John Duncan, were duly freed. In return Osei Yaw Akoto requested that several members of the royal family who had been captured at the Battle of Dodowa and were being held in Elmina should be released. Unfortunately, the Fante realising that the Asantes would be unable to launch another expedition to the coast in the foreseeable future, had taken the opportunity to besiege Asante allies at Elmina and it was therefore impossible, at that time, to accede to the king's request. In April 1828 Osei Yaw Akoto sent a formal protest to the British stating that they had not done enough to end the siege of Elmina and until they could control their Fante allies all peace negotiations would be placed on hold. Clearly the king felt the British were in cahoots with the Fante. Despite the best efforts of Major Ricketts, who acted as an arbiter, it took until the conclusion of 1829 for the siege to be lifted and by then the political situation on the Gold Coast had once again altered.

The Governorship of George Maclean

Conflict with the Asantes, prolonged peace negotiations and the behaviour of the Fantes had exasperated the British government, which had concluded that politically the Gold Coast was too problematic whilst financially it was becoming an ever-increasing drain on the public purse. The government was keen simply to walk away from its commitments, and this stimulated a debate in Britain over whether the benefits of trade were outweighed by the need and cost to protect. Many in government, as well as Parliament, felt that unprotected trade inevitably drew Britain into messy conflicts overseas. This view caused consternation amongst the African merchants and former members of the African Company. These individuals still possessed political weight and were able to call upon friends and associates in Parliament to ensure that there was a lively and hostile debate over the government's intentions. The result was that a compromise was reached in which the Gold Coast technically remained a dependency of Sierra Leone, whilst its administration was entrusted to a committee of merchants, based both on the coast and in London. This committee appointed Captain George Maclean as the African Company governor and he arrived on the Gold Coast to take over his responsibilities on 29 February 1830.

Maclean was born in Keith, Scotland, the son of a minister. He had had a short career in the British army in both the 27th and 91st Regiments of foot before poor health saw him resign his commission in 1821. He struggled to find a career in business before deciding to take the opportunity of a commission with the Royal African Colonial Corps, in which he served from 1826–8 in Sierra Leone. He possessed an awareness of the military situation in the Gold Coast for he was appointed as secretary to the military command in Sierra Leone. He was a popular officer who displayed enormous energy and had a unique ability to relate to both his men and the native tribes. His greatest gift was that he could quickly grasp the essence of a problem and he was a natural diplomat. Although many were surprised that he was chosen to be the new governor, he quickly rose to the challenge.

Maclean soon realised that the future prosperity of the Gold Coast was totally dependent on securing a definite peace treaty with the Asante nation and he made this his number one priority. Yet, he also understood that the secret to a long-lasting peace settlement was to ensure that the coastal tribes, and in particular the Fantes, were brought into the peace process so as to avoid any future confusion and misunderstanding turning to inevitable conflict. Maclean would need all his diplomatic skills to bring all the interested parties together, but this is just what he managed to do, and he genuinely seems to have been liked and respected by all the tribes.

After a year of frantic and dedicate diplomatic work Maclean, on 27 April 1831, was able to conclude a peace treaty signed by himself, the Asante nation and the kings of Fante, Assin, Denkyira and six other coastal tribes. In the treaty Osei Yaw Akoto agreed to deposit 600oz of gold at Cape Coast Castle, as well as delivering two members of the royal family, named Ossoo Ansah and Ossoo In Quantamissah, as security for Asante adherence to peace. In addition, all signatories agreed that trade and commerce should be open and free to all and crucially that 'the king of Ashantee has renounced all right or title of any tribute or homage from the Kings of Denkera, Assin, and others formerly his subjects, so on the other hand, these parties are strictly prohibited from insulting, by improper speaking or in any other way, their former master, such conduct being calculated to produce quarrels and war'.[15]

This treaty formed the basis of peace for decades to come and crucially its most important contribution was in adjudicating disputes. Maclean was able to introduce an element of fairness and equality in Anglo-Asante relations for the very first time and his success was recognised in future treaties. For all his peaceful overtures Maclean was not above using force if necessary, to maintain peace. In 1835 he even organised a military expedition against the king of Apollonia near Axim, who was accused of murdering traders in this area. In addition, by ensuring a peaceful settlement Maclean allowed economic activity to flourish and by 1840 exports from the Cape Coast had risen to £325,000 from £131,000 in 1831. This was largely seen in terms of increases in the gold and ivory trades, for the move away from subsistence agriculture to palm oil and cocoa production would not be seen until the 1860s onwards.[16]

Yet, Maclean's success brought jealousy and unfortunately his behaviour fuelled gossip and suspicion. The governor did not hide his night-time visits from Cape Coast Castle to his nearby 'country wives', which even continued after the arrival of his British wife, the celebrated novelist and poet Letitia

Elizabeth Landon, from London. When she died within just four months, the governor blamed the unforgiving climate of 'The White Man's Grave' yet rumours abounded of possible foul play. In addition, accusations that Maclean had not done enough to stop the slave trade and suppress domestic slavery undermined his reputation. Statements were made in Parliament that Cape Coast Castle was used a base for continued slavery and that Maclean had turned a blind eye. The government, embarrassed by such claims, and the governor's sensational private life, was quick to look for an excuse to remove Maclean from office and bring the administration back under the Crown. In 1841 the British government sent a commissioner, Dr R.R. Madden, to Cape Coast to investigate the charges against the governor. Although Madden's hostile findings were not accepted in full, the select committee appointed by Parliament did recommend that the governor's de facto rule of the area be given legality, and once more the Gold Coast was placed under the governor of Sierra Leone.

Maclean was made judicial assessor and magistrate in 1844 whilst Commander H.W. Hill, of the Royal Navy, took over responsibility for the Gold Coast forts and settlements as lieutenant governor. Together they negotiated various treaties with local Fante that came to be known as the Bond of 1844. Apart from recognizing the power and jurisdiction of British officials, the chiefs conceded the adjudication of serious crimes to British officials with the long-term purpose of establishing the general principles of British law in the country.

The Reign of Kwaku Dua I: Peace and Prosperity

Upon Osei Yaw Akoto's death in 1838, his nephew Kwaku Dua I succeeded him as *Asantehene*. The new king, whether governed by the new political circumstances of the Maclean treaty or by his own personal outlook, was far more willing to negotiate with the British than his predecessors had been. Governor Hill managed to upset Kwaku Dua on his arrival for Hill failed to tell him of his assumption of office and demotion of Maclean. Such an omission was considered a gross breach of etiquette and caused great resentment in Kumasi. Yet, Hill redeemed himself in Asante eyes by adjudicating in a case in which some Asante traders had been attacked whilst passing through Assin territory and an Asante woman had been murdered. Hill received an Asante delegation to listen to their claims and was later able to arrest the woman's murderer and, in the presence of the delegation, ensured that the culprit was sent to trial, found guilty and executed. This was the first of many examples in which various British governors arbitrated in disputes between the Asantes and various tribes through the 1840s and 1850s. Maclean's treaty stood the various tests that were thrown at it. This was a halcyon period in Anglo-Asante relations, although attempts by various British governors, including Governor Winniett's 1848 visit to Kumasi, failed to end the Asante practice of human sacrifice.

Largely good relations between the Asante, the British and the coastal tribes allowed mercantile trade to flourish. Asante traders visited the coast in large numbers, where they bartered produce for European goods. The geographical position of the nation allowed the Asantes to established themselves as middle-men for trade from the coast to those nations north of Asante. A large market was established by the Asantes at a town called Salaga and Muslim traders of the interior and the Sahara region were able to exchange sheep and cattle for kola nuts and European goods. Kwaku Dua was considered to be the wealthiest of the Asante kings. Although the *Asanthene* did not directly own any gold mines, any nuggets exceeding a certain size were his by law and this became a major source of income. All the property of a deceased *Abrempon*, or chief, was automatically the king's, paid as a sort of death duty. On the appointment of a new chief the king would return a proportion of the deceased chief's wealth. In addition, the king derived revenue from various fines, road taxes and Kwaku Dua had numerous trading ventures himself.

Of all European nations that had settlements along the coast, it was the British, with their role as legal arbiters, that secured the largest amount of the new trade which peace and a lack of political turmoil promoted. In 1850, the Danes decided to quit the Gold Coast and they sold their settlements along the coast to the British government for £10,000. The establishment of a supreme court in 1853, three years after the forts and settlements had become a separate colony from Sierra Leone, continued the process of legitimising both English common law in the colony and its political and economic authority.

A Collapse in Anglo-Asante Relations: Further Conflict

Anglo-Asante relations were severely tested in December 1862 when Kwaku Dua approached the new British governor, Governor Pine, who was a career diplomat having previously served as Lieutenant Governor of Natal before his appointment on the Gold Coast. Kwaku Dua asked Pine to extradite an Asante chief who had sought refuge with the British. The existing agreements were found wanting and failed to deal with this request and it could be argued that this dispute was at the heart of a British humiliation in 1864, which rumbled on to to a full-blown conflict in the following decade.

The dispute centred on a misunderstanding or miscommunication around the Maclean treaty. It began when an Asante chief named Kwasi Gyanin who, with one of his young slaves, fled Kumasi for he had been accused of not hand-ing over to the king gold nuggets, which by their very size should have become the property of Kwaku Dua by right. Kwasi Gyanin's flight to the coast seemed to many to indicate his guilt. The punishment for such a crime was death. The king clearly felt that a verbal agreement had been put in place between Osei Bonsu and Maclean which meant that runaways, prisoners and those accused of crimes must be returned to the respective authorities which had requested the extradition. The Dutch commissioner on the Gold Coast, Colonel Nagtglas, was adamant that such a verbal agreement did exist and certainly Kwaku Dua was convinced. Therefore, it was perhaps understandable that when Governor Pine refused to return the fugitives as requested the king was outraged. Pine was in a very difficult moral position for he realised that if Kwasi Gyanin and the boy slave were returned they would have both been certainly executed. He therefore told the Asante king that he would return the two if the king showed clear evidence of Kwasi Gyanin's guilt.

Up until now Kwaku Dua had been a relatively peaceful monarch, but Pine's refusal to cooperate with the extradition flew him into a rage. Arms, ammunition and powder were purchased from the king of Elmina and preparations were made for a large body of warriors to cross the Prah River and head for the coast. Although no formal declaration of war was made, in April 1863 three separate Asante armies invaded the British protectorate. Pine ordered Major Cockrane north to rally the loyal tribes against the latest Asante threat. One prong of the Asante army was used to hold in check the Wassa and Denkyira tribes, whilst a second marched down the centre of the protectorate. Both these armies were a feint for the main body, under the command of Awasu Koko, which entered the Akim tribal lands and marched on Essikuma where it surprised and routed the main allied force. Cockrane retired back to the region of the castle at Anomabu.

Although certainly surprised by the Asante plan and by the swiftness of the advance, Cochrane was in a relatively strong position. He had around 20,000 warriors at his disposal, a number almost double the enemy's force facing him. On 10 May 1863 the Asante army came to within half a mile of the allied force and some skirmishing took place, but the main battle was expected the following day. It seems evident that overnight Cochrane lost his nerve and much to the disgust of his allies he ordered a further retreat. As the allies moved back, Cochrane himself left his force and headed back to Cape Coast Castle. On the afternoon of 12 May the Asante army attacked in force the allied rear guard at the town of Bobikuma and completely routed the contingent there. However, now Awasu Koko wavered and rather than following up this success and attacking the larger allied army at Adijuma, the Asante commander restricted his action to destroying and plundering up to thirty towns in the area before retiring to Akim Swaidru, a town on the southern fringes of the Ashanti–Akim border.

From his new position at Akim Swaidru, Awasu Koko sent a messenger to Governor Pine stating that his quarrel was not with the British but that he had simply been sent by Kwaku Dua to recover the fugitives. In return Pine sent a message back stating that he would only negotiate with the king and that Awasu Koko must return with his force to Kumasi and compensation must be paid for any damage done by his troops. With the coming of the rains, and the likelihood of disease spreading through the ranks of the Asante army, the commander decided to retire across the Prah River. The Asante troops left a trail of destruction in their wake.

Having experienced the power of the Asante army, Governor Pine was now convinced that the British must be prepared to take the battle to the Asante nation. Pine strongly felt that the Asante military system had to be crushed if peace and prosperity could ever really be established on the Gold Coast. He thus petitioned the British government for the necessary troops to march and fight their way to Kumasi and plant the Union Jack there. Furthermore, Pine pointed out that without the military support from London, 'the most I can hope is, to drive the Ashantis from the Protectorate, without the chance of administrating that chastisement, or demanding that retribution, which is so justly due to its inhabitants, – and remain in constant dread of subsequent incursions of a powerful enemy'.[17] Yet, all Pine received from London was the government's sympathy for his predicament and no military help. The government was simply not going to risk the lives of British troops by sending them to 'The White Man's Grave'.

Bitterly disappointed, Pine felt that the local tribes would lose their confidence in British authority unless he took some decisive measures. Pine also felt that unless he acted aggressively then he would be inviting a further Asante attack the next year. All Asante troops re-crossed the Prah River by December 1863 and Pine used this as an opportunity to advance a body of troops, largely composed of men from the West Indies regiments stationed along the coast, north to the frontier. Pine hoped the very presence of British soldiers on his frontier would bring Kwaku Dua to his senses and that serious peace negotiations could then begin.

For the first ten weeks of 1864 the British on the frontier settled into a routine in which they constructed living quarters, laid the foundations for a bridge and built stockades against an Asante attack. However, as soon as the rains arrived the climate began to take its usual toll on victims. By the end of March 90 men out of 360 were hospitalised. The sick were escorted back to the coast and the number of fit troops halved. By early June only 100 men could stand for roll call and by the middle of the month all were withdrawn back to the coast and the camps were abandoned. Without a shot being fired, Pine's campaign had ended in utter failure. The returning troops were too weak to carry back their rifles and ammunition and these were unceremonially dumped into the Prah. On hearing of the British retreat, Kwaku Dua was heard to exult 'the white man may bring his cannon to the bush, but the bush is stronger than the cannon'.[18]

As a result of this debacle, both Pine's and the Britain's prestige were held in very low esteem by the local chiefs. Certainly, the Asante had won a moral victory and the belief that the British could not fight in the jungle was reinforced. One chief in particular, Aggery, king of the Cape Coast became very insubordinate towards the British after their recent loss of face, and he claimed jurisdiction over all grounds outside of Cape Coast Castle. Pine resisted Aggery's claim and the government refused to recognise him as king. Following his failure, Pine was replaced as governor by Colonel Edward Conran, who had previously served in Sierra Leone. Conran acted decisively and had the offending chief arrested and banished to Sierra Leone.

Governor Conran was also direct in his dealings with the Asante. A delegation was sent from the coast to Kumasi to begin peace talks and these progressed sufficiently for a delegation of Asantes to be sent to the coast. But here talks stalled. However, Conran was not to be deterred and in January 1866 he simply stated that as the Asante army had re-crossed the Prah a state of peace now existed. Kwaku Dua was once again indignant and he refused to take part in any further negotiations until the governor had handed over Kwasi Gyanin as earlier demanded.

Anglo-Asante relations now stalled and for the following months of Kwaku Dua's reign no negotiations took place. The king died in April 1867 after twenty-nine relatively peaceful years. He was succeeded by his great-nephew, Kofi Karikari, who would bring a very different and confrontational approach to Anglo-Asante relations. This year was also very significant as the Dutch finally abandoned their holdings on the Gold Coast, leaving the British as the only European nation able to face any future threat from the Asantes, and this would spark years of distrust and confrontation which would remain for the rest of the nineteenth century.

Part II

Empires Collide: Wolseley's Expedition of 1873–4

The humiliation endured by Governor Pine at the hands of the Asantes in 1864 had left a sour taste amongst officials not only on the Gold Coast but also in Britain. The first signs of disquiet in London were of a very personal nature as Admiral Hay, who had lost a brother to disease in the British camp on the banks of the Prah, almost carried a vote of censure through the House of Commons against Prime Minister Palmerston's government and his policies. As a result of the high loss of life to disease in the Pine debacle, the then Colonial Secretary, Edward Cardwell, announced that no British troops should ever be used in such a deadly climate and in future protectorate states would have to defend themselves. Sir Charles Adderley's Select Committee which investigated whether the protectorate should remain in British hands recommended though it was 'not possible to withdraw wholly or immediately all further extension of territory or assumption of government would be inexpedient and that the object should be more and more to transfer [to the local tribes] the administration with a view to our ultimate withdrawal'.[1]

Although these views were not government policy there definitely existed a waning of enthusiasm amongst politicians for the Gold Coast Protectorate. The financial situation did not inspire confidence either. Trade remained stable at around £500,000 per annum but the yearly cost of administering the region had tripled under Pine's tenure to over £170,000 per annum.[2] Indeed, Benjamin Disraeli even argued that the cost of £300,000 per annum to the Exchequer to manage the West African settlements was too high and that all should be relinquished to help balance the Crown's budget.[3]

With the publication of the select committee's views, Cardwell saw the opportunity for a compromise. Whilst there seemed no appetite for any further extensions of territory in West Africa, there was a recognition that there was a moral obligation not to abolish the protectorate, but no legal obligation to protect it either. Of course, such principles were contradictory but such a stance by Cardwell and his successors allowed for a fudge of policy for several years. It was only in 1872–3, in light of further Asante aggression, that the policy was reassessed and within nine years of the Prah camp disaster Britain would launch a major military expedition from its shores in which the Asante army would be defeated and Kumasi occupied, plundered and then burnt. The reason behind the switch from near indifference or disdain of the protectorate to it becoming yet another fixture of the ever-growing British Empire can be initially dated back to the events of 1867.

Transfer of Dutch Assets to the British

The Dutch had first traded on the Gold Coast in 1580 and in 1637 they had attacked the castle at Elmina and seized it from the Portuguese. From Elmina the Dutch continued the slave trade begun by its former owners and developed a strong relationship with both the king of Elmina, who controlled the surrounding lands, as well as the Asantes who supplied the Dutch with slaves in exchange for European goods and weapons. The king of Elmina had secured a supportive relationship with the Asantes over the years, which was based on trade and a mutual distrust of the British. The people of Elmina traded fish and salt to their immediate neighbours, in exchange for food stuffs, such as maize and cassava, as well as cattle. There was also an important trade with much of the Akan hinterland, including the Asante, in which the traders of Elmina exchanged goods, such as cotton cloth, leather goods, powder, ammunition and weapons for palm oil, food stuffs, animal skins and slaves.

Over the following centuries, the Dutch, working alongside Elmina traders, very much concentrated their efforts on economic activity. Although the abolition of slavery severely limited the trade in human cargo, it did not eradicate it and the Dutch continued to play a part in this trade, but not in such an overt manner as before. The Dutch maintained a neutrality in conflicts between the Asante nation and the British and their native allies and this can be partly explained by the fact that the Asantes, through conquest, held the 'Notes' to Elmina Castle and the Dutch would pay a yearly rent to the court at Kumasi in return for good relations between the two. Yet, this placid relationship was to alter as the nature of trade changed throughout the nineteenth century. The Dutch found it more and more difficult to make their economic activities along the Gold Coast financially viable and in the 1860s they began to negotiate with the British as to how both countries could benefit by working together.

In March 1867, in the hope of introducing and operating an effective tariff along the whole of the Gold Coast, and to reduce budgetary losses, the Dutch and the British agreed to consolidate their trading interests into two blocks. Elmina was used as the dividing line and the British took the area to the east and the Dutch to the west of the castle. In true imperial style, neither country gave any thought as to how the local population might react to a change in governance and none of the local chiefs were consulted. The treaty came into effect on 1 January 1868 and in its terms the British handed over control of the forts and trading posts of Apollonia, Dixcove, Sekondi and Kommenda and in return gained Dutch Accra, Moree, Apam and Kormantine. Crucially, the British also relinquished to the Dutch the protectorate over the peoples of Eastern and Western Wassa, Apollonia and Denkyira.

In the circumstances prevailing on the Gold Coast at the time it is perhaps hard to conceive of a worse division of lands, peoples and settlements than that agreed by the British and the Dutch and clearly little or no thought was given to the possible reaction or consequences. Disquiet centred on the transfers to the Dutch. The peoples of Dixcove objected to Dutch sovereignty and rioting occurred, whilst the townspeople of Kommenda had an even more violent reaction. A boat crew from a Dutch navy vessel was attacked as it tried to land at the settlement and had to flee for their lives. The Dutch responded by destroying the town with a naval cannonade. Yet, this violence was nothing compared with how the Wassa and Denkyira tribes reacted for these people had received some protection from possible Asante aggression by association with the British. They clearly feared that the Dutch, who had always been on friendly terms with the Asante nation, would not support these tribes in any future dispute they might have with the Asantes.

The immediate response to the Anglo-Dutch treaty amongst the Fante peoples was of disquiet and disbelief and then a realisation that they would have to galvanise themselves into some sort of coalition to face up to the strength of the Asante nation. A confederation of Fante states, excluding Elmina, was rapidly formed first as a defensive measure for at the end of 1868 the new *Asantehene*, Kofi Karikari, mounted a three-pronged attack on the coast; from the east, west and south. During the ceremonies surrounding Kofi Karikari's 'enstoolment' he was reported to have stated, whether correctly or not, that his first objective as the new king was war and it does seem that he was encouraged by many of his advisors and chiefs to pursue an aggressive policy, to benefit from the uncertainty caused by the disastrous Anglo-Dutch treaty.

The *Asantehene*'s uncle, Achiempon, commanded one of the invasion groups which followed a circuitous route west out of Kumasi to the coast and from there on to Elmina. Achiempon was renowned as being a cruel individual and the progress of his army was marked by a trail of atrocities that were remembered by the Fante with hurt and distress for decades to come. Yet, when Achiempon arrived at Elmina he was greeted by the king and the people there as a deliverer from the threat of a possible Fante attack.

Early the following year, the eastern Asante army, 30,000-strong and led by Edu Baffuo, crossed the Volta River and invaded the tribal area of Krepi with the aim of attacking the western area of the protectorate. However, under the inspired command of a man named Dompre, the Krepis were able to delay and frustrate the Asante advance. As Edu Baffuo moved forward slowly in the face of stubborn resistance he reached the town of Anum, on the banks of the Volta. Here the Basel Missionary Society had established a station and although the Revd and Mrs Ramseyer, with their infant son, knew of the impeding Asante attack, they refused to leave their post, and were captured. Edu Baffuo sent the unfortunate family to Kumasi as hostages, along with fellow missionary Mr Kuhne. The Ramseyer's child died during the arduous march to the capital and the missionaries were destined to spend nearly six years in captivity. For the British the fate of the Ramseyers was of great concern, although they were, of course, not British subjects. Yet, their capture and the aggressive march of the Asante armies led to a realisation that, at some point, the British and the Asante nations would clash once more. Fortunately, Edu Baffuo's attack was halted by the skilful Dompre, who not only defeated the Asantes in battle but captured their re-supply of ammunition which forced the Asantes to halt their plans for an attack on the protectorate.

The Fante Confederation had by now mustered support for an attack upon Elmina. For years the good relations between Asante and Elmina had been a thorn in the sides of the Fante and now with the recent treaty the Fante looked upon the Dutch and Elminas as one and decided to advance in force against them. The rage of the Fante was enhanced by the fact that Achiempon and his men, who had been so destructive in their march through Fantelands, were now guests of the king of Elmina and drawing food from the Dutch. In early 1870, the Fantes invaded Elmina territory and destroyed some sixty villages and laid waste to crops. The Dutch castle at Elmina was briefly besieged and although, under British political pressure, the Fantes did eventually withdraw, this was the last straw for the Dutch who had struggled to maintain their authority and peace since the treaty. The Dutch government began secret talks with the British to transfer the last of their holdings and responsibilities, including Elmina Castle, to them and finally to leave the Gold Coast after nearly 400 years of trading.

Initially, negotiations were at a local level between the Governor-General of the West African settlements, Sir Arthur Kennedy, and the Dutch Governor, Colonel Cornelis Nagtglas. To Kennedy's credit, the British seemed far more considerate of the position of the native tribes during these talks. First Kennedy sought an assurance that a transfer of Elmina Castle would not cause any disquiet with the Elminas people. He also sought clarification as to whether the Asante nation had a treaty or claim over the people of Elmina as well as seeking a definitive answer as to whether the ownership of the castle would require the British to pay an annual rent to Kumasi. In addition, the British Administrator of the Gold Coast, Herbert Taylor Ussher, stated that no serious negotiations could begin whilst Achiempon was still resident in Elmina and promised the Elminas the protection of the British flag once any transfer had taken place. On hearing of the Anglo-Dutch negotiations as to the future of Elmina, the Asante king wrote on 24 November 1870 to

Ussher to object to any possible transfer claiming that Elmina had 'from time immemorial paid annual tribute to my ancestors by right of arms' and that 'the Dutch delivered [Elmina] to Osei Tutu as his own'.[4] Naturally Ussher was perturbed to receive such a letter and again sought a reassurance from the Dutch that the Asante nation had no legal claim on Elmina or the castle there.

By the end of 1870 Nagtglas had responded to the points raised by the British and stated the Asante nation had no claim or treaty over Elmina. He claimed that the £80 paid annually to the Asante court was not paid as rent or a tribute, but as a gesture of friendship to encourage trade and that 'neither the King of Ashanti, nor his ancestor, have any right over the forts'.[5] Furthermore, Nagtglas stated that if the Elminas were given a small subsidy by the British that they would not object to the transfer. With these matters, apparently, resolved locally the negotiations moved to London and The Hague.

For the Dutch handing over suzerainty of their Gold Coast possessions to the British was part of a wider policy of entrenchment across the globe. The opening of the Suez Canal route in 1869 reinforced the Dutch government's view that colonial growth and expenditure should be concentrated upon the Dutch East Indies (modern day Indonesia) and that the Gold Coast was simply an unnecessary expense and distraction. The British continued to follow a contrary policy to its holdings in West Africa. With the members of the 1865 select committee, as well as other parliamentarians, still calling for entrenchment the government had made Sierra Leone the regional administrative hub and headquarters of the governor-in-chief for all the West African settlements with colonial administrators residing in the Gambia, Gold Coast and Lagos. Yet, despite the reduction in administration, when opportunities did arise for the British to leave the region they were not taken. The Colonial Secretary, Lord Kimberley, entered office in the summer of 1870, at a time when negotiations were well underway for Britain to cede the Gambia to France. Yet, Kimberley used the ongoing Franco-Prussian War as an excuse to suspend talks and later, in 1872, when there was a serious debate as to whether Britain should abandon Lagos, he sided with his Parliamentary Under Secretary at the Colonial Office, Edward Knatchbull-Hugessen, who stated that public opinion would not tolerate such a withdrawal.

Kimberley's predecessor as Colonial Secretary, Lord Granville, had, when the Liberal government under William Gladstone came to power in December 1868, seriously considered implementing the 1865 select committee's recommendation on withdrawal from the Gold Coast. Yet, the Anglo-Dutch partition had altered his mind and by 1871 the British were now set to sign a new treaty with the Dutch to take political and administrative control of the whole of the Gold Coast. Once reassurances were received from The Hague that Nagtglas's statements as to the positions of the Asante nation towards Elmina were indeed correct then the British government agreed to the Dutch proposal.

The convention for the transfer was signed on the 25 February 1871, but its ratification would take another year.

The Road to War

Although an agreement had been secured between London and The Hague there still remained several issues to resolve at a local level. There was concern over Asante intentions towards Elmina, the release of the captured missionaries from Kumasi and Britain's insistence that Achiempon be removed from Elmina before any formal ratification of the agreement could be made. To resolve these points would take several more months and, in retrospect, it seems apparent that the Asante king used this period to stall negotiations as much as possible to allow preparations for war to accelerate, and to resupply his army with arms and ammunition.

Having failed to persuade Achiempon to leave Elmina, the Dutch finally acted on 14 April 1871 and arrested him. The war chief was released the following month having sworn an oath to return to Kumasi within thirty days. He was rearrested in June having made no attempt to return to the Asante capital. Again, in retrospect, Achiempon was probably acting on the orders of the king to delay his return as long as possible and thereby frustrate the ratification of the treaty and allow his monarch more time to prepare for war. In January 1872, the patience of the Dutch, under pressure from the British, was finally exhausted and Achiempon was dragged on board a Dutch navy vessel and transported to Assin where it was hoped he would do no more mischief. Although this removed a major barrier to ratification, the war chief had no intention of easing the situation and in the following months he actively sought to spread dissatisfaction amongst the Dutch settlements in the west against the British takeover. In October the British reacted and under the orders of the Gold Coast Acting Administrator, C.S. Salmon, Colonel Foster, the Inspector General of Police, seized the chief and he was taken to Cape Coast Castle. Here he was held as a 'guest' of the British until early December. Achiempon was finally marched under a guard of armed police and conveyed across the frontier back into Asante where the British hoped he would cause no more difficulties.

At the same time as the Achiempon saga was playing out, the British were party to more theatre. To further reassure them that Kofi Karikari had no claim upon Elmina or the castle there, the Dutch produced 'An Apology', apparently with the monarch's official mark from the Kumasi court. In May 1871, the Dutch had sent Henry Plange, a native clerk in their employ, to the royal palace to try and secure a promise from the king to withdraw his claim to Elmina. Plange returned in September and presented the Dutch governor with the aforesaid 'Apology'. In turn the governor forwarded it to the Gold Coast Acting Administrator at Cape Castle, Salmon. The document was divided into six points and explained why Kofi Karikari had written to the British in 1870 to first announce his claim and went on to say that this had been incorrect and that he was now withdrawing his claim with an apology. Perhaps because they wanted the document to be genuine, the British were completely satisfied with it and the convention for the cession of the Dutch settlements was ratified on 17 February 1872. There is little doubt that the document was a forgery and it is interesting to speculate who would benefit from such an approach. There appear to be only two culprits; perhaps Plange wanting to enhance his own lowly position may have decided that his mission needed to be seen as a success when it had not been, or Plange could have been working directly under the orders of the Dutch authorities who were becoming more and more desperate to relinquish their responsibilities on the Gold Coast. Whatever was the truth behind the 'Apology', the one thing that is certain is that the British were convinced enough of its authenticity to agree to the treaty.

It was not only the British who were convinced by the 'Apology' for it also seems to have been a factor in reducing the dissatisfaction felt by the Elminas towards British rule, and their opposition diminished to something of a whimper. On 6 April 1872, the new Governor of the West African Settlements, John Pope Hennessy, arrived to formally take over the Dutch possession. For a payment of around £3,500 the British acquired Elmina Castle and its ordnance from the Dutch and with this payment the 274-year Dutch presence on the Gold Coast was brought to an end.

The new governor was immediately faced with enormous challenges; he had to pacify and reassure the people of Elmina that they would benefit from and receive the protection of British rule, he had to face up to growing demands from the Fante Confederation for some limited self-rule and determination which had come to the fore in 1871, and he had to stand up to any military threat from the Asante nation. Part of the latter problem, as he saw it, was to try and secure the release of the missionaries still held hostage in Kumasi. The government held a different view as the hostages were not British subjects and the governor would be criticised in London for involving the administration in such negotiations. In these issues Pope Hennessy miscalculated and displayed a high degree of incompetence in all his moves and deliberations. Indeed, it has been stated that he 'has strong claims to be regarded as the worst colonial governor of the nineteenth century'.[6]

Just when the political situation needed foresight and strength, Pope Hennessy decided upon a policy of appeasement, which was viewed by many, including the Asante, as weakness. On 20 April, the governor wrote to Kofi Karikari to inform him of the transfer of Dutch assets and responsibilities to the British and, on his own initiative, offered to double the annual payment previously made by the Dutch. Pope Hennessy followed this with gifts of lavish presents to the king as well as the release of Asante hostages, held at Cape Coast since the last Asante aggression of 1868. He even reversed C.S. Salmon's decision to close the trade route between the coast and Kumasi, which the colonial administrator had taken to limit the purchase and supply of arms to the Asante army. These gestures of appeasement by the governor seemed to have been designed to add and facilitate negotiations over the release of the missionaries. By doing so Pope Hennessy exceeded his own authority in the eyes of London. Furthermore, he showed poor judgement in sending Plange, previously in the pay of the Dutch and of dubious credentials, to Kumasi to lead the hostage negotiations.

Eight months of fruitless discussions now took place as to the price of the ransom. The amount initially demanded by Kofi Karikari was £4,000. This was later reduced to half that figure before an agreement of sorts was reached at £1,000. At one stage Pope Hennessy interjected and raised the issue as to whether the Basel Missionary Society should be paying, and this led to further delays all of which allowed the king more time for war preparations. At the point when the figure had been finally settled and the money was held at Cape Coast awaiting the arrival of the hostages, the Asante army was already beginning to plan its mobilisation for an invasion of the protectorate.

Kofi Karikari had never been in a strong position amongst his chiefs and advisors, or *Abrempon*, ever since he was appointed *Asantehene*. This weakness had initially stemmed from the funeral rituals that followed the death his predecessor, Kwaku Dua, at which, following centuries of tradition, a number of male slaves were executed to provide the king with attendants, or *Ahinkwa*, in the afterlife. At Kwaku Dua's funeral it is believed that up to 300 unfortunates were summarily executed. Accidentally, or more likely by design, Boachi Aso, a son of the dead king, arranged for the nephew of a rival, Asamoa Nkwanta, to be one of the unlucky 300. Asamoa Nkwanta was a powerful general who was thrown into a rage by the execution of his nephew and civil war was narrowly avoided by Boachi Aso's sudden departure from court. Kofi Karikari undoubtedly felt that to appease his generals he would need to strike a strong stance against the British. In addition, the missionary hostages provided him with a level of prestige amongst his chiefs and Pope Hennessy's weak negotiation style helped raise the Asante's perception of their own self-importance, which was additionally fuelled by rivalries amongst the chiefs for the king's favour, patronage and honour.

In the midst of a power struggle at court, in which the king was forced to play rivals off against each other to maintain his own authority, the transfer of Dutch possessions, particularly Elmina Castle, to the British was an opportunity for Kofi Karikari to assert his kingship. Not only did the Asantes feel humiliation at the loss of authority over Elmina they were concerned that, with the departure of the Dutch, they could lose vital trading outlets which would hinder their ability to purchase arms and ammunition. In addition, whilst the Dutch had not been averse to looking the other way when it came to the continued presence of slave trading, the abolitionist British would not, and this in itself threatened the power of the Asante nation. Of all the factors which led the Asantes to attack the protectorate, the transfer of Elmina to the British was the leading one.

Kofi Karikari had cleverly used the time bought by the hostage negotiations as well as the delays in removing his uncle, the warlike chief Achiempon, from the protectorate, to resupply his army with arms and ammunition. The king, surrounded as he was by chiefs spoiling for a chance of self-aggrandisement through war, was listening to confident voices. He was repeatedly reassured that the British could not fight in the jungle or survive the climate. At a council meeting on 22 October 1872, Kofi Karikari was confronted with demands from his chiefs that they must invade the protectorate to defend their position and honour. It was recorded that the king replied, 'If you go, I go with you.'[7]

Invasion

Even as the British were in the process of conveying Achiempon back to Asante, the king and his chiefs had begun the invasion. Having filled and then drained the skull of Sir Charles McCarthy in a symbolic toast to victory, Kofi Karikari ordered his armies to march. The plan was for a three-pronged attack. The first force, under the command of Edu Baffuo, had left Kumasi on 9 December and the 4–5,000 warriors marched on the western flank in a divisionary attack upon the Wassa and Denkyira tribes. The main army, of 12,000–20,000 troops, under the command of Amankwa Tia, marched south for the coast a week later. A third, smaller force, under the leadership of the king of Marawere, moved the following month, with orders to keep the Akim peoples engaged so that they might not join forces with the Fantes.

The invasion came as a complete surprise, not just for the politicians in London, but also those British officials at Cape Coast. The main Asante army reached the Prah River on 22 January 1873, where, due to the size of the force, the crossing took five days. News that the Asante force had been engaged by local tribes reached the British on 29 January and an emergency meeting of the legislative council was assembled by Colonel Harley, who had recently replaced Salmon. The council decided to despatch a meagre force of Hausa police north as a show of solidarity with the Fante chiefs and arrangements were made for the issue of a small number of arms, along with ammunition to the allied chiefs. Harley also recommended to Pope Hennessy that the small force of 171 professional soldiers from the West Indies Regiment should be reinforced from Sierra Leone. Yet, the governor did not immediately act on this request for, continuing his propensity for misreading situations, he declared that he thought the invasion had been exaggerated and wrote to London stating: 'I need scarcely convey the profound astonishment with which I have received these tidings, as nothing but the most amicable relations have existed between this Government and Ashanti for some time; and assurances of lasting peace and goodwill have been sent down by the king ever since my assumption of government'.[8] The British governor had been completely deceived by the Asante king. He was relieved of his post a few weeks later and was despatched as governor to a rather unfortunate Bahamas.

Pope Hennessy's successor, Major R.W. Keate also failed to act upon Harley's recommendations for he believed that the Asantes would not dare attack the British and informed the Fantes that they could not rely on British military support and that 'they must depend on their own exertions'.[9] Keate became yet another victim of 'The White Man's Grave' for he died on 17 March, within weeks of arriving on the Gold Coast. Harley became acting governor and, although he clearly showed a disdain bordering on racism towards the locals, his undiplomatic approach was, after the previous administrations, at least decisive. He arrested and then banished to Sierra Leone the King of Elmina, Kobina Gyan, whom he considered to be at the centre of pro-Asante elements in the area, and ordered troops and armed police to be sent from Sierra Leone and Lagos. Yet, despite dispiriting news of battlefield reversals the Colonial Office continued to procrastinate over whether more military support should be sent.

Amongst the Fantes it seems to have been accepted that it was the cession of Elmina Castle that had precipitated the war. The King of Abrah, near Cape Coast, stated that, 'the causes and purposes of these inroads of the Ashantis are the cession of the Elmina fort, and the Elminas having become British subjects; because the king of Ashanti says that from time immemorial his ancestors ate and drank at Elmina and that the fort is theres: therefore he will come and take it by force of arms'.[10] From the Asante point of view, considerations of pride, power and prestige all seemed to demand a challenge to the cession. Yet, for the *ultimate* cause of the war it may be necessary to look elsewhere. The Asantes still felt there was unfinished business from 1863–4 and there remained a desire to avenge the defeat of Dodowa, for this humiliation still burnt in Asante hearts.

The main Asante army was pedestrian in its southwards move towards the coast. The force included many wives and children of warriors, which slowed progress and retribution and pillaging became the priority. Towns were taken and burnt, yet crops were left to be gathered by the troops on their possible return. Skirmishes between scouts were frequent, but the hastily collected forces of Assin warriors fell back as the Asantes continued to head south. The first major engagement was on 9 February 1873 when the Assin camp at Yancommassie Assin was stormed and occupied. The allies now fell back and concentrated 35 miles further south at Yancommassie Fanti. Here the allies prepared to face the Asante invasion force.

On the morning of 10 March, the allies, including a Lieutenant Hopkins, who commanded a company of Hausas, awoke to see the Asante army in front of the camp. Completely surprised by the sudden presence of the enemy, the allies sent out scouts to probe the enemy's position. The Asantes failed to respond and sensing that an attack was not imminent the allied chiefs allowed their troops to prepare breakfast. Suddenly shots rang out and the main body of the Asante army rushed forward. This rapid move caused some of the forward allied troops to retreat in disorder and within minutes the Asantes had broken through and were attacking the allies from both front and rear. Only the Assin and Denkyira tribes, along with Hopkins and his small detachment, stood their ground. Eventually even these troops buckled, and the allied force fled back to the coast in disarray.

Fortunately, the Asante commander, Amankwa Tia, decided to now allow his army to rest and recuperate and the victory was not immediately followed up. Even so, the main Asante force was now encamped within just 30 miles of the coast. The allies had to act and, reinforced with 100 men of the West Indies Regiment, the forces reassembled and concentrated at the village of Dunkwa, just 4 miles south of the Asante position. Despite some not so polite urgings from Harley that the allies should attack, they remained on the defensive. This allowed Amankwa Tia to receive much-needed supplies of ammunition and Edu Baffuo and his troops, victorious from defeating the Wassa and Denkyira on their diversionary attack, to join the main army.

In the early morning of 8 April the Asantes attacked the Fante camp upon its whole 6-mile length, but on this occasion there was to be no retreat. The fighting was bitter but for the Fantes, who bore the brunt of the assault, it was the first time in their history that they successfully beat back an Asante attack. The Hausa company, who had received some criticism for their conduct at the Battle of Yancommassie Fanti, fought bravely and suffered seventeen killed and wounded. The battle was a stalemate and although the Asante withdrew slightly, the allies held the field. Hopkins pleaded with the allied chiefs to follow up their success and go on the offensive. Promises of such action were made, but no attack was forthcoming.

The two forces remained in place until the morning of 14 April when once again the Asantes attacked. Fierce fighting raged from 8am to 7pm and although severely pressed, the allies held their ground. The Asantes concentrated their assault upon the centre of the Fante line and it was indeed fortunate that the Acting Inspector of Police, a Mr Loggie, formerly of the Royal Artillery, had placed a battery of rockets there and these instruments tipped the battle in favour of the allies. Despite this success, Hopkins was still unable to get the allies to advance and darkness coupled with a lack of ammunition saw the battle grind to a stalemate. Both the allies and the Asantes had taken high casualties and it seems that Amankwa Tia was contemplating a withdrawal. Yet, daybreak revealed that the Fantes had decided to retreat en masse and Hopkins's protestations failed to stop the movement back towards the coast. He and his remaining Hausas formed a rear guard as the allies walked off the battlefield. Amankwa Tia now contented himself with forming a large camp at Dunkwa and here his force remained for nearly month during which it was resupplied.

News of the Dunkwa debacle reached London in early May and initiated an immediate change in the attitude of the British public to the Asante threat and a shift in the Colonial Office's approach to how the Asante menace should be contained. Ever since March a debate had been raging in Whitehall as to how the British government should respond to the Asante threat. On one hand, Knatchbull-Hugessen, the Parliamentary Under Secretary at the Colonial Office, was very bullish and felt strongly that the Asantes should 'receive a severe lesson' to deter future aggression.[11] However, the Colonial Secretary, Lord Kimberley, was weary of making any commitment that might detract from the 1865 policy of non-intervention. When questioned in the House of Lords on 7 March 1873, he simply stated that he did not know why the Asante had invaded.

On 10 March, inspired by Harley's more direct approach, Kimberley agreed that the Fante should be roused to more aggressive action and arranged for food supplies and arms to be sent by the Royal Navy to Cape Coast. Yet, he clung on to the policy of non-intervention, despite Knatchbull-Hugessen becoming even more vocal in his calls for direct action to be taken. By May, with news of the retreat at Dunkwa along with reports which seemed to indicate that other former Dutch settlements would rise up in rebellion if the Asantes appeared to be in ascendency, the need for some sort of action became more apparent. Kimberley received news from Harley that the Asante king had stated in writing that the cause of the invasion was the cession of Elmina and with this confirmation a conference was called in the War Office on 10 May. The principal attendees were Kimberley, Robert Herbert, the Permanent Under Secretary of the Colonial Office, Edward Cardwell, the Secretary of State for War, and George Goschen, the First Lord of the Admiralty. The meeting concluded with the decision to despatch immediately 100 Royal Marines to the Gold Coast and to transfer a further 4 companies of the West Indies Regiment from Barbados.

As the month progressed the need for a firm policy towards the Gold Coast became more pressing. The commanding officer at Cape Coast, Captain Brett, wrote to the War Office stating that defence of the forts along the coast was becoming more difficult as the surrounding lands were swollen with refugees from the Asante invasion. Brett sought clarification on the government's position as to military intervention and upon reading the correspondence Kimberley noted in his journal, 'The Ashantee war begins to look very troublesome', and furthermore he warned the Prime Minister, William Gladstone, that he felt the matter would need to be debated in the Cabinet.[12] Yet, Kimberley remained defiant that there would not be a change of policy and wrote on 28 May, 'If we wish to weaken ourselves we cannot adopt a better course than to spend a few millions in conquering Ashentee, and establishing a West African Empire. It is to be hoped that no Govt. will be mad enough to embark on so extravagant an enterprise.'[13] Brett was thus informed that the policy of non-intervention would remain.

For much of June the situation upon the Gold Coast, as seen from London, appeared to be much more stable. Little news was forthcoming, and the government seemed to be working on the assumption that 'no news is good news'. There were strong hopes that the Asante armies would retire, and that intervention would be avoided. Yet, in reality, events on the Gold Coast were very much turning against the British.

In early June, Amankwa Tia led the main Asante force on to Jukwa, 14 miles to the south west of Dunkwa. It seems clear that the Asante commander felt that in securing the town his troops would be able to obtain food from the nearby Elminas and the army would have an easy approach to Elmina itself and all the supplies that the coast would have to offer. Harley realised that this move should be opposed and with the assistance of Dr Rowe, the colonial surgeon who was acting as a liaison officer and special commissioner, the allied force, including the Cape Coast militia, concentrated at Jukwa on 4 June. The Asante army, reported to be up to 30,000-strong, attacked the following day and the allies buckled without offering any real resistance and fled to the coast. One of the first to flee the battlefield was Quasi Kaye, the king of the Denkyira tribe, and it was his actions that seems to have started a mass panic, which spread from the warriors to civilians. The roads to both Cape Coast Castle and Elmina Castle were soon packed as troops, men, women and children fled panic-stricken. The lands surrounding both forts were soon overwhelmed by thousands of refugees.

On 7 June, allied chiefs, government officials, Captain Blake, the senior naval officer present, and Captain Brett, commanding the 2nd West Indies Regiment, assembled at Cape Coast Castle for a meeting of the legislative council. Harley attempted to impress upon the chiefs that all was not lost, and that resistance must continue. He stated that they still had the support of the government, that arms and ammunitions would be forthcoming and that if they could form another camp, and resolved to fight, then he felt that the Asantees could still be beaten back. Little came from the meeting and certainly no decision was agreed to re-assemble the army. Later that day Harley received news from Elmina Castle that the locals were growing increasingly aggressive and that Asante scouts had been seen on the outskirts of the town.

Harley finally had some good news late on 7 June when HMS *Barracouta*, Captain Fremantle commanding, was seen off the coast. Onboard were the 110 Royal Marines, commanded by Lieutenant Colonel Francis Festing of the Royal Marine Artillery. Harley realised that at last he could go on the offensive. The Royal Marines were disembarked at Cape Coast Castle on 9 June and Festing assumed command of all troops on the coast. After talks with Harley it was agreed that Elmina was at biggest risk and on 10 June Festing, along with Dr Rowe and Captain Fremantle and the Royal Marine contingent, headed there to use the castle as their base of operations.

On arrival the British discovered those inhabitants loyal to the former king had been supplying the Asante army and the mood in the town was danger-ous and uncertain. On 12 June the British declared martial law in the town and its surrounds and a demand was made for the inhabitants in these areas to hand over any arms in their possession to the authorities. The operation to enforce martial law was planned for dawn on 13 June and Festing marched out of the castle with a detachment of Royal Marines, Hausas and troops from the 2nd West Indies Regiment. The proclamation was read out and required the delivery of arms within 2 hours. At 10.30am, with no arms forthcoming, a second proclamation was read aloud stating that the town had 1 hour for women, children and unarmed men to leave after which, and if arms had not been surrendered, a bombardment of the town would commence. At a little after noon, with the numbers of armed men in the town increasing, Festing gave the order to commence the bombardment. Artillery on the battlements of the castle opened fire and rockets shot out. In addition, shell fire from naval vessels, including the *Barracouta*, poured into the town.

The bombardment lasted for around 20 minutes and the town was set on fire in several places. Armed men were spotted running through the flames and orders were sent to the Hausas and West Indies troops to pursue them. These soldiers were soon under fire and in moments the commanding position of Fort St Jago, from where the Dutch had besieged the Portuguese in 1637, was full of Asante warriors, estimated at 2–3,000 in number. The enemy then descended through the bush to the west of the town and extended their right towards the sea. Festing saw his opportunity and with all the forces available, around 500 troops, he advanced out of the castle and along the beach towards the Asantes, before they could properly form up for an attack. Firing as they advanced, the British drove the Asantes for nearly 3 miles, killing between twenty and thirty of the enemy for the loss of one soldier.

The British retired to the castle where they were able to grab a meal. Yet, the Asante had not given up in their attempts and Festing soon received reports that a large enemy force was advancing from a northerly direction upon the loyal quarter of the town. Again, Festing led his men out and the

Asante were discovered boldly crossing a piece of open ground. Mr Loggie, who now commanded the Hausas, was directed to advance against the warriors, with support from the West Indies troops and the Royal Marines. The British were outnumbered six to one and it was not long before the British right flank was in danger. Fortunately, a Lieutenant Wells RN had disembarked sailors from the *Barracouta* and arrived on the extreme right just as the Asante were pushing forward. From the cover of a garden wall, Wells's men poured a heavy fire into the warriors who staggered back under the unexpected assault. Festing now ordered his whole line to advance and in a running fight the British pushed the Asante back across the plain. Although some warriors tried to make a stand, the British fire was too much and the main body fled back into the cover of the bush, leaving more than 200 of their dead comrades behind. The British had lost only one man and Festing had the sense not to pursue the enemy into the jungle. Although the British had secured Elmina, the Asante threat remained.

The lack of news from the Gold Coast had lulled London into thinking that the Asante problem had lessened. In truth, two mail ships had been lost on their return from West Africa and it was not until 10 July that the government learnt of the rout at Jukwa and fighting at Elmina. British troops had come directly under Asante attack and this was something that neither the government nor the British public could accept without some form retaliation. On hearing of the news from Elmina, Kimberley wrote, 'An end to all the peace and quiet for the unlucky Colonial Office.'[14]

British Plans and Preparations

Kimberley now realised that the time for action had come. At a meeting at the War Office on 15 July he pressed for the despatch of an additional 200 Royal Marines who duly sailed the following day. In a definite escalation of the situation the military authorities agreed to place an infantry battalion on standby. In parallel to government meetings, public opinion was being steered towards the possibility of direct military intervention. On the day the Royal Marines departed *The Times* questioned whether General Charles Gordon, 'Chinese Gordon', should be sent to the Gold Coast based on his proven ability in raising local forces.

Harley sent further despatches to the Colonial Office in which he described the difficulties of raising the local Fantes to oppose the Asante, and Kimberley instructed Harley to inform the loyal chiefs that they would receive further British support with which to defend themselves. On 26 July he wrote to the Minster of War, Edward Cardwell, seeking his advice and outlining the problematic nature of how a decision for intervention might be made:

The question seems to be: can active measures be taken against the Ashantee during the rainy season? If so, within what limits, and of what nature? Of course if the Ashantee attack our forts, the course is simple, to repel them, but if they do not attack what then? We cannot leave them quietly in occupation of the Protectorate. Public opinion would not allow us to do so, if we ourselves desired it: and all the trade of our settlements is practically destroyed by the presence of the invading force, so that if things are left in their present position, the settlements will be merely a heavy burden on the Imperial Treasury. Are we to contemplate an attack on Coomassie and could we assemble a force sufficient enough for the purpose?[15]

Cardwell and Kimberley met two days later to investigate various possible lines of action. Yet, when Kimberley wrote to Harley on 30 July he announced that the government had not yet committed to any course and that he should maintain the pressure upon the Fantes to resist the Asantes. Discussions had taken place between Commander John Glover RN and both the War Office and the Admiralty as to how supplies might be taken up the Prah River in the event of an assault upon Kumasi and Glover had met with Cardwell on 29 July. At this meeting Glover suggested to the War Office that he lead an expedition up the Volta to attack the Asantes in the flank and rear. The following day, probably with Cardwell's encouragement, Glover met with Kimberley to offer his services and two days later the Colonial Office received Cabinet approval for the Glover expedition. Kimberley again met with Glover on 4 August where he confirmed his appointment. Working with a budget of £15,000, he would utilise a small group of special service officers and local tribesmen for his expedition. Kimberley was aware that Glover's expedition would have to be kept from the House of Commons at this stage for fear of jeopardising military plans and Kimberley was also aware that a direct assault across the Prah River might soon need to be considered. Yet, for all these apparent behind the scenes moves, Glover's role would always be secondary to any direct assault upon Kumasi and here it seems that the plotting and planning was even more intriguing.

It appears that Cardwell and Kimberley were now working quietly to prepare for such a direct assault, without consulting the prime minister. Furthermore, it seems very likely that discussions had been taking place since the news of the Jukwa and Elmina battles was received on 10 July as to whether and how the government might intervene. Sir Garnet Wolseley had already achieved notoriety for successfully leading a campaign against the Metis rebels in Canada in 1870, known as the Red River Expedition. The campaign was seen as a model of logistical planning and one in which not one British soldier was lost. Wolseley was a veteran of the Second Burmese War, the Crimean War, the Indian Mutiny and the Second Opium War. He was the author of the *Soldier's Pocket Book*, which was first published in 1871. This work was basically a field manual for the British army. Wolseley later served in South Africa, Egypt and the Sudan, and would eventually become commander-in-chief of the British army. He was a rare breed in the Victorian army – a thinking soldier, who prided himself in ensuring every detail was considered, especially when on active service. During his incredibly successful and brave night-time assault upon the Egyptian position at Tel El Kebir (13 September 1882) Wolseley overlooked the fact that there was a brief lunar eclipse on that night which covered the ground in total darkness for a few moments and caused some confusion on the line of march. He never forgave himself for he strongly felt that he had let his men down.

Apart from being meticulous in his planning he was also a very ambitious man and he clearly saw the news from the Gold Coast as a personal opportunity. Evelyn Wood, who was to join Wolseley in the fight against the Asante, recorded in his autobiography that he visited Wolseley at the War Office in May 1873 and found him hunched over Dutch maps of Asante and the two men discussed the apparent logistical difficulties of crossing the Prah with a large force. Wolseley also stated to Wood that in Asante was 'a King there who required a lesson to bring him to a sense of the power of England'.[16] This was of course weeks before the Asante assault upon Elmina.

It seems clear that Wolseley was planning a direct assault upon Kumasi as early as May 1873 with the knowledge or approval of the War Office, and specifically of the minster, Cardwell. Indeed, in his own autobiography, *A Soldier's Life*, Wolseley wrote, 'Mr Cardwell had in confidence already informed me that he would like me to go there should it be determined to undertake active operations against the invading Ashanti . . . I submitted privately to Mr Cardwell a rough outline of a military scheme . . .'.[17] The plan assumed that Wolseley be appointed to the governorship of the Gold Coast and that he would be allowed to relinquish the position and return to England at the end of operations. He also requested that he should be able to pick a small group of special service officers with which to train and raise a force from the local tribes to drive the Asante army back across the Prah. Wolseley stated frankly that he envisaged the need for two battalions of British regulars to march upon Kumasi. Wolseley was to write in later life that he had felt a lasting peace with a warrior nation such as the Asantes could only be achieved once they had been utterly defeated in battle and any other solution 'was merely the wild dream of timid men'.[18]

Wolseley also strongly believed if the British did not beat the Asantes in battle and take Kumasi then they could expect further conflict in other West African settlements. Victory had to be secured by white troops or all the tribes would continue to believe that the British dare not push towards the Prah for fear of death and extermination in the jungle. Alan Lloyd has written that neither the Fantes or Asantes saw the British as great warriors and the idea of white men marching through the forest and going into battle like ordinary warriors seemed preposterous to the majority of the locals on the Gold Coast. Kofi Karikari is recorded as having asked one visitor to Kumasi, 'Do white men now how to travel to fight?'[19]

Cardwell sent the outline of the plan to Kimberley *before* the Cabinet meeting of 2 August at which the prime minister agreed to Glover's expedition and stated to Kimberley that Wolseley was ready to take Kumasi if the order was given.[20] For all the reluctance shown by Cardwell in 1865, when he was Colonial Secretary, to use British troops, and Kimberley earlier in 1873, both men had now realised that if Kumasi was to be taken it was highly probable that British soldiers would have to be deployed upon the Gold Coast. Both men knew the risks of the climate, and it says much for their trust and respect for Wolseley's plan that they would contemplate such a move. After the war Kimberley recorded that he never doubted for a moment that British troops would eventually be sent to the Gold Coast.[21]

Thus, the Wolseley plan had two firm supporters in Cardwell and Kimberley and both politicians gave Wolseley their tacit support to carry on planning the operation, whilst at the same time keeping their intrigues from the prime minister. Wolseley's plan was not the only one under consideration for Sir Andrew Clarke, the Director of Works at the Admiralty, had also submitted a proposal. Unlike the Wolseley plan, Clarke was adamantly against the use of British troops and asked that he be given a free hand to make a settlement with Kofi Karikari. Although the full details of the plan have been lost (perhaps deliberately), it seems that after any war Clarke proposed that the protectorate be handed back to the local tribes. Whilst Prime Minister Gladstone might have preferred such an approach, Clarke had left England in the early summer of 1873 to accept an overseas posting and was not at hand to promote his views in person and Kimberley was not about to bring the Clarke plan to the fore. The colonial secretary now had the difficult task of persuading Gladstone of the merits of the Wolseley plan.

Whilst it appears a tacit agreement had been made between Cardwell, Kimberley and Wolseley by early August 1873 it would take another two months before the despatch of British battalions to the Gold Coast was officially sanctioned. The Cabinet dispersed with the closing of Parliament for the summer recess and certainly most of its members were unaware of the Wolseley plan. Kimberley briefed Gladstone in early August and apparently the prime minister was most displeased that the plan had been so advanced. Whilst Wolseley had realised from the start that British troops would be required at some point, Cardwell and Kimberley hoped that a peace settlement might be reached before such an eventuality, but both politicians were under no illusions that the despatch of British soldiers was likely and Kimberley did have the grace to tell Gladstone so. The prime minister still insisted that Wolseley must only request British troops if he felt them to be absolutely necessary.

Whilst the political debate raged on for several more weeks, Wolseley, with the local rank of major general (the youngest general in the British army at the time), was officially appointed as administrator and commander-in-chief on the Gold Coast on 13 August, and now at least he had been given the green light to press on with his own plans for the first stage of the operation. He realised that if the British had any hope of transforming the local tribes into an effective force with which to help defeat the Asante he would require special service officers of the highest calibre in terms of physical strength, intelligence, commitment and ability to display initiative. As soon as his appointment was announced he was besieged with applications from officers who were desperate to join the expedition. Yet, it is clear from the final twenty-seven who were chosen that many had already been selected in Wolseley's mind at least, probably as early as May 1873. Although given free rein to pick from the officer corps as a whole, several had already served alongside Wolseley in the Red River Expedition. These included Captains Redvers Buller, George Huyshe and Colonel John McNeil VC, who would be Wolseley's chief of staff in Asante. Wolseley considered McNeil 'daring, determined, self-confident and indefatigable'.[22] These were just the qualities Wolseley was looking for in all of his special service officers.

In addition to these men, some, such as Evelyn Wood VC, had already come to Wolseley's attention and almost all were to distinguish themselves in future years. For example, Wood would reach the rank of field marshal whilst General Buller would later command British forces in South Africa in 1899. Four of the twenty-seven were or would become holders of the Victoria Cross. The careers of these men often followed Wolseley's patronage, so much so that they became known in later years as 'The Ashanti Ring'. However, not all those who journeyed out to the Gold Coast were so carefully selected. One in particular, Lieutenant Arthur Eyre of the 90th Regiment, was personally recommended by Wood to Wolseley as Eyre was 'the son of a good soldier, his mother is a Lady'.[23] This was apparently sufficient for Wolseley and Eyre did indeed join the expedition. Wood's other request that his soldier valet join him was politely rejected by Cardwell on the grounds of the dangerous climate.

Wolseley, perhaps with the certainty that British troops would be called upon, shared his views with Cardwell as to the composition of the two battalions he would require. He proposed to select the twelve best battalions then currently stationed in Britain and from these take only volunteers with no man under two years' service to be accepted. Every man would be medically inspected and only the strongest would be taken to face the rigours of the climate. Wolseley suggested that the engineers and artillery men be selected in a similar manner. He also requested that these men should be ready for service upon the Gold Coast from 1 December 1873. For once Wolseley did not get his own way for Cardwell would not accept either the date or the composition of the battalions. The minister of war argued there was no precedent for such a course, that the traditions of the British service were contrary to it and that such a scheme would undermine the very nature of the British regimental system. Wolseley was informed that the next two battalions on the roster for foreign service would be informed of the possible requirement for active service in West Africa and that they would be brought up to full strength and readiness for service. These were the 23rd Royal Welsh Fusiliers and the second battalion of the Rifle Brigade.

Not deterred, Wolseley submitted his requirements for supplies, which were of course extensive and detailed, and included 9lb rockets, 12-pounder mountain howitzers, 4,000 Snider rifles and 3,200,000 rounds of ammunition. The Snider rifle had first seen active service in Abyssinia in 1867–8 during the expedition against Emperor Tewodros who had taken European hostages and was holding them in the citadel at Magdala. It was an adaption of the highly successful Enfield rifle that had been so effective in the Crimean War and the Indian Mutiny, as well as seeing widespread service in the American Civil War. The Enfield displayed both an impressive range combined with accuracy, yet it was a muzzle-loading rifle and therefore slow to load and reload particularly in battle-field conditions. As Britain's European rivals began to introduce breech-loading rifles in the 1860s, which could be loaded faster, the British responded by mod-ifying their stocks of Enfield rifles by adapting them to breech loaders from a design by Jacob Snider. A 2.5in length was cut away from the Enfield breech and into the trough a right-handed steel block was inserted. This consisted of a claw extractor which was incorporated into the breech mechanism, with a striker operated by the original Enfield hammer. The extractor partially pulled the new centre-fire cartridge out of the open breech and with a swift arm movement, the used cartridge was discarded by turning the rifle upside down. Whilst the rate of fire from the Enfield was, at best, three or four rounds by minute, the Snider could achieve eight or ten aimed rounds by minute. The Asante army had already experienced the murderous fire of the Snider at Elmina and would suffer further from it in later battles. For the British the Snider gave them a huge technological advantage over the Asante's 'Long Danes'.

No mention was made in Wolseley's list of requirements for supply or pack animals as during his research Wolseley realised that both horses and mules would not survive the climate for long and that all stores would have to be carried by native porters. The need for large numbers of such, both men and women, was to become the largest logistical problem of the entire expedition. Wolseley also provided exact designs for kits and dress for the troops. He personally designed a simple grey uniform of strong serge for both officers and men which would allow for freer circulation of air than the traditional uniforms and would reduce the risk of heat exhaustion. The officers were to be provided with Norfolk jackets, pantaloons, gaiters and shooting boots, cork helmets and puggarees, with which to shield exposed necks from the worst of the sun. Swords were to remain in Britain and sword bayonets and revolvers alone were to be employed. Men were to be issued with helmets, smock-frocks, trousers and long sailors' boots. They were to be armed with the short Snider rifle and a sword bayonet. Wolseley even designed a special harness so that the artillery pieces could be efficiently and comfortably pulled through the bush by native allies.

Wolseley's in-depth planning and research convinced him that if British troops were to be deployed on the Gold Coast, which he was certain they would be, then the most serious enemy the British troops faced was to be the climate. He knew that any campaign must be completed during the healthiest months of the year, between December and March, when a hot dry wind blows down from the Sahara Desert and there is little or no rain. Wolseley also planned for his men to spend as little time as possible on land and envisaged that they would begin to march north from the coast on the day they disembarked. The route must be completed as far forward as possible, hopefully up to the Prah River, the boundary into the Asante nation. Staging posts, with enough raised beds and canteen facilities, would have to be constructed along the way. Sanitary precautions must be undertaken, and ammunition was to be taken forward of the advancing troops. There was to be no slow baggage convoy to hinder the march. This work was to be undertaken by local tribes, under the guidance of the special service officers so as to avoid any unnecessary delay or fatigue for the British troops, whose role would be to spearhead any attack across the Prah. A native carrier was to be assigned to every three soldiers to assist in the carrying of equipment, which included salt, veils and cholera belts (worn in an attempt to keep the stomach warm, which at the time was considered a way of warding off cholera and dysentery). A dose of quinine was given to each man before the start of the day's march in either his tea or hot chocolate, to deter malaria. When British battalions were eventually disembarked upon the Gold Coast strict health guidelines were issued to all men, which included the need to keep heads covered from the sun at all times, to avoid direct contact with damp earth and that sleeping just a few inches off the ground was essential to preserve health.

The reputation of the Gold Coast as 'The White Man's Grave' had clearly influenced Wolseley's planning and his precautions to preserve the health of his troops were dramatically justified when news of the fate of the Royal Marines who had fought at Elmina in June was learnt. Of these 104 troops, by 26 July only 44 were effective. It was decided to invalid home most of the detachment on board the *Himalaya*. Ten men unfortunately died during the transit back to England and a further fifty-eight were admitted to hospital on their arrival. Both Wolseley and the government must have been seriously concerned that they might be defeated by the climate rather than the Asantes.

Whilst Wolseley planned and Cardwell and Kimberley schemed to get Gladstone, their Cabinet colleagues and the British public to agree to the expedition, the situation on the Gold Coast remained chaotic. After the Asante army had clashed with British forces at Elmina it became clear to Amankwa Tia that his troops could not face the British Snider rifle fire in the open nor could they possibly storm Elmina Castle or Cape Coast Castle. The Elmina action also convinced the Elmina peoples of the supremacy of British firepower and they reconsidered their support for the Asantes. Amankwa Tia was forced to pull back his army from the coast and a main camp was established at Mampon. Both the Asante warriors and their adversaries upon the coast suffered during the months of July and August for the rains were unusually servere in 1873. Mampon camp was soon insanitary and smallpox and dysentery reduced and weakened the ranks of the Asante army, as many warriors either died or were invalided back to Kumasi. For the British, it was not only the Royal Marines who were struck down by sickness but even a large number of the West Indies and Hausa troops were ill due to the climate. Dr Home arrived on the coast on 28 June and he was very heavily engaged throughout the summer months as the casualty list rose higher and higher. Colonel Harley was even forced to hand over the drawing room in Government House at Cape Castle as a temporary hospital.

Yet, despite the dwindling number of effective troops Colonel Festing tried constantly to improve the military position he now faced, as well as demonstrating to the local allied tribes that the British were still very much committed to opposing the Asante invasion. The biggest difficulty he faced was the lack of accurate intelligence as to the whereabouts of the enemy. Small detachments were frequently sent out from both Elmina Castle and Cape Coast Castle to try and confirm reports about the whereabouts of Asante troops, but these missions were often unsuccessful as the local intelligence proved defective, if not totally useless. The British soon realised that the information received from Fante spies could not be relied upon because it was discovered these men would frequently hide in the bush and return days later having falsified their reports or would simply report back what they thought the British wished to hear. It was only with the arrival of the *Himalaya* with 13 officers and 360 men of the 2nd West Indies Regiment that Festing could really plan any sort of offensive action. With these troops came a Lieutenant A.H. Gordon of the 98th Foot who had volunteered for active service and had attached himself to the West Indies troops. On 10 July Gordon was appointed commandant of the Hausa troops and adjutant of armed police and he was soon to display enormous energy in these roles.

Within days Gordon was leading numerous marches to assess the strength and position of the Asantes along the coast. Although none of these reconnaissance missions made contact with the enemy in any large numbers, they did at least serve to harass the Asante constantly and many camps were discovered recently abandoned. Later, under the orders of Festing, Gordon raised two redoubts, 'Napoleon' and 'Abbaye', covering Cape Coast and Elmina, a distance of 6 miles from each respectively, which first and foremost offered an early warning of any possible Asante attack upon the castles. Both were completed by late August and manned by troops from the 2nd West Indies Regiment. Napoleon allowed Gordon to patrol the immediate area more readily and on a near daily basis Asante scouts were captured and forwarded to Cape Coast Castle for interrogation. Abbaye was strategically located to stop communication between the Asante camp at Mampon and Elmina and its construction restored a large portion of agricultural land back to the Fantes for cultivation.

In late August Harley wrote to Lord Kimberely to state that if the British were to reassert their authority and prestige upon the Gold Coast then they must go on the offensive and that Kumasi would have to be taken. Whilst the plan submitted by Harley was militarily somewhat naïve and clearly underestimated the distance and difficulty of the march to Kumasi, it did at least reaffirm the thinking of Kimberley, Cardwell and Wolseley that to asssert British sovereignty a march upon Kumasi would probably be essential. Harley's letter raised the need for British troops to be involved in the undertaking and this must also have pleased the triumvirate in London. Colonel Festing felt that he had to respond to some of the inconsistencies and errors in Harley's letter and his own musing stressed, again, the need for British troops and emphasized the difficulty the soldiers would face with the climate. Festing offered suggestions as to how the possible health risks might be overcome and when Wolseley finally arrived on the Gold Coast and reviewed Festing's plans he was struck how similar they were to his own.

Both Harley and Festing were determined to continue to take the fight to the Asantes and at a council meeting on 5 September, at which Captain Fremantle RN was also present, it was decided that Festing would lead a local force from Abbaye to attack Mampon, supported by Hausa and West Indies troops, as well as Royal Marines. Yet, this offensive never took place. Harley promised a native force of 5,000 warriors but scarcely a hundred could be raised and, with the arrival of Glover, Festing received orders to release the Hausa detachments into Glover's command for the latter's expedition up the Volta River. Furthermore, news was received from London of Wolseley's imminent departure and that he would be assuming command upon the Gold Coast. Wolseley requested that no major military activities were undertaken against the Asante army until he had arrived to assess the situation. Even though Harley and Festing had been frustrated, the British continued to do what they could to harass the Asantes, gather intelligence and prepare for Wolseley's arrival.

One point that Festing stressed in his own plan for the advance upon Kumasi was the need for a road to be constructed to ease the movement of British troops. Festing thus ordered Gordon to work with Fante labourers, to begin the road to Kumasi, widening the bush-path as far as Mansu, about halfway to the Prah. This was a most daring enterprise, for the Asantes might at any time have cut him off from the coast. On his arrival in early October, Wolseley was informed that the road had been constructed to within a mile of the former Fante camp at Yancommassie Fanti. On learning of Gordon's enterprise and endeavours, Sir Garnet at once placed Gordon on his list of special service officers.

In London, Kimberley and Cardwell still worked to gain the support of Cabinet colleagues, as well as the prime minster for the Wolseley plan. At a meeting in Whitehall in early September there was some minor disagreements over the terms of any likely peace treaty, which rather bizarrely focused on whether a deal should insist upon the ending of human sacrifice with Gladstone actually arguing that such acts were not recognised as crimes in Africa. The matter was resolved with Kimberley suggesting that Wolseley should urge the king to end such atrocities. Gladstone also felt that Wolseley would have too much discretion, but Cardwell argued that the general must have the widest latitude to deal with the situation upon his arrival, although Cardwell stated that of course Wolseley would have to report to the Cabinet. There were some concerns raised as to the likely cost of the expedition, and in particularly the need for a hospital ship to be provided, but these financial questions were not resolved before Wolseley sailed for the Gold Coast on 12 September.

With the transfer of Robert Lowe as Chancellor of the Exchequer to the Home Office in August, Gladstone had also assumed responsibilities at the Treasury and here he became fully aware of the full financial implications of the Wolseley plan. He also began to realise just how far Cardwell, in particular, had advanced those plans which seemed certain to involve the taking of Kumasi. The supply of equipment included 15 miles of railway to be sent to the Gold Coast, at, in Gladstone's opinion, a huge cost. Gladstone was indignant and required reassurance from Cardwell, which he received in a letter of 20 September:

> We have not involved the country in a war without calling Parliament together. We are in a war forced upon us . . . and existing long before Parliament broke up. I believe the steps we have taken have averted a storm of indignation, which would have burst forth if these ill-tidings had arrived and no such steps had already been taken. As regards the tramway . . . I do not regard it as pledging us to an expedition into Ashanti territory.[24]

For all the political and financial focus upon the railway, once Wolseley had seen the local conditions, he decided it was not feasible to utilise it.

Yet, despite reassurances, as September progressed both Cardwell and Kimberley sensed that the prime minister and Cabinet colleagues were either cooling or actively against the thought of British intervention. At a meeting at the War Office on 22 September, which finally agreed to the expense of the railway and the hospital ship, the two men had to agree and concede that the decision-making on all aspects of the Wolseley plan would have to enlarge to include the whole Cabinet. The matter was finally discussed in detail in a 5-hour long Cabinet meeting held on the afternoon of 4 October 1873. Opposition to the Kimberley-Cardwell policy was vocal with John Bright, Chancellor of the Duchy of Lancaster, the most outspoken critic. The following day, as a result of the meeting, the Cabinet sent a memorandum of instruction, largely drafted by Gladstone himself, to Wolseley. The general was warned against conducting desultory operations and informed that the government would be very reluctant to sanction the use of British battalions upon the Gold Coast. Furthermore, the letter stated that the government would now be satisfied with an honourable peace which chastised the Asantes for the invasion and saw them leave the protectorate.

This was the first real attempt by Gladstone to assert any authority upon the situation caused by the Asante invasion and it came too late to have any influence on future events. For as the letter was sent to Wolseley, the general had begun to assess matters on the ground in the Gold Coast and he had already reaffirmed in his own mind the need for British battalions to be sent and for Kumasi to be taken. Furthermore, the prime minister and some members of his Cabinet had failed to appreciate that public opinion was shifting very much towards the deployment of British troops and for the Asante nation to be taught a military lesson.

The public mood had changed during the summer when news of Asante attacks upon Royal Navy personnel reached Britain. On 7 August an intelligence report had arrived from Dixcove that the enemy was attempting to cross the Prah, two days' sailing from its mouth, into Wassa territory. From there this force was to converge with the main Asante army under the command of Achiempon. Together the combined force was then to attack the settlements of Dixcove and Secondee. Captain John Commerell VC of HMS *Rattlesnake*, and commodore of the West African squadron, felt that if the intelligence proved to be correct then everything must be done to impede the march south of this new Asante threat. He thus led a reconnaissance. At the town of Shama, at the mouth of the Prah, he landed to question the local chief and to impress upon him that his loyalty to the Crown would be beneficial to both him and his people. The chief professed his desire to remain neutral in any conflict between Britain and the Asante nation and denied that he had materially assisted the Asantes in any way. Although appearing to be friendly, the chief refused Commerell's request for two chiefs to help pilot the British boats up the river, but he advised the commodore to be wary of the Asantes and keep close to the right bank.

A procession of boats was lowered from HMS *Rattlesnake* and Commerell led them up the Prah. After about a mile-and-a-half up the river, without warning and without the enemy being seen, a heavy fire erupted from the riverbank from several hundred enemy muskets and tore into the small armada. Commerell was hit in the first salvo; a serious lung wound which forced him into unconsciousness. Before he faded, command was transferred to Captain Percy Luxmoore and an order given to sail to the midstream. Luxmoore was also severely wounded but was able to order a return of small arms fire from the boats which forced the unseen enemy to fade back into the jungle. Almost fainting through loss of blood, Luxmoore managed to return the boats back to the *Rattlesnake*. Nearly all the officers had been shot in the back from the first enemy salvo and a further six sailors were hit. Commerell's wound was so dangerous that he had to be evacuated back to England and was forced to relinquish his command to Captain Fremantle.

Whilst Commerell's party was being ambushed, a cutter was landed on a beach close to Shama. Sub Lieutenant Draffan and ten Fante policemen were immediately surrounded by a large hostile crowd and the men had to battle their way back to the boat. Unfortunately, the cutter had been overturned in the surf and the young midshipman in charge and the sailors were having difficulty in righting it. Whilst this was being attempted shots came from the crowd of natives which now rushed forward. Several of the Fante were wounded but Draffan and his command managed to hold the natives back whilst the sailors successfully relaunched the boat. As their shells ran out, Draffan and his men took to the water and the sailors were able to rescue the survivors. One man was spotted by coxswain Charles Godden and ordinary seaman William Sermon. These two brave men volunteered to swim back to shore and the man was rescued and dragged through the surf to the safety of the cutter. The headless bodies of three of the policemen and one ordinary sailor were left behind on the blood-soaked beach. In a separate incident another party was landed at the village of Takoradi and was similarly attacked. On this occasion fifteen soldiers and sailors were killed or wounded.

Such an affront to the Royal Navy was too much to bear without swift retaliation. The decks of Her Majesty's Ships, *Rattlesnake*, *Argus* and the *Barracouta*, were cleared for action and broadsides were poured on shore reducing Shama, Takoradi and several villages in-between to burning ruins and surely claiming many civilian lives. Yet, British honour had been seemingly restored and these incidents had a profound effect on public opinion. Apathy suddenly turned to

indignation and jingoism in the British press and editors looked to send report-
ers to the Gold Coast. Even the *New York Herald* despatched a reporter, one
named Henry Morton Stanley, who had achieved world fame when he located
the 'missing' Dr Livingstone in 1871. Wolseley and his officers first learnt of the
Royal Navy's clash of arms when on their passage to the Gold Coast. Calling on
route at Madeira, one of the officers recorded in his diary:

> Most of us declared it [the attack upon Commerell's command] was
> the reverse of a disaster for the expedition. Hitherto the British peo-
> ple had looked upon the war with languor and actual distrust: it was
> a war, said the world, which could bring us neither glory nor gain; it
> would cost money; many fine young men would perish ignobly from
> the climate, and victories gained over naked savages could not be
> viewed with satisfaction. But the disaster on the Pra was a blow in the
> face for Europe, and it stirred the spirit of the Nation.[25]

Public opinion was firmly on Wolseley's side now.

Whilst rumblings continued between Cabinet colleagues as to the cost and
goals of the expedition, Wolseley and his special service officers received instruction that they were to depart for the Gold Coast on the *Ambriz*, which was to
sail from Liverpool on 12 September. A few days before departure Wolseley
received two pieces of correspondence from Kimberley and one from Cardwell,
all of which attempted to outline Wolseley's tasks and aims for the expedition,
as well as setting out the terms which would be acceptable to the government
in any proposed peace treaty. Captain Henry Brackenbury, who was Wolseley's
military secretary on the expedition, was to write a two-volume 'official' account
of the campaign and described the instructions as 'like orders to make bricks
without straw'.[26]

In Kimberley's first seventeen-point letter he laid out the historical situation
between Britain and the Asantes, and stated that Wolseley should summon the
Asante king to withdraw his forces from the protectorate, to receive reparation
for injuries suffered by the native allies and to seek securities for the maintenance of peace. If these demands were not forthcoming Wolseley was instructed
to use native forces to secure them. Kimberley concluded,

> If you should find it necessary to ask for any considerable reinforce-
> ments of European troops, I have to request that you will enter into
> full explanation as to the circumstances in which you propose to
> employ them, and the reasons which may lead you to believe that
> they can be employed without an unjustifiable exposure, and with a
> well-grounded anticipation of success.[27]

In his second letter Kimberley, in eight separate points, outlined the peace terms that would be acceptable to the government in light of an Asante withdrawal. These included a call to the Asante king to renounce any claim upon the native kings and their lands as well as any claim on Elmina. Kimberley also wrote that a reasonable indemnity should be claimed against the Asante king for the expense of the war and the injuries suffered by Her Majesty's allies. The final point, stated, 'Lastly, the opportunity should not be lost for putting an end, if possible, to the human sacrifices and the slave-hunting which, with other barbarities, prevail in the Ashanti kingdom.'[28]

Cardwell in his letter to Wolseley confirmed his appointment as both military commander and head of the civilian administration on the Gold Coast. Cardwell also wrote of the dangers of the climate and insisted that Wolseley take into account, and act upon, any means by which European troops could be shielded from these dangers. Cardwell concluded:

> Nothing but a conviction of necessity would induce her Majesty's Government to engage in any operation involving the possibility of its requiring the service of Europeans at the Gold Coast. But it is far from my intention to fetter your judgement in the responsible and arduous duties which have been intrusted to you; and no one, I am sure, will be more sensible than yourself of the cardinal importance of the considerations to which I have invited your attention, or more desirous to spare to the upmost of your power the exposure of European soldiers or marines to the climate of the Gold Coast.[29]

Writing after the campaign, Brackenbury was particularly damming of the two politicians for he surmised that both called upon Wolseley to drive the Asante army out of the protectorate, secure a lasting peace and do so without the use of British troops. However, it is clear that both Cardwell and Kimberley knew that realistically British troops would be called upon at some point during the expedition and were simply, in writing at least, ensuring that any request for additional soldiers would be based on Wolseley's firm military judgement as to the situation and requirements on the ground and that they expected Wolseley to undertake every reasonable step to minimise the risk to troops from the climate. Like politicians throughout history, both men were simply covering themselves from any backlash from those who might have seen them as contriving to place Britain in a position where the use of regulars was the only alternative. Yet, it seems, that this was exactly what they were doing.

Wolseley had based his choice of special service officers on their cheerfulness, their ability to not be easily discouraged and their optimism. All these qualities rapidly disappeared when the men viewed with horror the vessel, *Ambriz*, which was to transport them to the Gold Coast. In the haste to sail, the ship had been repainted only the day before. Brackenbury described the condition in which they found the *Ambriz* and wrote of cabin floors oozing with bilge-water, for the ship had no bulwarks, and of foul smells which seemed to slowly poison the passengers. Brackenbury thought that the ship was barely seaworthy and stated, 'the discomforts suffered in the Bay of Biscay are looked back upon now as exceeding any that the campaign itself induced'.[30] Colonel Wood claimed that he thought on more than one occasion the ship would capsize in heavy seas, whilst Wolseley described the *Ambriz* as the most unhealthy and abominable craft he had ever sailed in. Brackenbury described the relief when they called into Madeira for 24 hours which he compared to finding an oasis in a desert, and also wrote of their arrival at Sierra Leone on 27 September when Wolseley formally assumed command of land forces in the West African settlements. Brackenbury was delighted by the tropical scenery and the unexpected beauty. The governor-in-chief of Sierra Leone, Mr Berkeley, endeavoured to assist Wolseley in his aim of raising local forces from along the coast and gave every service to Captain Furse and Lieutenant Saunders, who disembarked to travel to Bathurst on the River Gambia to encourage recruits from the Mandingo and Jollif tribes. A Lieutenant Gordon of the 93rd Highlanders remained in Sierra Leone to try and enlist local men there for the forthcoming campaign.

The *Ambriz* sailed on, finally arriving on the Gold Coast on 2 October. The voyage, although uncomfortable and unsanitary, had allowed the officers to bond together in adversity and certainly the time onboard had not been wasted. All attended lectures given by Wolseley and Brackenbury on the history of the Gold Coast and the maps that were available were poured over again and again. Books on the region, its history and geography and the customs of the tribes were read and re-read. Wolseley shared his thoughts as to how local forces were to be raised as well as how to use them; Colonel Evelyn Wood and Major Baker Russell were charged with forming, training and leading two native units and much would depend upon them to initially engage with the Asantes. As Wolseley, his staff and the special service officers finally disembarked on the Gold Coast they were as briefed upon the task ahead of them as much as possible and readied themselves to face the challenges that the expedition would present.

Wolseley's Arrival Upon the Gold Coast and First Shots

On the early morning of 2 October, Brackenbury gained his first view of Cape Coast Castle and he later wrote that it did not make a favourable impression. Indeed, he and some of his fellow officers thought they had arrived at Elmina for the castle in front of them displayed all the apparent ravages of shells and fire which it must have endured during the Asante assault. Yet, they soon discovered that the sight was just an example of the effect of the climate upon buildings.

The impact of the climate on the health of the troops was also evident. Wolseley's fears regarding the dangers of 'The White Man's Grave' were discovered to be well-founded. Of the 130 English officers and men in the country only 22 were fit for duty. British troops in the protectorate amounted to about 30 officers and 770 other ranks, comprising the 2nd West Indies Regiment and the Royal Marines contingent. Of these men, one-fifth were sick. In addition, Glover had taken on his Volta expedition the 300-strong Hausa detachment, along with their Snider rifles. Clearly much would depend on the ability not only to raise sufficient men from amongst the local tribes but also how well and how quickly these natives could be turned into a fighting force. However, it seems clear that Wolseley had already made up his own mind that the local natives would be unequal to the task. Writing to his wife during the voyage, and in a tone typical of the prejudice held by many at the time, Wolseley wrote, 'the Africans are like so many monkeys: they are a good-for-nothing race'.[31]

Disembarkation from the *Ambriz* carried on for most of the day. Major Baker Russell and his officers were bivouacked at Prospect House, whilst the head-quarter staff were housed in Government House. The engineer, artillery and medical officers were placed in the castle. Wolseley finally disembarked late in the afternoon, after having seen Festing, Home and Fremantle onboard to gain an understanding of the current situation. Sir Garnet was landed under the custom-ary salutes and was received at Government House by Colonel Harley and sworn in as the new governor of the Gold Coast. Harley hosted a dinner in the castle in Wolseley's honour to which most of his officers were invited. Colonel Wood and his officers had left earlier in the day by steam-pinnace for Elmina Castle where the reality of serving on the Gold Coast soon became apparent to them. Arriving in time for afternoon tea, Wood and his staff discovered that three of the officers in the garrison were sick with fever but the remaining three offered them a hospi-table welcome. Although tea was expected and hoped for, Wood and his men were told that tea had not been seen for several months and were offered traders' gin instead. Lieutenant Eyre declined and one of his hosts gratefully drank his glass as well as his own! Wood recorded that he found the experience very depressing.

Kimberley had written in advance to Harley to instruct him to summon the local chiefs to Cape Coast as soon as Wolseley and his officers had arrived. This Harley had duly done, and the meeting was scheduled for 4 October. Harley, now relieved of his duties, departed for England leaving Wolseley to his new role as governor. On 3 October, Wolseley appointed Captain Huyshe to survey and map the route north of the coast, whilst Lieutenant Hart was tasked with doing the same around Cape Coast and Elmina. Wolseley gave the important brief of intelligence-gathering to his old comrade from the Red River Expedition, Redvers Buller. This would prove to be an inspired appointment and Buller quickly rose to the challenge and worked tirelessly throughout the campaign.

Interpreters and spies were recruited and interrogation of captured Asantes, disaffected locals and escaped slaves became common practice. His new sources were able to inform Buller that the main Asante army was still based around Mampon and that Amankwa Tia was still in command. Yet, with his army suffering from dysentery and associated illnesses, the commander was considering a withdrawal across the Prah. To facilitate a quick march back to Kumasi, the Asantes had started to cut a new forest path to join the main route at Mansu. Buller also gleaned that the Asantes were reliant on provisions from Elmina and coastal settlements to the west, and that all the supplies where sent via Essaman.

To supplement his meagre forces, Wolseley decided to use his civilian powers to command the native armed police into his military command, yet, much to his disappointment, he discovered that this yielded only a further ten recruits. Much would depend upon how the local chiefs reacted to his call for troops. Wolseley decided to telegraph the War Office for an additional twelve special service officers to be sent, yet without a direct telegraph link the request would take two weeks to reach London. Any correspondence between the Gold Coast and London either had to travel by the regular mail packet ship service, which took around twenty days, or if it was urgent then a message could be taken to Madeira and then telegraphed to Lisbon and then on to London. Even this speedier approach took around two weeks so the answer to any request would not be received for about four weeks. Indeed, during the conflict, the cable broke between Madeira and Lisbon and the Royal Navy were forced to ferry important cables themselves to Portugal.

The meeting with local chiefs was not a great success. There were many promises but little enthusiasm to fight again amongst the Fante tribes. Wolseley was able to promise £10 per month to each chief for every thousand men he could put into the field and each of these men would be paid 1*s*. ½*d*. per day and be supplied with arms, ammunition and some rations. Wolseley spoke for several minutes to try and encourage support and was clear in his aims. He stated:

> I can assure you that if you place all your available resources at my disposal, and are loyally determined to fight your hereditary enemies [the Asantes] now, I will guarantee to you that I, with God's assistance, shall drive them out of your territory, and that I will inflict such a terrible punishment upon them, that for all time to come you can have nothing to dread from them. My intention is to chase them out of your country, and, if necessary, to pursue them into Ashanti territory.[32]

Despite this statement Wolseley could clearly see that the locals were reluctant to fight. The meeting ended with the chiefs departing with a gift of gin and a promise from them that they would respond to Wolseley's request as a matter of urgency. Wolseley was not surprised or deflated when he heard the news that the local natives were ready to work as porters but not as fighters. He wrote, 'Seeing that we left them entirely to themselves at the beginning it is scarcely to be expected that the whole of a much dispersed and dispirited people will suddenly come to believe in our serious intentions vigorously to aid them. To get the people to act with that rapidity which is essential we must act energetically ourselves.'[33] Wolseley was correct in his assessment for there did exist a belief amongst the locals that the British would be no match for the Asante in battle, particularly in the jungle. Wolseley believed that he must strike at the enemy as soon as practical in order to win back some confidence amongst the native allies.

Yet, whatever the outcome of Wolseley's recruitment drive amongst the local tribes, he had already written to his wife and confided in her that he would be asking for British troops to be despatched. His official request was sent to London on 13 October, where it arrived on 17 November. This was the day before British troops, Hausas and a few Fantes had engaged the Asantes for the first time.[34] Wolseley's request for two battalions was debated by the Cabinet on 17 November and it sanctioned the despatch of three battalions instead of two, and the Royal Welsh Fusiliers, the 42nd Royal Highland Regiment (the Black Watch) and the 2nd Battalion of the Rifles sailed between the 19 and 21 November. On 21 November the Cabinet again met when it considered the instructions on the use of the battalions. Gladstone reiterated his desire that Wolseley should make peace as soon as he could and that if he had to engage with the enemy it should be done as far from the Prah River and Kumasi as possible. John Bright again voiced his opposition to the sending of British troops and his opinion that the war was folly, but he was a lone voice. Gladstone also warned Wolseley that if he was to crush the Asante army and reach Kumasi that he might find that there was no one to negotiate a peace with, and this was precisely what was to happen. Queen Victoria, via her Secretary Lord Ponsonby, made it known that she hoped Gladstone was not trying to restrict Wolseley's freedom to act, and Gladstone's cautious remarks were the last attempt at interference in the expedition by the government. The time delay in sending despatches between London and the Gold Coast now worked in Wolseley's favour as he was free to act as he thought fit.

On the Gold Coast, Wolseley was acting vigorously upon local reports of Asante forces and against tribes that were appearing to offer material support to the invading army. On hearing reports that chiefs near to Elmina were still supplying the Asante army at Mampon with food, Wolseley summoned them to appear before him at Elmina Castle. The chief of Ampeene sent no answer but beheaded a native loyal to the British and displayed his severed head on the beach, another responded by saying that he had 'smallpox today but will come tomorrow', whilst the chief of Essaman wrote back with his own invitation, 'Come and fetch me if you dare. White man no dare go bush.'[35] Clearly Wolseley had to act against such insolence if Britain was to establish its authority with the local tribes.

Wolseley wanted a short and very sharp engagement to restore British morale and prestige throughout the protectorate and the disrespectful chiefs of the coastal settlements around Elmina offered an obvious target for his first punitive act. On 10 October a company of Hausa troops arrived from Lagos and with the addition of these men Wolseley was able to cobble together a force comprising 180 white troops; Royal Marines, several of the special service officers and around 50 sailors commanded by Captain Fremantle, and 330 black troops which were composed of men from the 2nd West Indies Regiment, the Hausa company and around 30 Fante labourers. At around 4am on 14 October the contingent slipped silently through the gates of Elmina. Such was the secrecy surrounding the preparations only Wolseley and Wood knew the target of the raid. The inhabitants of Essaman were in for an early morning shock.

After 3 hours of following a narrow bush path the party neared Essaman. A mile outside the village the column was hit by a volley of 'Long Dane' fire from an invisible enemy in front and close to the sides of the path. One of the Hausas was killed outright from a fire so close that Evelyn Wood recorded that the enemy's barrel must have almost been touching its victim, yet still the Asantes were not seen. The 2nd West Indies troops, led by Lieutenant Eyre, ascended a small hillock and there they attracted so much musketry from the Asantes that they were almost obscured by smoke. Although Wolseley was with the column, to show the locals that the new governor was a fighting man, command was in the hands of Wood who sent forward the special service officers. Buller led a detachment of thirty Fante axemen and they entered the bush and cut a new path at an angle to the village. He was able to report to Wood that armed men and drummers could be seen. Wolseley could not now control his instinct for command and without consulting Wood he ordered Brackenbury and Lieutenant Charteris to charge forward at the head of a detachment of Royal Marines. At the same time, the chief of staff, Colonel McNeil, led a party on a left flanking advance and Captain Fremantle was able to fire both a 7lb cannon and rockets into the village. Both men were wounded; Fremantle in the arm and McNeil in the wrist. The latter's wound was so severe that all the muscles and tendons on his wrist had been sliced and stood out like the threads of an unravelled rope. Although Fremantle had been badly injured, he quickly recovered but McNeil was so badly hurt that Wolseley's chief of staff had to be evacuated back to England. Wolseley would greatly miss the help and support of his friend and colleague.

Buller assumed command of McNeil's flanking advance and cleared the left side of Essaman. The Asantes employed their usual jungle tactics of attacking the flanks and they now fell upon troops from the 2nd West Indies Regiment. Although they made some initial inroads, Major Baker Russell and Wood rallied the troops and the Asantes were beaten back. In the meantime, Brackenbury, Charteris and the Royal Marines had stormed into the centre of Essaman to find that the Asantes, and the villagers, except for one small child, had fled.

Wood ordered the settlement to be burnt and the consequent explosions from many of the houses illustrated how much powder was being stored there. After an hour's rest the column marched 5 miles on to the town of Amquana. Clearly the sounds of fire and exploding powder had forewarned the inhabitants for Amquana was found to be deserted. Again, Wood ordered its destruction. It was now noon and the effects of the powerful sun began to take a toll. Wood was forced to let many of the European troops rest, but with 30 white and 250 native troops he moved on to to the villages of Akimfoo and Ampeene which were also burnt to the ground.

Although the men had carried as much water as possible, and despite receiving additional supplies from Royal Navy cutters that landed between Akimfoo and Ampeene, this had proved inadequate and they were left with none for much of the afternoon. Lieutenant Eyre collapsed from heat exhaustion and the column had to wait whilst he recovered. At one point the British had only advanced 4 miles in 3 hours. Brackenbury wrote of the day, 'The march was intensely fatiguing. The thick bush shut out every breath of air, and there were no forest trees to give shade. The path was rugged, and the way seemed never-ending. Then for the first time we learnt the terrible strain of performing staff duties on foot in such a climate.'[36] The column returned to Elmina in the early evening, having covered nearly 22 miles across varied and difficult terrain. The British casualties were two killed and twenty-three officers and men wounded. There was no record of the number of the enemy's casualties; very few bodies were seen, and the British were not going to venture into the bush to count the enemy fallen. Of the troops, the Hausas had shown themselves to be brave, but very excitable and they needed to be strictly controlled to prevent them from firing wildly. The West Indies troops had performed stoically, whilst the local Fantes, used as labourers and porters, had not reacted well under fire, dropping their loads and running back down the bush path. At one point the Royal Marines seemed to have been infected with the same rashness as the Hausas and their enthusiasm had to be reined in with a swift rebuke from their commanding officer, Captain John Crease.

Yet, this small punitive raid was a great success and did much to restore British morale and prestige throughout the protectorate. It also provided some useful lessons for all those that had taken part and Wolseley shared some of these in a letter to Cardwell. He commented that the uniforms of the West Indies troops had proven to be completely unsuitable for bush fighting, thus reaffirming his own decision to adapt the British tunics, and that due to the difficulty of maintaining contact in the bush a higher proportion of officers to men would be required in future engagements. Wolseley also stated:

> I have been shown how little reliance can be placed on even the best native troops in this bush-fighting. The Hausas showed undeniable courage and spirit; but their uncontrollable wildness, the way in which they fired volley after volley in the air, or at imaginary foes in the bush, expending their ammunition, shows how little use they are for the work we have in hand.[37]

Of course such statements, although undoubtedly correct, allowed Wolseley to further justify his call for British battalions.

Before additional British troops were to arrive, much had to be done to prepare for them, yet in October and early November Wolseley's most pressing concern was to keep harassing the invaders and encourage them to return across the Prah. By doing this he would continue to learn important lessons about bush fighting and the calibre of the troops then at his disposal, and such actions enhanced still further British prestige amongst the local chiefs. Wolseley was determined that this time the British would be seen to be resolute in their desire to defeat the Asantes.

Both Colonel Wood and Major Baker Russell set about training their respective regiments of native troops. Not only had the local Fantes failed to volunteer in significant numbers but the attempts to entice volunteers from Sierra Leone and other West African countries had largely been unsuccessful. As the campaign progressed the British would be forced more and more to 'pressgang' the local tribes into service, particularly as porters. Wood found the task of establishing his own regiment of native troops extremely frustrating. His four companies comprised men from Fante tribes as well as Bonny and Kossos men. The best Wood could say about the Bonny tribesmen was that they had an aptitude for basket work but not for war. Yet, Wood was later to admit that the native troops had been thrust together, with few understanding the language of the other companies or their British officers and it was not surprising that in battle they were found wanting.

Wolseley maintained the pressure upon the Asantes and on 27 October Colonel Festing led a company of the 2nd West Indies Regiment and about 600 local natives in an attack upon a small enemy camp at Escbio. The Asantes were totally surprised whilst cooking and initially they fled into the bush, but from there they returned a hot fire. Whilst the West Indies troops again behaved well, Festing lost control of the native troops and withdrew, having destroyed the camp. The following day, Wolseley led a reconnaissance force of 500 troops from Abakrampa to Assanchi and ordered Festing to move his force so that the two converged. However, Festing was unable to induce the native troops to advance at all and when Wolseley arrived at Assanchi he discovered that the enemy had fled into the bush.

November was a particularly difficult month for the British on the Gold Coast. The climate began to take a toll upon the newly arrived officers and within six weeks 70 per cent had fallen sick, many seriously. Lieutenant Charteris passed away on the hospital ship back to England after being evacuated suffering from fever and dysentery, and Wolseley himself was dangerous ill. He was moved to the hospital ship *Simoon* and when Wood visited there he was shocked at his commander's condition, although he found him coherent. Wood thought it unlikely that Wolseley would be fit enough to accompany a march on Kumasi, but he underestimated Wolseley who eventually was able to return to duty. In an action on 3 November the British had their first combat fatality. Colonel Festing led another reconnaissance in force, this time to Dunkwa but on this occasion the Asantes were waiting and the British march was stalled by heavy musket fire. A stalemate ensued for over 2 hours as troops of the 2nd West Indies Regiment returned the Asante fire. Lieutenant Eardley Wilmot of the Royal Artillery was wounded in the shoulder by the first Asante salvo and was later killed as he led an advance. Festing himself was hit in the back as he recovered Wilmot's body and a further four officers were wounded. Wilmot's death was felt keenly for he was the first of the *Ambriz* contingent to die and he had impressed all with his tireless work with the Hausa recruits.

In November it was the turn of the Asantes to go on the offensive at the village of Abakrampa. This was the furthermost western settlement which had been garrisoned by the British, but Wolseley had decided that with the area apparently quiet a detachment of sixty men and an officer from the Naval Brigade could be deployed elsewhere. These men were actually on parade and ready to move off on the afternoon of 5 November when a large Asante force attacked. Major Baker Russell and Captain Huyshe had ensured that the ground surrounding the village had been cleared of undergrowth and sentry posts established in the nearby scrub. As the Asantes advanced, with their usual shouts and drums, the sentries fell back to the village. As the enemy appeared in the open and were within 60m of the British defences, the 2nd West Indies Regiment fired a devasting volley and then charged with the bayonet. The surviving Asantes sought refuge in the bush from where they continued a heavy fire. The defenders were largely in trenches and only one sailor was seriously injured in the eye, although many were hit with slugs but with the distance too great from the Asante powder these resulting in bruises rather than wounds.

The enemy now switched its direction of attack and a determined assault was launched over the cleared ground to the left and rear of the defences. Again, the firepower of the Snider rifle was decisive, and each attempt was repelled. The Asantes continued to attack until midnight and sniping fire kept the defenders awake until this too ceased at about 4am the following morning. The battle was resumed at about midday, but the enthusiasm and determination of the Asantes on the previous day was not apparent.

Baker Russell had been able to inform Wolseley of the Asante assault via a telegraphic link to Cape Coast Castle. Although 200 miles of cable had been despatched from England, it had not yet arrived but due to the initiative of Lieutenant Jekyll, who personally brought out 20 miles of cable in his baggage and then set abut erecting poles and laying the cable, a link had been established as far as Accroful. The news was received by Wolseley and his staff with almost disbelief but once the full implication of the attack was appreciated the general reacted swiftly to reinforce Abakrampa. All the available sailors and marines onboard the five Royal Navy ships off the coast were commandeered and Wolseley was able to cobble together a further 300 men and 22 officers, as well as a detachment of rockets. With these men Wolseley set off towards Abakrampa. Unfortunately, many of the men had been long on vessels and their fitness levels were not high, nor were the sailors equipped with suitable head gear to shade themselves from the hot sun and there was very little shade on the line of march. In the extreme heat over a tenth of the force fell out suffering from heat stroke and exhaustion. After only 10 miles the whole column had to rest for some hours, and it was not until nearly dark that Wolseley led his force into the village. Although they were met by enemy small-arms fire, they were able to enter the defences and collapse for the night.

Wolseley also ordered Wood to support Baker Russell and, with 1,000 new recruits from the coastal tribes, the colonel led his regiment on an equally gruelling march through the bush. They arrived on the morning of 7 November and despite the efforts of Wood and his officers and the warlike Kossos, the new recruits could not be persuaded to attack. Without exception they lay down and simply refused to move. One of Wood's officers even broke his umbrella over one of the chiefs who would not cooperate. The Hausas engaged the Asantes and at the sound of gunfire the recruits fled the battle. Fortunately, the Asantes felt it prudent to withdraw back into the jungle but the engagement had been something of an embarrassment for Wood and again showed that any thought of crossing the Prah into Asante territory would have to wait for the arrival of British troops and this view was reinforced by further smaller actions.

The British continued to harass the Asante army as it inched, roughly 5 miles a day, north towards the Prah. There were frequent clashes between the Asante rear guard and various detachments of natives, such as the Hausas led by Lieutenant Gordon and the Abra tribesmen commanded by Captain Charles Bromhead of the 24th Regiment. Both officers continued to struggle to control their men in action for they would fire wildly at both the enemy and in their excitement each other. On 8 November Bromhead, commanding a combined force of Hausas, Kossos and Cape Coast men, engaged the rear of the Asante army at the village of Ainsa. Here they met determined resistance from the Asante and were driven back. Bromhead thought it prudent to withdraw, but the Fante panicked and fired wildly, killing twenty of their own and then, fleeing across a stream, they rushed over the Hausas and drowned one, trampling him under the water. They continued to run until they reached the safety of their own homes on the coast where they dispersed. Wolseley was furious at their cowardly behaviour.

The British officers now lost sight of the Asante army for nearly three weeks. Although nearly 3,000 native allies were in place between Dunkwa and Mansu, without the presence of British troops they refused to engage the enemy. Buller was able to continue in his role of intelligence-gathering and ascertained that Amankwa Tia was cutting fresh jungle paths parallel to those main tracks being used by the British.

The British were to be in action again on 27 November at the village of Faysowah. The skirmish was later to be magnified into something of a defeat for the irregular forces. Again, Wood led his newly formed regiment. A captured Asante warrior informed Wood that Amankwa Tia and several important chiefs were resting at Faysowah with a large body of troops. All were celebrating an *Adai*, or holy day, and Wood thought it a great opportunity to attack the enemy whilst he was so engrossed. Initially the engagement went well. The Hausa and Kossos advanced in skirmish order and pushed back the Asante pickets. However, once they came up against the main Asante camp the advance stalled and the enemy quickly reacted by adopting its usual battlefield flanking movements. Wood thought it best to withdraw. Unfortunately, the men from the coastal tribes once again panicked and ran off without offering any resistance, and this panic spread to both the Hausas and Kossos and the orderly withdrawal became a rout as weapons and ammunition and baggage were lost in the confusion. Only a spirited rear-guard action by Wood, Eyre, Gordon and the other special service officers, firing their Snider rifles to keep the enemy at bay, saved what could have become a disaster.

Although once again humiliated by the poor performance of the local tribesmen, both Wood and Wolseley were fortunate in that the action convinced Amankwa Tia to take the last of his army, ravaged by sickness, disease and malnutrition, back across the Prah. In less than two months Wolseley could congratulate himself and his officers that the invaders had been forced back to their homeland. Although how much credit can be attributed to the harassing stance taken by the British is difficult to determine, yet the fact remained that the invading army had left the protectorate. No one knows what casualties the Asante army had suffered. It is supposed that around half of the invading army perished on the campaign, mainly from smallpox and dysentery. One of the captive Europeans, Mr Kuhne, held in Kumasi witnessed the return to the city of 79 boxes containing the remains of 280 chiefs who had died in the protectorate and this alone indicates the level of loss to the army.[38] It was at this point that Wolseley might have pursued a policy of peace and appeasement. The invaders had been driven back across the Prah and the war party at the Asante court had been weakened by events and even suggested that some financial compensation might be considered for the act of invasion. With up to half of the army lost, the *Asantehene* clearly hoped that the British might consider calling off the campaign and tentative peace feelers were put out from the Kumasi court. Yet, Wolseley now knew he had public opinion firmly on his side; a lesson had to be taught to these African barbarians for passions were running high at home and these increased with every story of Asante savagery and tales of human sacrifice. The government could not ignore public opinion and more importantly Wolseley knew how to use it to his advantage. Queen Victoria was also firmly on his side and Wolseley was not going to let peace interfere with the prospect of a successful and brilliant campaign which would further enhance his own standing and reputation.

Wolseley and his officers could now turn to the logistical problems of preparing for the arrival of the British battalions and of making sure their eventual passage through the jungle to Kumasi would be as quick as possible. Road-making, bush-cutting and the construction of bases along the eventual line of march were the priority for December. The herculean task of ensuring that the British battalions could arrive at the base of Prahsu in relative comfort rested with the energy and planning of Wolseley and the efficiency and dedication of Major Robert Home of the Royal Engineers. Even though Wolseley had chosen the dry season for his expedition he knew that with the troops needing to march the 70 miles from the coast to the staging post of Prahsu high losses from heat exhaustion could jeopardise not only lives but the success of the campaign. Working in extremely difficult conditions, Home built seven stations at roughly 10-mile intervals. Each had accommodation for 400 men, as well as a hospital, storage sheds and water purifiers. Two of these stations had bakeries and four abattoirs. Although Gordon had managed to extend the path up to Yancommassie Fanti before Wolseley's arrival, there remained around 50 miles of paths to widen and improve before the British troops arrived. In addition, 237 footbridges had to be constructed along this route, including a 200m bridge across the Prah River from which the British would launch their assault into the Asante nation.

The forward base at Prahsu was particularly elaborate. Accommodation for 4,000 troops was built, along with a hospital for a hundred patients, a battery and magazine, canteen, post office and headquarters for Wolseley and his staff. Both Baker Russell's and Wood's regiments of native troops were employed in the widening of the path and on 16 December, they began to clear the area for the Prahsu base. Work continued for a month and the surroundings were denuded of palm leaves, which were to be used for thatching both walls and roofs. Thousands of poles were cut for uprights and supports, and all were transformed into the buildings of the camp. Raised beds with bamboo frames were also made to ensure the troops did not have to sleep on damp ground. Wolseley and his staff arrived at Prahsu on 2 January 1874 and surely must have been impressed by the work of Home, Wood and Baker Russell. Yet, for all the incredible efforts and feats there remained one huge logistical problem that threatened the success of the expedition.

Although Home's feat to build the road to Prahsu was outstanding, it was not without difficulties which would become Wolseley's main concern as the year came to an end. North of the town of Mansu the construction of the road, with its waystations and many bridges, slowed considerably and this was primarily due to manpower. The further the British moved from the coast the greater the issue of recruiting and keeping local tribesmen to help with construction became. With the Asante army now back across the Prah, the Fante viewed the war as a European war and not their affair. In despair Wolseley was driven to characterise his Fante allies as 'too cowardly to fight their own battles and too lazy, even when well paid, to help those who are risking their lives in their cause'.[39]

Yet, all the blame in securing sufficient manpower did not rest with the Fante chiefs alone for the army commissariat, with civilian administrators, lacked an understanding of how their work could adversely affect or positively enhance a campaign. Whilst stores could be efficiently offloaded at the coast, the mechanism and urgent need for these to be transported forward was not always operationally understood and nor were the needs of the porters themselves. Men from different tribes, often with long-standing historical grievances, were forced to work alongside each other. Some were paid twice for the same job whilst others received nothing. Many were overworked to the point of exhaustion and often it was only the threat of physical violence that got the men to work. Hundreds deserted because they were not fed, for the British relied on food subsistence payments for the men to buy their own provisions. Whilst this worked on the coast, they could hardly eat this money in the jungle where there was nothing to purchase. The British, and indeed Wolseley himself, seem to have been guilty of thinking that the local populace would be grateful to work for them and that this alone would suffice. The British could not understand why the natives did not relish the opportunity of carrying 50lb loads on their heads for over 70 miles. It would take a brilliant individual to ensure that the campaign was not to be jeopardised by logistical hurdles.

That individual was the Professor of Military Administration at the Staff College, Colonel Pomeroy Colley. Wolseley had specifically requested the assistance of his friend who as soon as he arrived on the Gold Coast in December was appointed to his staff as commander of transport. Colley had a brilliant brain and an acute eye for detail and his appointment effected an almost immediate transformation. Yet, he had arrived late to the problem and although the situation improved immensely under Colley's watchful eye, the porterage of supplies would remain one of Wolseley's most pressing problems.

On assuming his role, Colley calculated once the British battalions had arrived and had begun their march towards Kumasi that at least 8,500 porters would be required. Of this figure, 2,500 would be required for daily provisions, 3,500 for the transport of regimental supplies and equipment and the remaining would be needed just to maintain supplies at Prahsu. To illustrate the immense challenge, the porters had to move over a million rounds of Snider ammunition and 400 tons of food rations which was the equivalent of 30 days' rations for 6,500 men. The daily ration for each soldier was fixed a 1½lb of bread or biscuit, 1½lb of salted or fresh meat, 2oz of rice or peas, ½oz of salt, ¾oz of tea and 3oz of sugar.

Colley took over his new role just before Christmas and systematically set about improving the porterage system, based on the basic premise of providing the carriers with reasonable working conditions. Colley divided the line of communication into sections, with specific porters allocated to their own sections and they would not be expected to work in other sections. Allocation would be by tribes, with their own headmen reporting to a British officer who would individually pay each porter after the work had been completed. When possible, each porter would be given a day's rest after every four days' work. It was hoped that this humane approach would lessen desertions and although it proved successful to some degree, the loss of porters remained a problem.

At Wolseley's request for British battalions the Cabinet had authorised their despatch and the troops had left promptly for the Gold Coast. Unfortunately, in the haste surrounding the decision the need to inform Wolseley had been overlooked. The general was expecting the reinforcements to be seen towards the end of the year, but the first he was made aware of the imminent arrival of the men was when the *Himalaya* arrived at Cape Coast on 9 December, bringing the 2nd Battalion of the Rifle Brigade. Two days later the *Senegal* brought the Royal Welsh Fusiliers and, on 17 December, the *Sarmatian* appeared with the last battalion, the 42nd Highlanders. With the problems of sufficient porters to bring supplies, and the camp at Prahsu still not constructed, Wolseley issued the only practical order and each of the vessels was sent back to sea to cruise back and forth along the coast until the facilities required for their safe passage and accommodation north from the coast had been completed.

Lieutenant Joseph Hammond Thomas, of the Rifles, left a vivid account of his voyage to the Gold Coast onboard the *Himalaya*. The battalion was stationed in Ireland when it received notification to board special trains from Cork to Queenstown from where the men sailed on the afternoon of 21 November. After several rough days at sea, the *Himalaya* arrived at Madeira on 26 November for a brief stop of a few hours during which the men traded tobacco and spare clothes with the locals for fresh fruit and cheeses. By 1 December the ship had reached the island of St Vincent, which Thomas found bare and desolate. On the evening of 9 December the *Himalaya* arrived off Cape Coast, although the men had to wait until the following morning for their first view of the Gold Coast. A message was sent from Wolseley informing the men that arrangements for the landing of troops were not complete and the next day news was sent that the battalion would have to go on a 'cruise'. Over the next two days the reserve stores were sent on shore and a detachment of Engineers, Army Service Corps and Army Hospital Corp were disembarked. On 13 December the *Himalaya* weighed anchor and was not to return until 30 December. Thomas was clearly frustrated at the delay; his diary describes the repeated parades and the regular practising of packing and repacking tents and clothing into convenient bundles for the porters to carry. Thomas described how one of the officers, using a piece of pork as bait, caught a 2m shark which was added to the daily ration. Thomas stated he did not admire the flavour of shark but that the sailors onboard enjoyed it immensely.

The weather was, according to Thomas, delightful and the troops were able to relax on deck during the day, although boredom became a problem and steps were taken to relieve the monotony of the extended cruise. A newspaper was started, and readings and theatre productions were held. As the battalion's band had been left in Ireland an improvised band was formed and this played daily. At night it was too hot to sleep below so blankets were laid on deck and the men slept under the stars. Christmas morning saw a parade at 10am after which the chaplain led a service. Thomas wrote:

> Our Christmas dinner was not a very enviable one; it consisted of boiled pork, pea soup, soft bread and pickles, with our usual allowance of Stout (one pint). An extra pint was served out in the evening, and the men formed themselves into groups, chatted and sung quite merrily, until the last post sounded at 9 pm, when hammocks were swung and we all turned in.[40]

On its return to the coast on 30 December, the men onboard the *Himalaya* were told that they were begin to disembark on 1 January 1874.

With his usual attention to detail, Wolseley had issued a hundred pamphlets printed with guidelines on how best to maintain health whilst in the jungle as well as a detailed description of what troops could expect when fighting in this alien environment. These pamphlets were distributed amongst the troops and read before they reached the coast. Wolseley was clearly trying to convey to the men what they could expect both in the jungle and from the likely fighting with the Asantes, and, in addition, health guidelines were given, such as not exposing the head to the sun and never to drink water until it had been filtered. The pamphlet stressed independence of action for small units of men in skirmish order and stated that self-confidence and reliance on comrades would be required in the dark, dense jungle. Wolseley wrote of how difficult it would be to maintain contact through the bush and along narrow jungle paths and that bugle calls would be essential to maintain cohesion. The pamphlet was, in essence, the first detailed description of jungle warfare.

Wolseley concluded the pamphlet with what can only be described as a rousing Victorian call to arms, or in modern language something of a pep talk. He wrote:

> It must never be forgotten by our soldiers that Providence has implemented in the heart of every native of Africa a superstitious awe and dread of the white man that prevent the negro from daring to meet us face to face in combat. A steady advance or charge, no matter how partial, if made with determination, always means the retreat of the enemy. Although when at a distance, and even when under heavy fire, the Ashantis seem brave enough, from their practice of yelling and singing, and beating drums, in order to frighten the enemies of their own colour, with whom they are accustomed to make war, they will not stand against the advance of the white man. English soldiers and sailors are accustomed to fight against immense odds in all parts of the world; it is scarcely necessary to remind them that when in our battles beyond the Pra they find themselves surrounded on all sides by hordes of howling enemies, they must rely on their own British courage and discipline, and upon the courage of their comrades. Soldiers and sailors, remember that the black man holds you in superstitious awe; be cool; fire low; fire slow and charge home; the more numerous your enemy the greater will be the loss inflicted upon him, and the greater your honour in defeating him.[41]

Even though Wolseley was not from the usual background of Britain's officer class he held, like many of them, a social Darwinist view on Britain's racial superiority over other races and nationalities and Africans were viewed as being vastly inferior to the British. Today, these thoughts and words are clearly viewed as racist and offensive. Whether Wolseley's troops remembered these words at the height of their battles with the Asante is unknown. What is clear is that by the end of the war, all, even Wolseley, would view their enemy with respect for his bravery and tenacity.

In a letter to Lieutenant Gordon, Captain Buller, commenting on Wolseley's desire for order and procedure, wrote, 'Sir Garnet is most anxious that everything should be done methodically upon a fixed plan.'[42] Although Buller was commenting on the work of the intelligence department, these sentiments could have equally applied to all aspects of Wolseley's planning. This was clearly seen in the methods and systems that Wolseley had approved to deal with any sick and wounded troops. With the reputation of the region for sickness, and with Cardwell impressing upon Wolseley the need to minimise the risk and to deal quickly and efficiently with any cases of illness or battlefield wounds, the general turned his mind for detail and order on this area. Each of the stations along the line of march had designated buildings for the sick and a separate hut for infectious cases. At the Prahsu and Mansu sites, as well as at Cape Coast, there were hospitals for up to 500 patients. The system in place for moving the sick was a conveyor belt of hammocks with native bearers working in relays between each of the way stations until the patients were delivered, in relative comfort, to the coast. A total of 150 hammocks and 85 cots were sent out with the troops and it was envisaged that around 200 men could be moved speedily at any one time.

Once at the coast the sick and wounded became the responsibility of the government. The vessel HMS *Victor Emmanuel* was sent from England as a hospital ship for 240 patients. In addition, the *Himalaya* and *Tamar* were moored offshore with an additional 100 beds each. A steamer service was established from Cape Coast back to St Vincent, where the *Simoom* was stationed as a floating nursing home for patients awaiting transfer back to England on the regular Cape Town to Southampton mail boats. Every ship that the government chartered for the Asante Expedition, whether as a troop or supply ship, was also fitted with additional sick cots. All these measures would be tested to the limit during the months of January and February 1874 as both the climate and the fierce fighting took a heavy toll upon the British troops. Ironically, the two men responsible for medical arrangements in the Gold Coast, Dr Home and Surgeon Major Albert Gore, suffered from the climate and both were invalided back to England before the British battalions had disembarked. Surgeon Major William Mackinnon arrived in December and acted as principal medical officer throughout the reminder of the campaign.

The British are Coming

As vessels arrived from England throughout December Wolseley's staff was strengthened. Colonel George Greaves arrived on the same ship as Colley and he replaced Colonel McNeil as chief of staff. Also onboard was Brigadier General Sir Archibald Alison, a veteran of the Indian Mutiny, who was given command of the British brigade in the expedition. Although senior to Wolseley, he would defer to him, though Alison would lead the battalions in action. Wolseley was clearly not pleased with Alison's appointment for he wrote in his journal on 10 December, 'Heard from Horse Gds that Sir A. Alison is coming here as Brigadier General & second in command. I am very sorry for this as I don't care much for him & don't think he is the man I want.'[43] Despite Wolseley's misgivings the two generals would work together and their cooperation in battle was crucial in later battlefield success.

Wolseley gave Alison responsibility for the disembarkation of the British battalions. The first men to arrive on shore were sailors from the so-called Naval Brigade. All 251 men were carefully selected volunteers from all the ships anchored off the coast, and Wolseley described them as splendid physical specimens in his journal. The detachment left the coast on 27 December and they covered the 70 miles to Prahsu without mishap by 3 January. The disembarkation of the troops began with the Rifle Brigade at 2am on 1 January which was divided into two 'wings', left and right, with the left the first to disembark from the *Himalaya*. With the way stations designed to accommodate roughly half a battalion at any one time, Alison had planned that all three battalions would be divided in half and would move up north towards the Prah in such a fashion.

Lieutenant Thomas of the Rifles recorded in his diary both the disembarkation and the subsequent march to the Prahsu camp. He described how the troops transferred to launches which were then towed by a steam launch to within 300m of the shore. With much difficulty the troops then had to board surfboats, manned by local Fantes, who struggled through the high and powerful surf to deposit the men at the base of Cape Castle's walls. It would take seven days for this first half battalion to march to the camp at Barraco, a distance of 67 miles. Here they rested for ten days until entering Prahsu on 17 January. Thomas described the march as 'fearfully oppressive, and the seventy rounds of ammunition hung very heavily around our waists, and very much retarded our progress'.[44] At both the Barraco and Yancommassie Assin stations the men were employed in sanitary fatigues which involved the cutting down of the jungle and bush for roughly 500yd around each encampment so as to clear the air of the innumerable swarms of insects. Fever and dysentery first made an appearance amongst the men at these two camps and the worst cases had to be carried back to the coast.

It was now the turn of the 42nd Highlanders, the Black Watch to disembark, followed by the 23rd Royal Welsh Fusiliers. At first the march went well, but the appearance of the British troops led to a realisation that a fight might be imminent, and this resulted in a significant increase in the desertion rate amongst the porters. Alison recognised that there was a real risk that not enough food and supplies could be carried forward for all three battalions so, acting on his own initiative, he stopped the disembarkation of the remaining half of the 23rd as well as the gunners from the Royal Artillery. When Wolseley assessed the supply and porter situation he agreed with Alison's assessment and ordered the leading half of the 23rd, which had already marched 13 miles to the Accroful station to return to the coast and re-embark. Naturally, the officers and men of the regiment were bitterly disappointed at being denied their part in the campaign and after protestations from the commanding officer, Colonel Savage Mostyn, Wolseley relented slightly. Although there could be no question of the supply situation allowing more than two battalions to go forward, Wolseley did agree that 100 of the least fit officers and men of the 42nd would be replaced by troops from the 23rd. The gunners did not receive any such concession and they saw no active service. Indeed, Wolseley had been so impressed with how Captain Arthur Rait of the Royal Artillery, one of his initial special service officers, had trained and instructed his sixty Hausa gunners that the general realised that any additional Royal Artillery personnel would be superfluous. Furthermore, Wolseley conceded that the Hausa's ability to dismantle and carry their guns through the jungle meant that they offered a great advantage over British gunners.

As an intermediate solution to the immediate porterage problem, men from Wood's and Baker Russell's commands, as well as troops from the 1st and 2nd West Indies Regiment were added to the porterage detachment. Wolseley's ingrained racism towards the men of the local regiments meant that he had no hesitation in transferring these men from a fighting unit to more menial duties and despite the men of the West Indies regiments showing a reliability in battle these too would be used as porters and later as guards for baggage and supplies. In his journal of 3 December, Wolseley recorded that he had inspected the 2nd West Indies Regiment and described them as rotten to the core and a melancholy sight. Troops from the 42nd took it upon themselves to move stores but when Wolseley heard of this, he forbade it for he wanted these men fresh for the fight and didn't want to jeopardise their health by such exertions.

Wolseley took direct punitive action to secure more locals. He harangued local chiefs, threatening that the British soldiers would withdraw from the Gold Coast and thus leave the local tribes at the mercy of Asante retribution. Colley led a reconnaissance to the villages around Dunkwa and Agoonal from where porters had deserted en masse. As an example, Colley and his men burnt the

British cannon held in Kumasi Military Museum, reportedly captured by the Asante army at the Battle of Nsamankow, 22 January 1824.

British troops and sailors lead an assault on the Asante centre during the latter stages of the Battle of Dodowa, 7 August 1826.

The interior of Cape Coast Castle today.

The battlements of Cape Coast Castle today.

A cross in the Commonwealth War Graves Cemetery near Kumasi Fort in remembrance of Captain George Marshall who died during the flight from Kumasi.

The grave of Captain Maguire located in the Commonwealth War Graves Cemetery near Kumasi Fort.

Kumasi Fort, October 2019.

Kumasi Fort today, home of the Ghana Military Museum.

settlements to the ground. Within a few days this tough stance had worked, and the number of porters was back to what was required. The most direct action owed nothing to Colley's scientific assessment but more to eighteenth-century practice of the 'pressgang'. One of Wolseley's biographers wrote:

> Desperate for carriers, Wolseley cast [aside] all forms of legality. Kidnapping began on a large scale . . . The commandant of Accra, with a man-of-war at his disposal, went up and down the coast collecting carriers. If the chiefs were unco-operative, a party of sailors would land at night, surround his village and carry off the entire adult population, leaving only a few old women to care for the infants.[45]

Women porters were also recruited, particularly from Anomabu, and they were found to complain less and smile more than the men. Although the porterage system did not collapse it would always remain a constant cause of concern for Wolseley and his staff.

With the return of porters to something like the levels required, the march of the British battalions continued. The Rifle Brigade, after their enforced stays at the Yancoommassie Assin and Barraco stations, arrived at Prahsu on 20 January and the Highlanders arrived two days later. As the British moved from the coast so the realisation dawned upon the Asante king that war was indeed likely. Envoys from the Kumasi court arrived at Prahsu on 2 January and it was clear that Kofi Karikari was not totally aware of the situation. The representatives carried two letters from the king, although it seems that the court did not know of Wolseley's appointment as both were addressed to his predecessor, Colonel Harley. The first letter, dated late November, was somewhat conciliatory in tone, although it did state the missionaries and other Europeans held in Kumasi, including a Mr Dawson, would not be released unless a ransom was paid. The second letter, dated 26 December 1873, was much firmer in its demands and it would appear that the king had been convinced by Amankwa Tia and other chiefs that the skirmish at Faysowah had been a great victory and that militarily the Asantes were in a strong position. Kofi Karikari thus renewed his claim upon the Assin and Denkyira peoples and demanded an explanation for the British aggression.

Wolseley was in no hurry to respond to the king's letters but when he did, he not only pointed out that Faysowah, rather than a great victory, was a small skirmish which resulted in the Asante army retreating back across the Prah. Wolseley also 'educated' the king by stating that Amankwa Tia had attacked Elmina and Abakrampa and had been decisively defeated on both occasions. Wolseley refused to acknowledge the Asante claims to the Assin and Denkyira peoples and demanded that the hostages be released immediately. Furthermore, the general stated as the Asantes had waged an unjust war by invading the protectorate that the British sought 50,000oz of gold in compensation and that royal hostages would have to be provided to guarantee future good behaviour. If Wolseley's terms were not met, then the British would advance upon Kumasi on four fronts. The Asante envoys stayed at Prahsu until 6 January, whilst Major Home completed the bridge across the Prah, and were then marched across and escorted by Buller for a few miles and then sent on their way to deliver Wolseley's terms to the king. The British did not slow their plans for invasion as they waited for Kofi Karikari's response. It seems most likely that by seeking such high-value compensation as well as royal personages as guarantors that Wolseley knew the terms would be too costly for the king to accept and then be able to maintain his own authority. Wolseley was in command of a powerful force and he was not willing to simply turn it around in the face of Asante promises.

The Four-Pronged Attack

Whilst Wolseley had been working to bring British battalions to a position at which an assault across the Prah could be launched, three other detachments had been endeavouring to harass the Asantes and ultimately head for Kumasi. Captains Butler and Dalrymple were tasked with leading forces of natives in diversionary movements. Butler was appointed to enlist an army of Akims and lead them in a march east of and parallel to Wolseley's main army, whilst Dalrymple was to raise a force from amongst the Wassa tribe and invade into western Asante, via the Ofin River. Both operations failed in their initial aspirations for lack of volunteers amongst the tribes. Butler did manage to recruit 1,400 Akims and crossed the Prah with them on 15 January. When he was just 15 miles from Kumasi, and only 5 miles to the west of Wolseley as he attacked the main Asante army, his force evaporated when it was opposed by what was undoubtedly an imaginary enemy. Butler was to spend two months in hospital in England recovering from the exertions of his ordeal and later wrote a book of his exploits which was aptly entitled *Akim-Foo (Ashantee 1874) – The History of a Failure*. Dalrymple was even less successful and only managed to recruit 50 of the required 1,000 Wassa tribesmen and was then unable to persuade this meagre force to cross the Ofin and by the end of January he abandoned his mission. All that can be said of these two operations is they at least kept the Asantes wondering what they had planned and this alone diverted some warriors away from those opposing Wolseley's main force. In the case of Dalrymple, the king of Bekwai had to assemble a force to repel an expected invasion whilst Butler's exploits kept the king of Kokofu from bringing his army to oppose Wolseley's main advance.

The largest of the operations was led by Captain Glover RN and his ambitious plan was first submitted to Kimberley in July 1873. Glover, with ten special by him to you . . . he must count upon your using the ordinary precautions of a military commander of troops in the field'.[49]

Wolseley realised, as he probably had all along, that Glover's much-reduced military operation would have little or no effect upon the result of the battles he would face as he moved on Kumasi. Although Glover's much smaller force would indeed eventually cross the Prah and even reach Kumasi, it had very much become a sideshow to Wolseley's main advance. With the battalions now marching towards the Prahsu base and the general and his staff already there, it was time for Buller and his intelligence department to cross the Prah and to scout ahead in preparation for the main British invasion.

Buller had collected a fine team around him. Over the next month, Lieutenant Lord Gifford would frequently be at the head of a band of scouts, which had been recruited from the local Assins. These men were natural forest dwellers and hunters and could speak the dialect of the Asantes without an accent. Even the hard to please Wolseley was impressed with these men. The rest of the scouts were composed of other special service officers and Hausas, Kossos and a few West Indies troops. Covered by the scouts, Baker Russell's regiment crossed the Prah on 5 January, followed by Wood's regiment ten days later. Each of these native regiments also carried eight to ten days of supplies forward which would have been impossible if Wolseley's plans had been opposed.

Amankwa Tia and his fellow war chiefs had devised a strategy to be used against the British once the battalions had crossed into Asante territory. It called for scouts and forward units of the army to carry out a fighting withdrawal to coax Wolseley's force deep into the jungle and then strike at a place of their choosing. Yet, initially Gifford and his scouts saw very little of the Asantes. There was a reliance upon various fetishes left along the trail to deter Wolseley's advance. These included half-buried kid goats, a mutilated body and white thread strung between the trees, which seemed to imitate the British telegraph wires, which the Asantes seemed to assume was a white man's fetish.

The next round of diplomacy began on 12 January when Gifford's party met a senior envoy along the path from Kumasi who was accompanied by one of the missionaries, Mr Kuhne, whom the king had decided to release as a gesture of goodwill. Kuhne was able to inform the British that the Asante army had not yet been fully mobilized, and that the king was unwilling to fight. Kuhne also stated that the king was unable to pay the high indemnity Wolseley demanded but had asked for the British to halt their advance. This Wolseley refused to do and the British marched on. Wolseley received Kofi Karikari's response on 21 January, which was delivered by another senior court official who was accompanied by the last hostages, the Ramseyers and Mr Bonnat (likely another missionary who had been kidnapped at the same time as the Ramseyers). Mr Dawson was still held in his role as an interpreter.

Wolseley felt that the news of the release of the hostages merited extraordinary action to get the information to the government as soon as possible and a chain of runners and the telegraph got the news to the coast on 24 January to meet the *Sarmatian*, which was tasked that night to sail to Gibraltar. Such prompt action saw the news reach London by 5 February. Although this costly move displayed Wolseley's flair for publicity, it somewhat backfired in that unbeknown to him Gladstone had sought a dissolution of Parliament and a general election was underway, and the expensive gesture and the news of the hostage release did not have the impact he was hoping for.

The king's latest negotiation stance was again dismissed by Wolseley. Even though Kofi Karikari indicated that Amankwa Tia would be required to pay an indemnity for the invasion, the released hostages confirmed that the king was not able to pay the 50,000oz of gold. Yet, with the release of the hostages and with the withdrawal of the invading army most of the original needs for the campaign had been settled and a moment probably existed for the peaceful entry into Kumasi of perhaps a token force. However, Wolseley was not going to let the opportunity for a military victory be missed and for a settlement to be imposed. Indeed, there is a strong argument that British public opinion expected a decisive defeat of the 'savages' and even stronger one that the Asantes had to be taught a firm lesson to ensure that the protectorate would not be threatened by a further invasion. Thus, Wolseley in replying to the king's pleas to halt demanded that all Fante prisoners were also released, for half of the gold should be paid immediately and for six hostages to guarantee Asante behaviour be handed over to the British at Cape Coast Castle. These were to include the *Asantehemaa*, queen mother, as well as the king's brother and designated heir. There is no knowing if Wolseley had demanded other hostages whether Kofi Karikari would have conceded but the king simply could not handover such royal personages and maintain his own throne. Wolseley would have known this and that as he pressed his men on towards Kumasi confrontation was inevitable.

There is also reason to believe that the king was deceitful in his negotiations. For Buller's spies had informed him that the Asante army was now gathering en masse to oppose Wolseley's advance and that the negotiations were simply attempts to slow the British and allow more time for the army to assemble. When two further letters were received on 29 January from the king asking once more for the British to halt they also came with a coded message from Dawson, 'Please see 2 Corinthians, chap.ii, ver.II'. Wolseley obtained a Bible and read the highlighted text, 'Lest Satan should get an advantage of us: for we are not ignorant of his devices.'[50] Wolseley took the message as a warning that the king was trying to delay the advance so as to gather his forces and that a battle was imminent.

Lieutenant Thomas also recorded in his diary the march of the Rifle Brigade after it had crossed the Prah. Gone were the comfortable way stations and now the men had tents and groundsheets for their accommodation. The battalion reached Prahsu on 20 January and was met with a mournful sound as three volleys were fired over the grave of Captain Huyshe of the 1st Battalion who had died of fever the day before. Many of the officers, including Thomas, would have known Huyshe so it must have been a sobering time for them all. The battalion crossed the Prah on 21 January and marched nearly 14 miles to Essiamau where they found no huts, just long open sheds, covered with palm leaves. The strength of the battalion was 27 officers and 583 men, having already lost 6 officers and 69 men to fever and dysentery who had to be carried back to the coast. The following day saw another march of around 14 miles, during which fifteen men fell out with exhaustion. Thomas and his comrades finally reached Accrofoomu where 'lean-tos' had to be constructed and tents pitched. On 23 January the march to Moinsey was just 8 miles but here the men had to clear the bush and build huts. The march continued until the battalion reached Fomena on 25 January and it waited here for four nights whilst further supplies were brought up. Sickness returned to the battalion during this halt and Captain Slade had to be invalided back to the coast suffering from dysentery. On 29 January the Rifles marched 10 miles to Ahkankuassie, where the men built huts and the officers found accommodation in village dwellings, which were described as filthy places, overrun with lizards. Rations were served to the men for the following day when they marched just 4 miles to Insarfu. Throughout the march from the coast the Rifle Brigade had formed the rear-guard of the advance and here they were informed that a battle was expected on the following day and that once again they would be the rear of any assault.

In the days leading up to the Battle of Amoaful the British patrols had had more contacts with the Asante scouts and Buller's intelligence reported that the main army would likely oppose the British close to the village of Amoaful. The British increasingly came under sniping fire, although they were ordered only to fire upon the Asantes if they had been attacked first. There was some controversy about this when a most popular officer, Captain James Nicol, was killed during a reconnaissance towards Borborasi, where the king of Adanse's forces were thought to be assembling. Nicol was formerly an officer in the 13th Regiment and the Hampshire Militia who had fallen upon hard times. He had volunteered for the expedition hoping that it would be a means by which he could re-join the regular army as a full-time officer. He was commanding the Anamabo tribesmen from Baker Russell's regiment when he was killed. Some of the newspaper correspondents attempted to claim that Nicol died as a result of following the order to wait to be fired upon before returning fire and in this vein Winwood Reade even went so far as to claim that Nicol was a 'human sacrifice'.[51] Yet, according to Evelyn Wood, Nicol died as he approached a group of villagers to whom he was trying to convey the need for them to retire, when he was shot by a native who was hiding behind a house. Wood clearly felt that the 'no shoot' order was not to blame and furthermore stated, 'Neither could so brave and humane a man as Captain Nicol, with or without orders, have fired into a crowd of unresisting men.'[52] Wolseley and his officers were much affected by Nicol's death and a fund for his widow and children raised £80, of which Wolseley gave £20. In addition, when the Grocer's Company of the City of London gifted Wolseley £250 for him to distribute to those who had suffered as a result of the campaign, Nicol's widow received half.

On the death of Nicol, the British force opened fire and cleared the village of Asantes and captured in the process the state umbrella of the veteran Asante general, Asamoa Nkwanta. The presence of such an important figure suggested that a major battle was close and indeed Asamoa Nkwanta and the king of Adanse were trying to lure Wolseley on to the main Asante army, which, as Buller's spies confirmed, was holding a reversed arrow head-shaped defensive zone on raised ground around the village of Amoaful. The plan to oppose the British seemed to have followed the normal battlefield tactics of the Asante army. With Amankwa Tia out of favour, command was given to the *Mamponhene*, or the king of Mampon, a man named Kwabena Dwumo, who usually led the army's right wing. Amankwa Tia was reportedly so incensed by this slur that he swore not to return alive from the forthcoming battle. It was envisaged that as the main Asante force pinned down the British advance the traditional flanking movements would pass to the British rear, destroy the bridge across the Prah and thus cut off the main British army from the sea, supplies and reinforcements. Such tactics had worked so well against African foes and had also prevailed against Governor McCarthy. However, Wolseley had researched Asante tactics and had read every piece of writing about McCarthy's disastrous campaign and was thus ready for such an approach. He was to place one of his best units, the Rifle Brigade, on the rear to counter this Asante tactic. Wolseley accepted the challenge laid down by Kwabena Dwumo for, hoping to avoid more than one engagement, he saw the coming battle as an opportunity to destroy the enemy, although he had hoped that the battle would be nearer Kumasi.

The Battle of Amoaful, 31 January 1874

The battle Wolseley was so intent on was now almost upon him and his troops. Although the Asante position was a strong one, it had been weakened at the last minute by the need to divert the forces of the king of Dwaben, Asafo Agyei, to oppose Captain Glover's advance, which had finally made some progress in its march on Kumasi. The night before the battle Wolseley called together all his battalion and regimental officers and outlined his plan of attack. He reiterated how the jungle would mean that close control of men would be essential and reaffirmed the expected Asante plan of attack. Wolseley stated that to counter the Asante flanking movements he resolved to advance as a large open square formation, or parallelogram, with each side having its own selected commander. The position to be occupied by each battalion and regiment was explained in detail to each of the commanders (see below). The front fighting line was to be 600–700m wide, with its centre marked by Captain Rait's two 7-pounders, which would move forward on the Kumasi road, surrounded by the Highlanders of the 42nd, commanded by Major Duncan Macpherson, with Alison in overall command of the front face. The rockets were deployed on the front two angles of the square.

The left and right faces, commanded by Colonels McLeod and Wood respectively, would initially cut at 90 degrees to the front of the square, at a maximum distance of 300m from the road and then turn and cut a path parallel to the main path. Wolseley, his staff, the newspaper correspondents, the medical orderlies and the reserve of a detachment of the 23rd Royal Welsh Fusiliers were placed in the centre of the square. The baggage was held at Ahkankuassie under the guard of a sick Baker Russell and one company of his regiment, whilst the West Indies troops guarded the field hospital and reserve ammunition held at Insarfu. Wolseley knew that his force of 1,508 Europeans and 708 native troops was too small to prevent the enemy, estimated at between 15,000 and 20,000 warriors, from surrounding it and that they would be much more mobile moving through the jungle than the British could ever hope to be. Wolseley impressed upon the officers that the Asantes were a formidable enemy who would use drums, horns and screams to try and intimidate the troops and that to prevail the British needed to be brave, confident and highly disciplined. He stressed that all faces of the square were equally important in honour and importance.

Gifford's scouts were in advance of the British square as it pushed forward at about 8am on the morning of 31 January 1874. They passed through the village of Quarman without seeing the enemy but ¾ mile further on, as they approached Egginassie they came under long-range but ineffective musket fire. Gifford, leading from the front, urged his men on, passed an attempted ambush in the village and took possession of it without further resistance. However, a large body of Asantes was across and around the road leading out of Egginassie. It was now time for the British infantry to be deployed and Alison ordered forward two companies of Highlanders and they pushed on through the scouts to engage the main Asante army.

Almost immediately after moving forward, the two leading companies of the 42nd had to be reinforced by a third and all became hotly engaged with the enemy. It soon became clear that the Asantes were endeavouring to turn the left flank of the Highlanders and in order to meet this movement two more companies were sent up a narrow bush path branching off to the left, but with firm orders not to lose contact with the three leading companies. Now the Highlanders were not facing ineffective spent bullets but close-range fire from Asantes lying flat on the ground. These warriors were virtually invisible until they fired their 'Long Danes' and this point-blank fire hit a number of troops, including the commanding officer, Major Macpherson, and Major Baird, who was severely wounded.

In his report after the battle, Alison wrote of this period:

> We were in the midst of a semi-circle of hostile fire, and we hardly caught sight of a man. As company after company of the 42nd descended, with their pipes playing, into the ravine, they were almost immediately lost sight of in the bush, and their positions could only be judged from the sharp crack of the rifles in contradistinction to the loud dull roar of the Ashanti musketry.[53]

By 10am Alison reported back to Wolseley that the enemy were holding their ground determinedly and that he was suffering many wounded. This Wolseley already knew from the steady stream of Highlanders returning to seek medical attention. Wolseley sent forward more surgeons and Alison called for reinforcements of half a battalion of the Rifle Brigade. Wolseley could not spare such numbers but sent the eighty-three-strong detachment of the Welsh Fusiliers and later one company of the Rifles.

The front column consisted of:

Two 7-pounder guns,
The 42nd Highlanders,
{ Brigadier - General
Sir A. Alison,
Bart., C.B.

Left Column.

100 men of the Naval Brigade,
Russell's Regiment,
Two rocket detachments,
} Colonel
McLeod,
C.B.

Right Column.

100 men Naval Brigade,
Wood's Regiment,
Two rocket detachments,
} Lieut.-Colonel
Evelyn Wood,
V.C.

Reserve

One company 23rd Regiment,
{ Lieut.-Colonel
Mostyn.

Rear Column.

2nd Battalion Rifle
Brigade,
{ Lieut.-Colonel
Warren.

Taken from E. Wood, *British Battles of Land & Sea*, Vol. II.

This was no battle of structured or defined troop movements but rather one of noise and confusion. The reporter and popular novelist George Henty left a vivid description of the battle: '. . . there was no manoeuvring, no brilliant charges, no general concentration of troops; but [the battle] which consisted simply of five hours of lying down, of creeping through the bush of gaining ground foot by foot, and of pouring a ceaseless fire into every bush in front which might contain an invisible foe'.[54] Other accounts dwell on the noise of drums, war cries, tom-tom and horns as well as the enormous noise that the Asantes's muskets made as they discharged. All of which at least gave the British some idea of where the invisible enemy might be.

For the Asantes too this was a battle like no other. At such close quarters the Sniders and Rait's 7-pounders left heaps of Asante dead and wounded. The Asantes soon realised that they were seriously outgunned, and their only hope of success was to infiltrate the British square. Asante skirmishers were particularly skilled at slipping between two British units and firing upon both. Frequently the British did not know where the firing was coming from and simply fired back in the general direction from whence it had come and at least one wounded officer had a Snider bullet extracted from him. Officers from the Naval Brigade complained that they were fired upon by men of the Welsh Fusiliers who had been sent to reinforce the Highlanders, as well as by the Highlanders themselves whilst both these regiments claimed that the Naval Brigade had fired upon them.

The British flanks were now attacked with the normal Asante battlefield tactic. Wolseley was prepared for this and had warned his troops to expect it. He ensured that the Welsh Fusiliers he sent forward maintained contact with the Highlanders, whilst the Rifle Brigade had the responsibility of linking with the rear of the Welshmen. Even this deployment did not stop the British centre coming under close-range attack from all sides. The enemy fire was so intense that Asante black powder hung in the air making the already poor jungle visibility significantly worse. Even some of the newspaper correspondents, men such as Winwood Reade and Henry Stanley, joined the firing line and made effective use of the Snider. In this confusion, Wolseley willed himself to display calmness to his men and he walked around the central position chain-smoking cigars.

As the Highlanders edged forward so the British flanks tried to join this general movement. This was the responsibility of Wood's and Baker Russell's irregulars, supported by the 200-strong Naval Brigade, split evenly between each regiment. Baker Russell's men advanced with some Highlanders under the command of Colonel McLeod to the right of the centre, but this was stalled by fierce Asante fire. It was in this attempted advance that Captain Richard Buckle of the Royal Engineers received a mortal wound whilst leading labourers from Sierra Leone who had been tasked with cutting a path. Wood's advance on the left also stalled. The men found themselves unable to move under intense fire and Wood ordered his men to cut a clearing in which they laid down and returned fire. After an hour, Wood became aware of fire coming over his men's heads from the rear and fearing it was 'friendly fire' from the Highlanders, he shouted, '42nd don't fire this way'. On hearing no reply, he angrily advanced to the edge of the clearing and was just about to part the bush with his hands when he was dragged back by Lieutenant Eyre who said, 'It is really not your place', and pushed in front of Wood. Eyre was met by the fire from a 'Long Dane', the shot of which just passed over his head. A shocked Eyre returned to Wood's side to inform him, 'There are no 42nd men there; the fellow who fired at us is black and quite naked.' Wood ordered his men to fire a series of volleys into the bush and this immediate threat was nullified.[55]

Captain Luxmoore was part of Wood's wing and he later described the confusion of the battle:

> My men lying down to escape the enemy's storm of bullets and slugs, and there we had to remain over four hours without being able to advance . . . We ourselves fired into the 23rd Regiment once I afterward found out, but the bush was so dense that one could scarcely see one's own men . . . The whole day I only saw one living Ashantee about 50 yards from me . . .[56]

Luxmoore had to assume command when Wood was hit by an Asante nail fired into him, just above his heart and it would be the naval man who would later move the irregulars forward.

Just before noon, the Asante fire began to slacken and Rait and his Hausa gunners used the opportunity to carry forward the 7-pounder to support the Highlanders. This weapon, firing over open sights at a mere 50m range, inflicted serious casualties upon the enemy and after each firing the Highlanders were able to advance a few extra metres under cover of the confusion and destruction. After fifteen rounds of this pulverising fire the Highlanders were able to stand up and charge forward. They poured into a now vacated Asante camp but as they continued onwards they were met by a renewed resistance from the ridge behind it. Rait's gun was again brought forward and this combined with Snider fire lessened the Asante threat. A fresh charge was made, and the last serious stand of the enemy was broken. A little after 12.30pm Sir Archibald Alison was able to report to Wolseley, 'The village of Amoaful is occupied by the 42nd. Major Home, R.E., has gone onto strengthen it, and clear the bush with his sappers immediately around it. All is quiet on my front, but there is heavy firing going on my right rear.'[57]

The capture of Amoaful was certainly not the end of the day's fighting. As the Welsh Fusiliers advanced to join the Highlanders, they met resistance from

Asantes who had infiltrated behind the Scotsmen. Having lost the centre, the enemy broke off their attacks on the flanks, allowing the centre and irregulars to move forward, the latter with war cries. Yet, the Asantes continued to attack and now focused their attention upon the line of communication and the stores at Quarman. This was held by a detachment of the 2nd West Indies under the command of a sickly officer, Captain Burnett of the 15th Foot. On hearing the Asante musketry, Burnett rose from his sick bed and rallied his command sufficiently to hold back the Asante attack until companies from the Rifle Brigade could be rushed from the rear to support Quarman. Even with these additional troops Quarman was hard pressed for 2 hours. As Colley approached the harassed base with fresh supplies in a convoy of porters nearly 5 miles long, he too was attacked from the bush and many of his carriers fled. A company of the Rifles sallied forth from Quarman and rescued Colley from immediate danger before returning to the base. Colley salvaged what supplies and porters he could and fell back to Insarfu.

The maintenance of the line of supply, Egginassie to Quarman to Insarfu, was now critical and the Asantes would continue to harass it in subsequent days and indeed temporarily it was halted by Asante action. Wolseley moved forward and established his command in Amoaful. After several hours of severe fighting the exhausted troops secured a perimeter defence as best they could and tried to gain some rest. Considering the high level of Asante fire, the casualty toll was remarkably light: 21 officers, 144 troops and 29 irregulars had been wounded, whilst 1 officer and 2 men of the 42nd were dead and in addition 1 irregular had been killed. Yet, these figures do not tell the whole story for one in four of every Highlander became a casualty and Wolseley realised that although fatalities had been thankfully few, he would still probably have to fight another pitched battle before reaching Kumasi with a much-weakened force. It is not known how many Asante warriors were committed to the battle or how many were killed, for the Asantes's practice of carrying off their dead from the battlefield meant that numbers were impossible to establish, although it is likely to have been in excess of 1,500. As he had promised, Amankwa Tia died in battle, shot by a private of the 42nd, and several more senior chiefs also fell. The bravery of the Asante warriors had been conclusively proven at Amoaful as had the inferiority of their weapons.

The Dash to Kumasi

Wolseley must have had a fitful night's sleep as he contemplated his next move. Although the Asante army had been comprehensively beaten, it was still offering resistance and threatening the British supply line which was a real concern for the general. The British were still 16 miles from Kumasi, with a much-reduced force which could expect another pitched battle before the city could be entered and furthermore the rains were due at any time. In Kumasi the fearful number of dead and the sight of the wounded returning from the battlefield had brought the peace party to the fore in the king's council. Again, attempts were made to negotiate with Wolseley, but the commander held his ground and his insistence that royal hostages must be provided was just too great a demand for the royal court to accept. The council was forced to take the unpopular measure of remobilising an already beaten army. The role of commander was accepted by Asamoa Nkwanta, a key member of the peace party, and it says much for the respect in which the veteran commander was held that he was able to bring the army together once more to oppose Wolseley.

Wolseley concluded that the real threat to reaching Kumasi was delay. Colley was doing his upmost to ensure supplies were brought forward but repeated enemy attacks on the lines of supply, even as far south as the supply depot at Fomena, had so frightened most of the porters that they simply refused to work. In these circumstances, Colley informed the general that it would be several days before he would be able guarantee enough supplies could be brought up. Wolseley knew his force only had four days' rations and a march on Kumasi and then a return to Ajimamu, where Colley assured the general food would be waiting, would take six days. Wolseley thus instructed the captains of the companies to ask their men if they would take the limited rations for the work ahead. All agreed, whether out of duty or loyalty it is not known, but what is certain is that the troops, like the general, were keen to get the job done and return to the coast before the arrival of the rains. On his return to England Colonel Wood had a meeting with the Duke of Cambridge, as well as the adjutant-general and military secretary. He informed them that if Sir Garnet Wolseley had not been appointed to lead the Asante Expedition Kumasi would never have been taken for nobody else would have ventured to enter the Asante capital with only one day's food in hand and it was indeed a risky move by a brave and determined commander.

Ajimamu was quickly converted into a base ready for Colley's supplies, with strong entrenchments. A small garrison, comprising the sick and wounded, was left behind and on the morning of 2 February the British continued their march on Kumasi. Although there were no serious engagements with the enemy on this day, Gifford's scouts, supported by Baker Russell's men and the Rifles, had to shoot their way past numerous ambuscades. It is worth considering if the Asantes had adopted a guerrilla-style warfare as soon as Wolseley had crossed the Prah whether they would have slowed the British advance sufficiently for the rains and logistical problems to have forced Wolseley to retire. Yet, such tactics were contrary to the martial confrontation pitched battle tactics of the Asante army which had been so successful in the past and of course Wolseley knew this.

The hard fighting of the previous days and the constant demands of the march were finally beginning to take their toll on the troops. Men were becoming increasingly trigger happy, firing at shadows and their nerves were not helped by the Asante practice of human sacrifice. At each settlement the British passed through either the body of a young man or woman was laid out, feet in the direction of Kumasi and their severed heads directed towards the troops.

As the day progressed so the Asante resistance increased. Rait's guns were used to soften up any significant Asante opposition and at times Gifford and his scouts were dangerously exposed. By the end of the day the British had reached the River Oda and here they rested for the night and were able to count the cost of the day. Of the eleven Hausas serving Rait's guns, seven had been wounded by Asante skirmishers and there were a further thirty-three casualties amongst Baker Russell's irregulars and the Rifles. Wolseley received another deputation from the Asante king which stated that all Fante prisoners would be freed if Wolseley would only halt his advance. Needing a day for his engineers to build a bridge to cross the Oda, Wolseley bluffed and agreed to the halt for one day but wrote to Kofi Karikari stating that he still expected the royal hostages to be sent to him.

The British had a horrendous night for shortly before sunset a torrential rain storm struck the improvised camp and the men with no tents or cover of any sort were soon drenched. The rain was so intense that fires could not be lit, and few men gained any sleep. Daybreak brought relief and sunshine. The engineers had worked their usual miracle and despite the rain a bridge had been finished and the advance commenced once more. Buller's intelligence team captured an Asante who under interrogation revealed that there were up to 10,000 warriors ready to oppose the British at the village of Ordashu.

From 6.30am, the British began their march in single column with Wood's irregulars leading the advance. Wood had dragged himself out of his sick bed, with the Asante rusty nail still embedded in his chest where it remained until he died aged nearly 82. He had travelled through the downpours of the night before to be with his men at the vanguard. Wood was followed by three companies of Rifles and the remaining native regiments all under the command of Colonel McLeod. The rest of the Rifles, Rait's artillery and the dwindling band of Welsh Fusiliers and Highlanders formed the main body, again commanded by Archibald Alison. Wolseley followed with his staff whilst the Naval Brigade was tasked with the safe crossing of the baggage across the Oda and then to form a protective rear to the column.

Within minutes Wood's men were under accurate fire from Asante pickets and to his dismay the natives flung themselves to the ground and fired widely into the air, without even looking up. Wood tried to set an example for his reluctant men and stood in full view of the enemy. Lieutenant Eyre tried to encourage

Wood to at least crouch down and as he was doing so Eyre was hit in the bladder by an Asante shot. The young lieutenant died 2 hours later in excruciating pain, despite having been administered morphine. Wood was devasted by the loss. Wolseley relinquished the vanguard from Wood's petrified troops and the three companies of rifles, with the support of one 7-pounder, pushed forward.

The opposition from the Asante force stiffened and McLeod was forced to deploy more and more troops forward and he called upon Wolseley for support. At 9.30am, after nearly 2 hours of hard fighting, the Rifles gave a cheer and McLeod led them forward in a sudden rush which carried Ordashu. By 11am Wolseley had established his headquarters in the village but at this moment the position was attacked on all sides in an inferno of musketry for the Asantes were determined to retake the village. The Naval Brigade in the rear was also attacked in some force and they and the baggage had to rush forward to seek the relative sanctuary of the village. There is some confusion as to whether Kofi Karikari was actually present at the Battle of Ordashu or sat with the Golden Stool a couple of miles further back, but what is clear is that at this point in the battle the Asantes fought with renewed determination and vigour.

The sound of war drums, the screams of the warriors and crash of incessant musketry from an invisible foe finally began to take its toll on the British troops who had now endured three weeks of privations in the jungle with their nerves on edge. The Asante moved closer to the British and the right and rear was initially under much strain and soon the left was also pressed. Some men of the Rifles began firing indiscriminately and had to be rebuked, whilst the warriors encroached nearer and nearer. It was Henry Brackenbury who wrote of the unsteadiness of the Rifles in his official history of the war and his comments caused both anger and dismay amongst the officers of the Rifles who sought redress. Brackenbury stood by his comments, though it is felt by some historians this may have hindered his career.

Suddenly Wolseley himself was down, bowled over by an Asante slug that hit him on his helmet. His staff jumped to his aid and Colonel Greaves, who had replaced O'Neill as chief of staff, emptied his revolver in the direction of where the shot had come from. Fortunately, the folds of the puggaree on Wolseley's helmet had taken most of the impact. The general was helped to his feet and although he suffered from a bad headache for the rest of the day, he was otherwise unharmed.

Having regained his composure, Wolseley realised that the advance had stalled badly and it was only the steady volleys of the Snider that was keeping the determined Asantes from overrunning the British position. Wolseley called upon McLeod and the remaining 340 men of the 42nd to charge in rushes towards Kumasi. With pipers playing and a hearty cheer the Highlanders made a dash for the capital. Firing volleys by companies the Highlanders took turns to run forward and reload, without stopping. The first obstacle in the path was a huge silk–cotton tree which had been felled to block the advance. From behind this natural barrier Asante marksmen knocked over six Scotsmen but firing in rapid succession the Highlanders carried the position and charged on.

The Asantes were bewildered by this rapid advance. Each ambuscade was simply brushed past in the pursuit of the target of Kumasi. As they marched in double time or even ran along the path, the Highlanders ignored each flank attack. Rait's artillery could not possibly keep up with this wild charge as the men of the 42nd dashed through village after village. The Asantes had never seen an enemy behave in such a manner and their surprise shifted to fear and many broke and fled. Within little over an hour the now exhausted Highlanders reached the outskirts of the village of Karsi, the last remaining settlement before the capital. Here they rested and Alison, who had accompanied the mad advance, sent word back to the hard-pressed Wolseley that the 42nd would be in Kumasi before nightfall. The general at once ensured that this good news was communicated to all his troops, both European and native, and all raised ringing cheers at the news. This sound made the Asantes cease firing. They seemed instinctively to know what it meant, and this was reinforced when Asante speakers in the native regiments confirmed their fears with taunts. The warriors withdrew in silence and the battle was over.

Realising that he now had a great opportunity, Wolseley ordered a rapid advance of his whole force upon Kumasi. Leaving a small garrison at Ordashu, the general himself soon passed through the leading troops of the Rifles and overtaking them he smiled and said, 'Come on, my lads, you will have a house to sleep in tonight, perhaps a palace.'[58] The march was largely unhindered by Asante opposition. As Wolseley neared the capital a note was received from Dawson warning him that if the British pressed on to Kumasi that he and the remaining Fante prisoners were likely to be executed. The general's only comment to his troops was for them to quicken their pace. McLeod, waiting with his Highlanders at Karsi, also received an even more desperate plea from Dawson. This was duly sent back to Wolseley, but McLeod knew that his duty was to reach Kumasi and so he roused his tired Highlanders for one last effort and led them forward for the last 4 miles. Two hostages, one a woman, were forced to walk in front of the advancing Scotsmen and they shouted, 'Shanti fo! Shanti fo!', meaning 'Asante people' and this seems to have deterred any enemy fire. The troops came across some gruesome sights, including a newly decapitated young man and they managed to stop a group of warriors from inflicting a similar fate upon another victim. As they approached Kumasi the path widened and the jungle thinned. More and more Asantes appeared, some carrying their musket butts forward in submission whilst others remained sullen and aggressive-looking. One man, dressed in leopard skins, and apparently a commander of some importance, rebuked the British troops for both the rapid nature of the advance which had caught the Asantes by surprise and for continuing when the king still wanting to talk peace.

At about 5.30pm McLeod led his weary troops down the wide streets of Kumasi, without facing any opposition from large numbers of Asante warriors and civilians who stared at them with curiosity and astonishment. The Highlanders positioned themselves in the main market square where, an hour later, just before dusk, they were joined by Wolseley and the rest of the contingent. The general ordered his men to give three hearty cheers for Her Majesty, which must have caused some confusion amongst the locals. Most peculiarly the fierce warriors who had so fervently opposed the British wandered amongst the crowds of civilians embracing relatives and friends, seemingly relieved that the fight was over, whilst the British received water and handshakes from many of the townspeople. Although Wolseley must have been hugely satisfied that he had reached the capital, he knew his position was a delicate one. His men were hungry, wounded or sick and all were utterly exhausted, and he needed to find shelter for them quickly. At the same time there were literally hundreds of sullen, armed warriors on the streets and he was aware that if he tried to disarm them a violent incident might ensue, which in the confines of the city could quickly become a bloodbath. Wolseley was also keen to negotiate a peace treaty with Kofi Karikari who seemingly had fled the capital and was now in a country residence a few miles north. The general had to content himself with placing his artillery in the main square which would allow his men to sweep the streets surrounding it if violence broke out. He also positioned pickets to alert him of any danger and to discourage looting.

Both Dawson and the Fante prisoners had not been executed and Wolseley instructed Dawson to write a note to the king demanding that he come to Kumasi first thing the following day to secure a peace treaty, and he announced that his demand for the queen mother and the heir to be handed over as hostages had been waivered. If the king did not appear, then great harm would come to his kingdom and furthermore if a single shot was fired upon the British then Kumasi would be destroyed. The troops camped along the chief avenues of the capital and were served with gin, large quantities of which had been found in one of the palace buildings. Wolseley and his staff found a billet overlooking the main square and a bottle of champagne was retrieved from the general's baggage and all solemnly drank Queen Victoria's health.

During the night one of the men from the irregular regiments was hung for looting whilst many fires broke out around the capital, probably started by other looters and revenge-filled Fantes. The sappers from the engineers were again called upon to pull down buildings that were adjacent to those on fire to

control the blaze. In the resulting confusion many Asantes took the opportunity
to gather together their own belongings and slipped out of the city.

The British awoke to find Kumasi deserted. The thousands of civilians and
warriors that had thronged the city the evening before had vanished into the
bush and the British were left to explore their prize. Kumasi left those British
who had journeyed there with mixed emotions and images. Frank Boyle of
the *Daily Telegraph* wrote that Kumasi was 'a town over which the smell of
death hangs everywhere, and pulsates on each sickly breath of wind . . .'.[59]
Dr Mackinnon, the chief medical officer for the expedition, wrote that he had
been billeted in the house of the king's executioner who told Mackinnon that
he usually executed two or three people a day but as the British neared he had
lost count of his victims. Wolseley and others wrote of a grove of trees where
the bodies of those unfortunate enough to become human sacrifices had been
dumped and that many had been physically sick at the sights there.

Alternatively, Henry Stanley who, as he demonstrated during his search for
Dr Livingstone, and in his later service for the king of the Belgians in the Belgian
Congo, was no lover of Africans or their cultures. Stanley had accompanied the
expedition and wrote:

> We were anxious and curious to see . . . the King's palace, the place
> of execution, the great market, the town square. The streets were
> numerous; some half a dozen of them were broad and uniform. The
> main avenue on which the British and local troops bivouacked during
> the night was about 70 yards wide; here and there were great shade
> trees. The houses in the principal street were wattled structures,
> with alcoves and stuccoed facades, embellished with Arabic patterns.
> Behind each of the big buildings were groups of huts for the women,
> children and slaves, enclosing small courtyards. By the general order
> and neatness . . . I was compelled to the conclusion that they were a
> very clean people.

Winwood Reade of *The London Times* also wrote of Kumasi; 'The King's
palace consists of many courtyards, each surrounded with alcoves and verandas
having two gates or doors secured by padlocks. The rooms upstairs reminded
me of Wardour Street in London.' He found books in many languages, the
17 October 1873 issue of his own newspaper, Persian rugs, Kidderminster car-
pets, Bohemian glass, a sword inscribed from Queen Victoria, gold-studded
sandals, caps of beaten gold covered with leopard skin, velvet umbrellas and
other treasures 'too numerous to describe or even catalogue'.[60] Wolseley himself
commented: 'I visited the royal palace and was surprised to find it though not
imposing in character yet well laid out, clean and fairly well kept. Some of its

buildings were of substantial masonry, and most of it was solidly constructed and admirably roofed in.'[61]

Wolseley knew that he and his men could not stay long in Kumasi for the rains were threatening, the arrival of which could seriously jeopardise the return march to the coast. The casualties of the Battle of Ordashu were not as severe as at Amoaful; only Eyre and one native troop had been killed but six officers and sixty men had been wounded. All those who were able to walk were sent back down the line and the general realised that he could not risk another clash of arms with so many troops sick or wounded. His organisation for handling such men was already stretched to its limits and he knew he would have to head south soon. Frustratingly, the correspondence he received from the king promised his imminent arrival which never happened and although he waited another night, Wolseley knew the king would never appear.

In the early morning of 6 February a rather sullen force assembled to leave Kumasi for Wolseley had let it be known to the men that they were marching in pursuit of Kofi Karikari and his army, whereas this was simply a ruse to deceive any spies that might be in the vicinity. Spirits lifted noticeably when the men soon realised that were heading south and back to the coast. The British forces had looted the royal palace the day before. The captured booty was carried by thirty porters to Cape Coast Castle and some of this has subsequently found a home in the British Museum. Major Home and his engineers blew up the royal palace and set fires across the capital. The Naval Brigade led the march south and McLeod and the Highlanders were the last to leave the smoking ruins of Kumasi as they took the rear of the column.

Glover's Expedition

As ordered, Glover crossed the Prah on 15 January with 750 Hausas and Yorubas. His force lost touch with Wolseley's column by the end of the month and both men marched on not knowing the whereabouts of each other. Glover's advance was over difficult, mountainous jungle terrain and his small force suffered from want of supplies, yet its very presence diverted the king of Dwaben's sizeable force from Amoaful. Glover, and, in particular, one of his special service officers, Captain Reginald Sartorius of the 6th Bengal Cavalry, were engaged in skirmishes with the Dwaben. At the village of Odumase an enemy force about 1,000-strong were routed and for his leadership here and in other engagements Sartorius was later awarded the Victoria Cross.

After Kumasi had fallen Glover was astonished to receive a deputation from the Dwaben king requesting an armistice. Glover was not empowered to negotiate but realised that Wolseley must have reached Kumasi. He told the envoys to seek out Wolseley, and at the same time decided to despatch Sartorius with a small escort to try and contact the general. Sartorius set out on 10 February, without provisions, carrying a report from Glover to Wolseley. In it Glover gave his position as the village of Essiamimpon and wrote that he could not continue further with his force of now 700 troops because supplies were desperately low. He stated, 'My men have had only one ounce of salt meat per man since the 18th January, and that one four days since.'[62] Sartorius had been told by Glover that Kumasi was only 7 miles away, but he learnt to his cost that the actual distance was double that and as a consequence he was forced to spend an uncomfortable night lying in an abandoned village whilst Asante soldiers moved about in the jungle surrounding him.

The following day his small force of twenty Hausas entered an almost deserted Kumasi and the few Asantes that emerged from the remaining build-ings demonstrated no antagonism and reported that Wolseley's men had left. Sartorius had no difficulty in following the mud-trodden path of Wolseley's force and as the rains had eased, he and his men had little trouble fording the various streams en route. The battlefield of Amoaful possessed the dreadful smell of decaying unburied bodies and although Sartorius's detachment did pass isolated groups of Asante warriors, none offered any resistance. At noon on 13 February Wolseley's camp at Fomena was astonished to see an exhausted Sartorius ride in on a starving pony, followed by twenty footsore Hausas. Sartorius was able to deliver Glover's report to Wolseley in person before nearly collapsing. His force had achieved the remarkable feat of marching 55 miles through jungle terrain in enemy held territory to deliver the news of Glover's column. In his report to the Duke of Cambridge Wolseley was able to turn Sartorius's endeavours in his favour to demonstrate his own success for he wrote, 'There could be no greater proof of how thoroughly the enemy's army has been beaten and dispersed than the fact of one white man [Sartorius] with only 20 black soldiers being able to traverse the country in safety.'[63] Wolseley immediately sent a despatch to Glover ordering him to fall back across the Prah and thence to his base at Accra. After such high expectations of Glover's enterprise, especially at Cabinet level, many, including Glover himself, must have been disappointed at the limited success of this operation, as well as those of Butler and Dalrymple, yet each to some degree had at least managed to divert enemy warriors from opposing Wolseley's advance.

Peace and Laurels

Wolseley's decision to make a dash for Kumasi after the Battle of Amouful proved to be not only a brave one but also a correct one for the threatened rains arrived on the night of 6 February and the early days of the return march were severely hampered. The road which had been dry and firm only a few days before was now a swamp with mud that was so deep the men frequently disappeared up to their waists. The bridge built over the Ordah was found to be 2ft under the level of the swollen river, and it was with great difficulty in these early days that the troops wearily marched on. On 8 February the Rifle Brigade reached the battlefield of Amoaful on their march back to the coast. Lieutenant Thomas wrote in his diary on that day, 'The appearance of the battalion was really startling. Men who had landed six weeks previous, strong, robust and healthy, were reduced to mere skeletons, and had lost that soldier-like smartness and activity they had displayed on the march up country.'[64] On this day a proclamation from Wolseley was read out to all the returning troops which praised them for their efforts and reaffirmed that their mission had been to tame a 'savage' peoples:

> After five days' very hard fighting, under very trying circumstances, your courage and devotion have been rewarded with complete success . . . You have repeatedly defeated a very numerous and most courageous enemy, fighting on its own ground, in well selected positions. British pluck, and the discipline common to Her Majesty's land and sea forces, have enabled you thus to overcome all difficulties . . . and you have proved to this barbarous people that England is able to punish her enemies, no matter what their strength in numbers be, or the position they hold.[65]

The return to the coast was a more sombre affair for Wolseley than a victor might have expected. The casualty rate amongst the officers was disproportionately heavy and there were too many 'empty spaces'. Captain Brackenbury was the only surviving member of the thirty-five special services officers who had journeyed with Wolseley from England to accompany the general back to the coast. The remainder were either dead, like Charteris and Huyshe, wounded, like Wood, or sick with fever. Of about 2,500 white troops who had set out for Kumasi, 71 had died, 394 were wounded and a total of 1,018 were invalided home. Thus 59 per cent of the combined strength was either killed, wounded or succumbed to sickness. In the two months of the main campaign sickness affected 71 per cent of the total force in one way or another and this was despite the most careful preparations for dealing with the climate.

Wolseley had satisfied his own inclinations; the Asantes had been decisively defeated, Kumasi taken and the king humiliated, and all these were required to enhance Britain's reputation on the Gold Coast and ensure that the threat of a future invasion of the protectorate was nullified. Yet, Wolseley had not achieved his aim for, as Gladstone predicted and Kimberley had feared, the *Asantehene* had fled Kumasi and no one was there to sign a peace treaty; Wolseley was forced to turn his army around and head for the coast without one. The king's envoys did not reach Wolseley until 13 February when the draft of the Treaty of Fomena was handed to him and he had already left for home when the treaty was signed and ratified by the administrator at Cape Coast on 14 March 1874. The new treaty replaced the 1831 treaty with a few important additions. The *Asantehene* agreed to renounce all allegiance from the Denkyira, Assin, Akim and Adansi, as well as his claim on Elmina and the rent for the British forts. The king also agreed to pay the 50,000oz of gold Wolseley had demanded. However, this was never fully paid and would be used as an excuse for future conflict. Gladstone stated in his Greenwich manifesto, at the start of the 1874 general election campaign, that it was never the British government's policy to destroy the Asante nation, but it was to secure a treaty which would result in long-term peaceful relations. The Treaty of Fomena did nothing to secure good relations between the Asantes and the British, only resentment. The treaty was to undermine political stability in Kumasi, resulting in years of turmoil and would lead to further British intervention within twenty-five years. Wolseley, as he would do in the 1879 political settlement between Britain and the Zulu nation, was able to claim success and raise his own personal standing whilst leaving others to deal with the consequences.

Lieutenant Thomas and his comrades finally reached the coast on 21 February and were delighted to be served cocoa in Cape Coast Castle as their baggage was conveyed onboard the *Himalaya*. Sixty men were too ill to join the remainder of the battalion as it sailed for England on 23 February. En route Thomas wrote that few of the men availed themselves of the opportunity to read the numerous library books which had been sent out for the troops for all were so utterly worn out that all they cared for was sleep. Tragically the battalion had to attend the very poignant funeral of one of the men who died of dysentery aboard and his body was consigned to the waves. The *Himalaya* steamed into Portsmouth on 26 March to be greeted by the mayor and a 'perfect hurricane of cheers' from the locals. In Winchester Thomas found:

> The old city was astir, and every available nook was secured by the inhabitants to catch the first glimpse of the 'Ashanti heroes'. The streets were covered with bunting, triumphal arches, garlands of flowers, and brilliantly illuminated. Marching was out of the question; we made the best of our way through the crowds of people, headed by our band, to the Barracks, and here everything was made as comfortable as possible.[66]

The celebrations carried on for a further week; the battalion was inspected by the Commander-in-Chief, The Duke of Cambridge and later Queen Victoria reviewed the troops at a march-past in Windsor Great Park. Winchester further honoured the battalion with a banquet at the city's Guildhall.

Wolseley was to receive even greater thanks and plaudits. The queen presented him with an honorary knighthood, but he modestly declined a baronetcy. Wolseley did accept a sword of honour from the lord mayor of London and a lavish banquet at the Guildhall, as well as honorary degrees from both Oxford and Cambridge universities. Finally, the House of Commons awarded Wolseley a vote of thanks and a personal grant of £25,000. According to the War Office, the cost of the campaign had been £660,978, under the budgeted £800,000, and if this is compared with the figure of £23,412,223 for the Second Afghan War of 1878–80 it can clearly be seen why it was considered an inexpensive conflict.[67] The performance of the British troops reflected well upon Edward Cardwell and his contentious reforms to the battalion system and this and the fact that the campaign was low in cost and casualties was also viewed as a personal triumph for him. Clearly, he and Kimberley had chosen the right man in Wolseley and they showed their political bravery in backing him to assume military, operational and administrative responsibility once on the Gold Coast.

Wolseley drew huge praise for his logistical and operational skills which in turn had kept the feared high levels of loss amongst the troops to a relatively low level. The phrase 'All Sir Garnet' became synonymous for many years with something that was well planned or organised or going well. His fame was such that in 1879 he was caricatured as the very model of a modern major general by W.S. Gilbert in the comic opera *The Pirates of Penzance*. Thus ended the Anglo-Asante War of 1873–4. Wolseley would continue to further fame and fortune, as would many of those who had served alongside him. Yet, the comparatively low casualty rates hid many personal tragedies of young aspiring lives cut short and this is undoubtedly why Wolseley was later to write in his autobiography that the Anglo-Asante War of 1873–4 was 'the most horrible war I ever took part in'.[68]

Part III

The British Dictate

The Anglo-Asante War of 1873–4, or the 'Segrenti War', as the Asantes called it (this being a corruption of 'Sir Garnet'), was a decisive British victory. Although Wolseley's logistical and operational planning was inspired, some luck, as in all wars, played a part in the final result. Undoubtedly the vast technological superiority the British possessed was an important factor, but equally poor Asante ammunition and gunpowder meant that despite high numbers of wounded, battlefield fatalities amongst the British were mercifully low. Wolseley could have been dealing with large numbers of dead troops if the Asantes had been well resourced in munitions and this alone could have swung the war in the Asantes's favour.

Yet, the critical factor in the Asante defeat was that the nation's leadership was badly divided between the war and peace party and the king's decisions swung back and forth depending on who was in the ascendency in the council. A more united and vigorous defence as soon as the British had crossed the Prah, perhaps even guerrilla warfare, may have succeeded in delaying the advance of the British until the rains arrived and then Wolseley would have had little alternative but to retire to the coast, and Britain's military and political reputation on the Gold Coast would have been in tatters.

The Asante nation had been beaten and humbled and as it had been built by conquest and annexation, so it now began to crumble and the confederation of tribes broke apart. States like Kwahu, Gyaman, Sefwi, Banda and some of the northern tribes such as Bono, Dagbon and Gonja declared their independence, whilst the chiefs of Mampon, Nsuta, Bekwai, Kokofu, Dwaben and Aguna distanced themselves from Kumasi. According to Ghanaian historian Augustine Kofi Tieku, the nation was more or less reduced to its original metropolitan area by the defeat. Kofi Karikari was deposed seven months after the war's conclusion for he was found guilty of taking gold dust, trinkets, rings and chains off the bodies in the royal mausoleum without seeking the permission of the elders as a means to restock the royal treasury. He tried to hide his actions and even bribed those he ordered to act on his behalf. He was denounced by his own mother, Afua Kobi, and his brother, Nana Osei Mensa Bonsu, was appointed as the new *Asantehene*. The new king saw his main task as restoring the states that had deserted the confederation. Yet, the result was further political and military turmoil.

Britain's New Role

Despite Britain's military triumph there were still many influential Members of Parliament who advocated a complete withdrawal from the protectorate. Even the official historian for the campaign, Henry Brackenbury, claimed that Britain had no moral obligation to protect the Fantes and saw no advantage in retaining a settlement that was not financially self-supporting.[1] Yet, there is no doubt that there would have been dishonour in a withdrawal and this was pointed out by the *Gold Coast Times*, which claimed that it doubted whether the Asantes would keep to the terms of the Treaty of Fomena and urged the British government to lay down a clear future policy for the protectorate so that it could thrive economically and be in a position to defend itself from any further Asante aggression. *The Times* of London wrote, 'The King of Ashanti has bound us to the Gold Coast by the ties of honour and reputation.'[2]

In the Colonial Office the conclusion of the campaign brought a realisation of Britain's new responsibility. James Lowther, the Parliamentary Under Secretary at the Colonial Office stated, 'Complete annexation or total abandonment are I fear the only sound alternatives. The former is too ghastly a scheme to contemplate, the latter too charming to be capable of execution.'[3] Lord Carnarvon, the Secretary of State for the Colonies in Benjamin Disraeli's new Conservative government, saw Britain's responsibility towards the Gold Coast as 'A very evil choice to have to make.'[4]

Within the House of Commons there was a strong minority opinion for withdrawal which was certainly very vocal. Questions were raised as to the need for the campaign whilst the destruction of Kumasi was labelled as vandalism and that the Treaty of Fomena was worthless. Yet, the general mood had changed since 1865 and even those who had favoured withdrawal then, now favoured Britain remaining on the Gold Coast to define its role, obligations and territory. Disraeli, an expansionist prime minster, aimed to devise a firm policy and after a few months of deliberation letters patent and an Order in Council were issued on 24 July 1874 which transformed the Gold Coast Settlements into the Gold Coast Colony. Along with Lagos, it was to have its own administration, separate once more from Sierra Leone. Immediate security was to be provided by a Hausa police force led by British officers. On 6 August 1874 the Legislative Council of the Colony was empowered to legislate for adjacent protected territories. The Gold Coast Colony had thus secured its own position within the British Empire, yet the politicians were happy in that the new policy did not define the exact territorial limit of the colony or what degree of protection it could expect from London. This ambiguity was so that the Colonial Office could distance itself from the continuing practices of slavery and human sacrifice in the interior and in particular in Asante. Yet, in August 1874, under pressure from the Aborigines Protection Society and the new Governor, Sir George Strahan, who took a strong personal stance, Carnarvon was forced to declare domestic slavery illegal in the new colony. Although the policy was never properly enforced in the interior, it did have a negative effect on the general economy within Asante and added to the level of chaos in a troubled Asante nation. As Asante weakened and fractured after the 1873–4 war, the British government was not sorry to witness it and neither was it immediately willing to take any further action to either encourage or prevent turmoil in Asante.

The Weakening of the Asante Nation

The new *Asantehene* Mensa Bonsu saw that his first priority as king was to rebuild his shattered capital. Thus, a major project of construction began and within a year most of the royal palace had been rebuilt, although it would take three years of hard work for Kumasi to be largely restored to the commercial and political hub it had been. Mensa Bonsu also turned his attention upon those states who had used the military defeat at the hands of the British to distance themselves from Kumasi. His first target was Dwaben, which had secured an alliance with the Asokore, Nsuta, Effiduase and Oyoko tribes. Months of negotiation came to nothing and indeed Kumasi traders were frequently abused, killed or imprisoned by the Dwaben. Mensa Bonsu now switched to a military option. Realising that he needed modern rifles, the king secured several hundred Sniders and with the help of a German mercenary named Neilson formed a corps of Hausas to help transform the Asante army.

In October 1875 Mensa Bonsu attacked Dwaben, aided by states such as Kokofu, Bekwai and Asumegya. Initially the Dwaben held back the invasion and at Aseremaso they were able to inflict a reversal upon the Asante force. The following month a fresh Asante army under the command of Kobina Ewua was able to engage the main Dwaben army and after three days of heavy fighting, in which the Dwaben warriors were constantly pushed back, and with their ammunition nearly exhausted the Dwabens broke and fled. In the army's flight many Dwabens fell into Asante captivity and they were sold as slaves to the French in the adjacent territories in exchange for arms and ammunition. For the Asante nation the price of victory was high for the veteran commander Asamoa Nkwanta, who had led the army so well at Ordashu, was killed in the final battle.

The Dwaben chief, Asafo Agyei, fled for sanctuary to the Akim tribal area and from here he plotted for the next two years to lead an army of Dwaben, Asokore, Oyoko and Effiduase people, as well as some coastal tribes, against the Asantes. The new British Governor, Sir Sanford Freeling, hearing of Asafo Agyei's plans warned him to desist. This was a rare example of British intervention at this time and when the chief continued to plot, the governor ordered him to be deported to Lagos.

Although successful against the Dwaben, Mensa Bonsu realised that his army would never be strong enough to oppose the British and he did his utmost to maintain cordial relations with the various governors. On one occasion, in 1881, the king decided to send a golden axe by envoy as a gesture of goodwill. Unfortunately, such was the military reputation of the Asantes that the British misconstrued the meaning and took it as a sign of aggression. Another new Governor, Sir Samuel Rowe, reacted to rumours and scaremongering from traders, administrators and chiefs on the coast and on 13 April left Cape Coast Castle to join a hastily assembled force at the Prah River. It would take an intervention by Boatchi Tintin, husband of the respected queen mother, to finally persuade the British that everything had been a misunderstanding. Later in the month Mensa Bonsu offered 2,000oz of gold to the British as further proof of his friendship. Although a completely unnecessary war had been avoided, many in Kumasi saw the whole incident as deeply humiliating for the Asante nation and the king's hold on the Golden Stool was undoubtedly weakened.

The British governor, in search of increased trading opportunities in the interior, despatched Captain Rupert La Trobe Lonsdale to Kumasi and then further north. The British government was particularly anxious to end the Asante monopoly over the northern transit trade and on his return to the coast in early 1882 Lonsdale was able to report success. He discovered that particularly in the north east the tribes such as Gonjas, the Krachis and the Brong had formed a defensive alliance against the Asante and they would be more than happy to trade directly with the coast. The following year Lonsdale was despatched to the north west and here he found trade routes could be opened, but the biggest hinderance to trade was the molesting of traders. Lord Kimberley, Colonial Secretary once again, agreed with Lonsdale's report that the Asante threat to prosperous northern trade was a real one and that 'till they [the Asantes] have changed their nature it is better for us that they should be "down" and not "up"'.[5] Kimberley's words were something of a premonition of the next few years of Asante history, although some on the coast were hoping that Mensa Bonsu could be enticed to become a good British citizen.

The *Gold Coast Times* suggested that it was time for a permanent British consul at the royal court and in a series of articles entitled the 'Future of the Gold Coast' was so bold as to suggest that, 'The Kingdom of Ashantee can be fairly and without dispute be called a Gold Coast country, for putting aside the little peculiarities observable in the inhabitants of its nations they speak a common language and they come from one and the same stock or progenitor.'[6] Such an enlightened view was not yet held by many upon the coast and when Lonsdale suggested to Kimberley that British officers should be appointed as consuls in various parts of the Asante nations he was told that such a proposal would be firmly rejected.

The British were now to watch as any remaining power and threat the Asante nation had disappeared in internal disputes and civil war. Mensa Bonsu, already weakened by the perceived humiliation of the 'golden axe' incident, now made the fatal decision to refer a dispute between Kumasi and the Gyaman states to the British. Whilst Lonsdale was despatched once more to Kumasi to arbitrate, he was able to witness the internal dissension within the Asante nation that was beginning to tear it apart. The 'war party' in the council considered Mensa Bonsu's decision to defer to the British as a sign of weakness and thought war could bring both the Gyaman and Banda states back into the Asante fold. Other groups such as disaffected traders as well as influential commoners were despairing of the king's weak stance. Using the excuses of perceived cruelty and unfairness at court by Mensa Bonsu and excessive taxes levied by the king, they acted and Mensa Bonsu was deposed by thirty-three chiefs and had to flee Kumasi on 8 March 1883. Power rested with two chiefs, Asafo Boakye and Owusu Koko, whilst the search for the new *Asantehene* began.

Although he had to flee, Mensa Bonsu still maintained support and many wanted him back on the stool. The 'war party' had other ideas and proposed that the previous and disgraced king, Kofi Karikari, be restored. Conflict erupted and in a bloody clash at Breman between the two groups most of the pro-Kofi chiefs were killed or later committed suicide. Kofi Karikari was pursued through the jungle and was finally captured in a terrible physical state and imprisoned in Kumasi. A third and perhaps a compromise candidate was announced, Kwaku Dua, the nephew of the two previous kings. The people, tired of bloodshed, rallied to support him and he was duly enstooled in April 1884 as Nana Kwaku Dua I. Kumasi chiefs had sent messages to the governor imploring him to attend the enstoolment ceremony to enhance the new king's legitimacy, but the British ignored the requests, perhaps preferring a weak Asante nation. Tragically, within just forty-four days the young king died, a victim of smallpox. Kofi Karikari now once again came to the fore as the only likely successor, but the nation was plunged into confusion and uncertainty. Historians now dispute what occurred next. Europeans such as Alan Lloyd and Sir Francis Fuller claim that Kofi Karikari was murdered on 24 June 1884, whereas Ghanaian academics such as Osei Kwadwo state that he died as a result of his poor physical condition and of dysentery. Either way, the result was the same; the Asante nation descended into civil war.

Without direction, the nation descended into tribal feuds and anarchy prevailed. The economy collapsed and Kumasi was once again deserted. Jungle paths and roads fell into disuse and quickly disappeared into the foliage. Amidst this crisis the Queen Mother, Nana Yaa Akyaa, Kofi Karikari's sister and mother of Kwaku Dua I, decided to act. She summoned all the chiefs to unite in a stirring appeal for unity, and to elect a new *Asantehene* to save the kingdom. Most agreed but stipulated that the election and enstoolment should be witnessed and approved by a British official to legitimise the appointment and thus unite the nation once more. The queen mother proposed that her sister's son, Kwessi Kwissi, be enstooled. An envoy was duly sent to the governor and he arrived at the coast on 16 October 1884. Although the request was made, bizarrely the British failed to act for two years, during which time the envoy waited with increasing impatience. The British gave numerous excuses as to why no officer was available to be despatched, all of which look, in retrospect, to have been contrived. It seems clear that the governor believed much could be gained by procrastination for as long as the political turmoil remained the military threat from the Asantes was nullified.

Finally, in late 1886, the governor sent a C.W. Badger, an African interpreter, to Kumasi to assess the situation there. In the intervening two years Kwessi Kwissi had died and Badger found the Asante chiefs deeply divided into two factions, each supporting rival candidates for the Golden Stool. One was the 18-year-old son of the queen mother, named Agyeman Prempeh, and the other was a cousin of Mensa Bonsu called Yaw Achiriboanda. The excessive delay by the British had undoubtedly contributed to the tension in Kumasi which Badger reported back to the governor. Criticism was laid at the governor's feet by such diverse bodies as the *Gold Coast Methodist* newspaper and the Manchester Chamber of Commerce, both of which strongly attacked the governor, and hence the government, for a failure to show authority and leadership. Badger left Kumasi with a promise that an official would be sent soon.

It was not until the following year that Lonsdale journeyed to Kumasi with Captain E.A. Barnett and by this time blood had once more began to flow between the two rival factions. The officers were tasked with bringing, by arbitration, some normality and central government to Asante. Lonsdale returned to the coast without securing a permanent settlement, but Barnett remained and was persuaded that sufficient support could be secured for the enstoolment of Prempeh. However, the kings of Mampon and Kokofu could not be convinced to attend the enstoolment ceremony which was essential for its legitimacy. However, Barnett received reassurances from the two kings' representatives that they did support Prempeh. The young man was chosen as king-elect in March 1888, under the title of Kwaku Dua III. Barnett was present at the preliminary ceremony when Prempeh was given both the title of King of Asante and the 'royal stool'. Yet, despite the theatrical display of unity the Kokofus and the Mampon soon rebelled and Prempeh's first act as king was to crush rebellion, and civil war again struck Asante. The Kokofus were driven across the Prah in a bloody pursuit whilst the king of Mampon had to flee and Prempeh's rival for the stool, Achiriboanda, sought refuge on the coast, where he continued to intrigue against the new king.

In the Colonial Office the general feeling during this extended period of unrest was of hope that the new king could provide peace and security, without placing any more demands upon the British. In contrast, Barnett had advocated in his report to the new Governor, William Brandford Griffith, that a British officer be permanently based in Kumasi and this suggestion was supported by the merchants of Cape Coast. London was opposed for two main reasons; the cost and the fact that the Colonial Office held the view that the logical and ultimate result of such an appointment would be the inclusion of the Asante nation into the colony, and no one in Whitehall wished to present that to Parliament. Yet, within months the British policy had been completely altered to one of direct intervention.

The Scramble for Africa

When examining the British government's actions before 1895, it seems evident that ministers felt no urgent requirement to expand British influence in West Africa. They were not interested in using imperial power and capital to work in West Africa for the purpose of investing in new markets and resources. It is often thought that the empire existed to create more business for Britain, yet, according to Robinson and Gallagher in the seminal work *Africa and the Victorians*, in the Gold Coast, before 1895, it would be truer to say that the merchants were expected to create empire and that the British government expected them to do so without imperial rule, to make do with the limited protection and to pioneer their own way inland.

The 'Scramble for Africa' was to change that thinking. This term refers to a period in the late 1880s and 1890s during which many European powers, including Britain, France, Belgium and Germany, sought to expand their own empires or spheres of influence across the African continent. The motives behind such actions were often economic enhancement or dominance, but the nations were equally driven by the desire for their European rivals to be excluded from a region. Although this was true across Africa, West Africa was to be dominated by a strong rivalry between the British and the French.

At the height of the Scramble it was common that local officials were several steps ahead or even led opinion as to what action should be taken. Often the Colonial Office in London was slow in offering definitive guidance and policy could be made by the officials in situ. This was certainly true of the Gold Coast. The Governor Brandford Griffith had already alerted London that French colonial ambitions were being extended by exploration westwards into the hinterland of the Gold Coast, from their colony of the Ivory Coast. In 1886 a French officer, Captain Louis-Gustave Binger, had been tasked by the

French government to lead a reconnaissance mission along the Niger River. To avoid arousing British suspicions he started from the interior and by 1889 he had covered a huge area between Bamako, Kong and Wagadugu and he encroached on British influence in Salaga and Kintampo. In 1888, Binger even managed to secure a treaty of protection with the Bontuku under the noses of a British mission. Brandford Griffith feared that the French might even penetrate into northern Asante and so in 1886 he informed the Colonial Office that Asante territory should be quickly brought under British jurisdiction.

The following year the governor gave a further warning to London of German encroachment into Asante from Togo in the east. These warnings were not, initially, taken very seriously and the secretary of state, Henry Holland, 1st Baron of Knutsford, even wrote, 'If Ashanti is to be annexed to any European power let it be by the Germans.'[7] However, over the next few years such complacency disappeared from the Colonial Office in light of further European penetration of the interior of West Africa and diplomatic disagreements in Europe. It was felt that some action, at least to the north of Asante, would have to be considered. Here diplomacy within Europe secured two important agreements. The Anglo–French Agreement of 1889 defined the western boundary of the Gold Coast according to treaties made with the local chiefs. Similarly, the Anglo–German Treaty of 1890 established a neutral zone to the north east of Asante in which European nations bound themselves not to acquire protectorates. The treaty also defined the southern Gold Coast–Togoland boundary in general terms, but detailed interpretation on the ground aroused local resentment and the king of Krepi was outraged that the new boundary split his lands. Furthermore, the creation of the neutral zone merely heightened colonial rivalries in the adjacent territories. When the king of Attabubu approached the British seeking protection from German encroachment, the governor was delighted to recommend that a treaty of friendship and protection should be drawn up and this was executed in 1890, much to the annoyance of the Germans.

Although the Colonial Office was finally beginning to realise that the northern hinterland was very much up for grabs in the Scramble, it still could not bring itself to commit to bringing Asante into a protectorate. In late 1890, the new Colonial Secretary, Viscount Knutsford, advised Brandford Griffith to organise another fact-finding mission to Kumasi. In March 1891 the governor despatched one of his officers to the royal court and he exceeded his local authority by submitting a draft treaty of protection with a letter to Prempeh urging him to accept it. Brandford Griffith neglected to inform Knutsford of his initiative until two months later and on the governor's return to London, he was reprimanded for having broached so important a matter without the authority of the secretary of state. Yet, in May 1891, the governor reported: 'Ashanti as a whole, besides being gradually broken up, is steadily retrograding, both in its entirety . . . and in portions which have separated themselves from the nominal Government at Kumasi, which is powerless to check the downward tendency . . .'.[8] Brandford Griffith insisted that Asante must be pacified. This again was an example of a local official pre-empting a strategy that London was soon to follow. But the Colonial Office wanted no such commitment. Knutsford held that the colony had no resources to spare for what might prove a large military task. His Liberal successor, the Earl of Ripon, upheld the veto against moving across the Prah, although the merchants and officials of the Gold Coast still pressed for action. The colony could not foot the bill, and London would not underwrite it.

Brandford Griffith's move was slightly premature for at that moment many of the internal wars in Asante had been settled and the state of anarchy that had existed had been reduced. Prempeh felt sufficiently secure to be able to firmly decline the governor's offer and wrote a courteous response, 'I am happy to say we have arrived at this conclusion, that my Kingdom of Ashanti must remain independent as of old, at the same time to be friendly with all white men. Believe me, Governor, that I am happy to inform you, that the cause of Ashanti is progressing.'[9]

For the next five years the Colonial Office followed a contrary policy. Whilst still refusing to entertain direct rule in Asante, it continued further expansion to the north, which included the region of Dagombaland, which would eventually make the inclusion of Asante into the British sphere inevitable. When in 1893 it seemed that Asante would attack the Attabubu the British honoured their treaty of protection signed in 1890 and a force of Hausas, commanded by Sir Francis Scott, commander of the West African Police, was sent to Attabubu itself to deter Asante aggression. Whilst in the region, Scott used the opportunity conclude treaties of friendship and trade with several neighbouring tribes who wished to distance themselves from the Asantes. These included the important area of Nkoranza.

Frederick Hodgson assumed the role of acting governor in the absence of Brandford Griffith and he quickly determined that Asante must be annexed. He argued that a settlement would avoid the constant expense of maintaining a force to deal with a possible Asante threat and see an increase in trade which would justify the annual cost of a resident in Kumasi. During Scott's northern travels he found many, including the Nkoranza, the Dwaben and the Agogos, seeking British protection. He argued the time was now right to settle the Asante threat by sending Prempeh an ultimatum to bring Asante itself under British protection and this would also ensure that any German or French claims on the territory would be nullified. Scott felt that this could be achieved without bloodshed, a view supported by the missionary Henry Ramseyer, who had returned to Kumasi after Wolseley's victory and was living there with his wife. Hodgson welcomed Scott's views but was reluctant to act without at least the reassurance that he could count on British troops if required.

In March 1894, Hodgson attempted to force the pace towards a settlement, and he sent Hendrick Vroom, an African commissioner, to Kumasi. Armed with a letter from Hodgson, Vroom was tasked with persuading Prempeh to accept a British officer in Kumasi as an agent of the government. Financial incentives of £600 per annum were offered to Prempeh to accept Hodgson's offer. The king delayed replying as he was observing the funeral customs for his sister and later wrote to say that a formal response would have to wait until he had discussed the matter with all his chiefs. Vroom suggested to the governor that Prempeh was delaying in the hope of more favourable terms after he was formally enstooled as *Asantehene* in June 1894.

Whilst the mood was generally shifting in the Colonial Office towards intervention in Asante, Ripon would not countenance such drastic action and it would take a change of government and secretary of state for British policy to be dramatically altered. In the meantime, activity amongst the three powers, Britain, France and Germany, was increasing in the interior of West Africa. George Ekem Ferguson, also known as Ekow Atta, was a Fante civil servant, surveyor and cartographer who worked for the British colonial administration in the Gold Coast. During 1894 Ferguson journeyed throughout the north and secured treaties in a belt to the west and north of the neutral zone with such tribes as the Dagaris and the Mossis. Later that year he entered the neutral zone and secured a number of friendship treaties amongst the tribes there, thus contravening the treaty with Germany. At the same time a German expedition reached the northern reaches of Togo and in 1895 the French penetrated the Kong region and declared a protectorate over Dahomey. Yet, despite such posturing by the Europeans, the Colonial Office was still reluctant to directly challenge Prempeh.

News of Prempeh's enstoolment was accompanied with stories of atrocities and it seems highly likely that human sacrifices were made as part of the ceremony. There was outrage on the coast and Brandford Griffith, returned from London, refused to recognise the enstoolment. The governor took this opportunity to deny Prempeh's title and began merely to refer to him as the 'King of Kumasi'. The governor continued to lobby the Colonial Office for direct intervention in Asante and his language became increasingly bellicose. His stance received support from various bodies. In Accra the *Gold Coast Chronicle* wrote in an editorial, 'we must go straight to Kumasi and occupy or annex it, declaring Ashantee a British protectorate . . . It is a reproach moreover to the civilization of this country, that any savage King should be suffered by the British Government to do what King Prempeh is daily doing.'[10] In December 1894 The Cape Coast Chamber of Commerce sent a deputation to the governor demanding that Asante be brought into the British sphere of influence and it used its strong trading links with the chambers of commerce in Liverpool, London and Glasgow to petition the secretary of state.

With pressure building for British annexation Prempeh decided that he must assert his own position. The king did not trust the governor for he instinctively felt that his proposal for a resident would inevitably lead to a loss of independence. Prempeh was persuaded that a deputation, led by John Ansa, an English-speaking nobleman, needed to be sent to London to ensure that both the secretary of state and Queen Victoria realised that the Asante were friends of the British and presented no military threat. Such a proposed trip was not welcomed by the Colonial Office. It was feared that their presence in London might be used by the Opposition in Parliament to harass the government, or worse the Asantes might travel to Paris to stir up anti-British sentiment. When the deputation arrived at the coast it had several audiences with the governor in which Brandford Griffith was unable to disguise his disdain for the diplomats. He maintained that they would never receive an audience with Queen Victoria and that they were wasting their efforts and furthermore as the government's representative on the Gold Coast it was the governor with whom they should properly negotiate. After months of obstacles placed in their path, the deputation finally sailed in April 1895, which was just a few days before the arrival of the new Governor, Sir William Edward Maxwell. Their arrival in London caused a brief stir in the newspapers but they were refused a hearing with either the Colonial Office or the queen and to their dismay they discovered that the British were apparently planning military action to enforce their demands for a resident.

Maxwell had been busy formulating his views upon the Asante problem in his first few weeks as governor and they were to differ significantly from those of his predecessor. He suggested that all Asante tribes should accept British protection, with guarantees for the freedom of trade between the coast and the interior, and of the safety of missionaries. Furthermore, all human sacrifices must be abolished. If protection was refused and all the guarantees not accepted, then an ultimatum threatening military action would be sent to Prempeh. This was such a departure from just the acceptance of a resident in Kumasi as a 'friend and advisor' and in addition Maxwell, with the promoting of Hodgson, suggested to London that as a prerequisite for any possible military action the government might raise the unfulfilled Treaty of Fomena of 1874. According to that agreement the fact that human sacrifices were still commonplace and that the indemnity of 50,000oz of gold was still outstanding provided a reason for military intervention.

A change of government saw the appointment of Joseph Chamberlain as the new Colonial Secretary. Chamberlain was arguably the most expansionist secretary the Colonial Office had ever seen, and he was a devotee of all the political intrigue that surrounded the Scramble for Africa. He saw events in Asante as being part of the process by which Britain would extend its influence and empire. Chamberlain had anticipated a French challenge into Asante and this he was not going to permit. Thus, he latched onto Maxwell's proposal and replied by cable in September 1895 that Prempeh must be told that the government now expected the 1874 treaty to be met and honoured in full. In addition, he informed Maxwell that Prempeh must also be told that Asante must refrain from attacking neighbouring tribes and that he had to accept a British resident at Kumasi. Crucially, Chamberlain was prepared to back his words with military intervention.

This tougher stance was fully supported by the British Chamber of Commerce as well as many of the British newspapers. For example, *The Times* of 21 January 1896 claimed that Asante had long formed a block of savagery between the British coast and the interior. This had prevented trade and that the French were taking advantage of the situation by opening their own markets, which may now be lost to Britain.

On receiving Chamberlain's instructions, the governor despatched Vroom to Kumasi with an ultimatum for Prempeh which required of him either a written reply or a personal interview with the governor before the end of October. Although treated with courtesy, Vroom received no direct answer from Prempeh, and he returned to the coast. It seems Prempeh was putting all his hope in his deputation that had been sent to London and he sent a sword bearer and court crier to the coast to inform the British that he was awaiting a response from his messengers to Queen Victoria. As no written response was received to the ultimatum it was taken by Maxwell, Scott and Chamberlain as a rejection.

Maxwell had already informed Scott that he would be in command of the proposed military expedition and preparations were well under way. Chamberlain had already warned the Cabinet in November 1895 that private enterprise was now inadequate for opening Britain's vast 'underdeveloped estates', and that the government must lead the way with money and troops. Without consulting the prime minister, he announced a punitive expedition to Asante.

The Bloodless War

Wolseley's expedition of 1873–4 had taught the British many lessons, which surprisingly were remembered in 1895–6, although perhaps not always followed. The region's reputation as 'The White Man's Grave' was still very apt. Although the risks to the British were understood, it was thought that medical science had moved on apace since 1874 and that troops could be better supplied and instructed on the dangers of the climate. The benefit of using British soldiers for a rapid movement from the coast to Kumasi would outweigh the perils of the weather.

Therefore, following Chamberlain's announcement, the 2nd Battalion of the West Yorkshire Regiment, which was homeward bound after seventeen years' service in the East, which included India, Burma and Aden, was informed on its way home at Malta that they were to be diverted to the Gold Coast. The War Office thought that these men would endure the harsh climate of West Africa better than troops sent fresh from England. However, the constitutions of the Yorkshiremen had probably been weakened by their long foreign service and many were undoubtedly suffering from previously contracted fevers. The battalion was disembarked at Gibraltar and issued with suitable clothing for their march to Kumasi.

A second British battalion was raised by following Wolseley's suggestion of 1873 which Cardwell had then dismissed. This unit was formed of volunteers selected from those infantry regiments, including the Guards, that were stationed in Britain at the time. These men formed the Special Service Corp. To qualify all had to be at least 24 years of age with over four years' service, be good shots and capable of passing a pretty stiff medical examination. They were armed, like all the rest of the regular troops which took part in the expedition, with the single-shot Martini–Enfield carbine and the Elcho sword bayonet. It is of interest that a rifle was selected which was then not the current front-line weapon. This choice was made to minimise the weight of rifle to be carried by the men in the jungle terrain, for the carbine was significantly lighter and shorter than the Martini rifle which made it more manoeuvrable in the restricted environment of the bush. The decision also allowed for the ready supply and issue of ammunition as the expedition would comprise diverse units that would have carried different calibre rifles, yet by taking the Martini–Enfield carbine all would be using the same ammunition.

The Special Service Corp was formed at Aldershot on 27 November 1895, consisting of 250 men from the Coldstream and Grenadier Guards, Royal Irish & Northumberland Fusiliers, Yorkshire and Shropshire Light Infantry, Leinster and Devon Regiment and 60th Rifles & Rifle Brigade. Gunners, engineers and medical services were also provided, and the British contingent was completed by a naval brigade from the warships then in West African waters. A local element was composed of the Gold Coast Constabulary, an 800-strong unit made up of Hausas, as well as considerable force of friendly natives under British officers, with a body of scouts, commanded by Captain Robert Baden-Powell of the 13th Hussars. This officer was later to achieve national fame as the defender of Mafeking, during the Second Anglo-Boer War, and as the founder of the Boy Scout movement. As in 1874, the 2nd Battalion of the West Indies Regiment also took part in the expedition.

The British contingent embarked from the Albert Docks on P&O vessel *Coramandel* on 7 December 1895. Just before it sailed Lord Wolseley reviewed the troops and according to one of them, Lieutenant Ackland Hood of The Rifles, Wolseley stated that he had, 'never seen such a fine body of men'.[11] The expedition was joined by royal personages. Queen Victoria's son-in-law, Prince Henry of Battenberg, received the queen's permission to accompany Sir Francis Scott as his military secretary and he sailed with the main contingent onboard the *Coramandel*. Prince Henry was joined by one of the queen's grandsons, His Highness Prince Christian Victor of Schleswig-Holstein, as his aide-de-camp.

Lieutenant Hood left a diary of the expedition and it is clear from his early entries that the British took the threat of the climate very seriously:

> The doctors – we had a good many of them on board – now began to tell us of the many horrors and dangers of the climate we were going to, and they fairly made one's hair stand on end. After several lectures, I came to the conclusion that we must on no account wash, except in water that had been boiled and filtered, for fear of chaw-chaws and grunia worms, never walk about without shoes on for fear of jiggers, which burrow under the toe nails and lay their eggs there; never drink water for fear of dysentery, or eat fruit for the same cause; never drink spirits for fear of heat apoplexy and other aliments; only eat meat once a day; never go out in the sun for fear of sunstroke; and put on everything you could lay your hands on at night for fear of getting a chill, etc.etc.[12]

In November the *British Medical Journal* even joined the debate when it stated that the war would be to a large extent a 'doctor's war' and that, 'Much will depend on preventive measures, the choice of camping ground, a proper commissariat and especially on pure water.'[13] Events would show that such measures were not always adhered to.

Whilst Hood was still in transit advance British units had already arrived at Cape Coast Castle. Lieutenant Llewelyn Atcherley of the Army Service Corp had landed on 13 December. In a letter to his Aunt Lucy, dated 17 December, he wrote, 'I arrived here on the 13th and am now working very hard organising the 10,000 Carriers for the Expedition to carry the stores – The heat is intense and very hard to get sleep as the climate is so enervating . . .'.[14] What Atcherley's letter shows was how, once again, the march to Kumasi would be a major logistical undertaking and how the climate would be a significant factor in the performance of the troops.

The *Coramandel* arrived on the Gold Coast on 28 December 1895. As each company landed, it drew seventy rounds per man and an emergency ration and marched off to Jaykuma, a distance of 7 miles. For men straight off the ship, Hood described it as a very hot and trying march. There was dense scrub on either side of the road and no shade. Hood wrote of a very powerful smell of the worst description which permeated everything. Both Sergeant Arkinstall of the Scots Guards and Corporal Dickeson of the Army Service Corp expired from heat apoplexy after just 5 miles on the road and were buried in the bush at the side of the path. Hood stated that the water at the Jaykuma camp was very dark in colour and smelt horribly, as the water filters which the men brought with them could not be made to work and that he and his fellow officers survived on quinine and champagne on the first night. Obtaining clean water was a constant problem on the line of march. Fortunately, in one of the camps, a correspondent for *The Lancet* was at hand to warn the men queueing for water that it was severely contaminated, and they should not touch it. This was confirmed by the chief medical officer who journeyed up the line, and who then condemned the whole camp, probably saving several lives.

The West Yorks arrived a few days after the Special Service Battalion and like the troops before them all were given seventy rounds and told to march straight from the ship the 7 miles to the Jaykuma camp. It soon became apparent that the War Office was wrong in their assumption that these veterans would cope well with the demands of the Gold Coast climate. On the first day 30 men fell out and by the time the troops reached the Prahsu camp nearly 250 were sick and the *Coromandel* had been transformed into a hospital ship to accommodate them. By the time the battalion finally sailed for England only sixty-eight men were fit for duty.

Hood wrote of the march to Kumasi and left details of how much of the day's exertions were undertaken in the early hours to avoid the worst of the climate. He also outlined the monotony and described how reliant the men were on the efforts of the porters:

> One camp was much like another, and one march very much like another – one day – 31st January – Reveillie at 12.45am and cocoa at 1.15am, paraded at 1.45am, and marched off at 2am. A good moon, which enabled us to see our way more or less, but it was impossible to see the roots and rocks which one kept stumbling over. After marching about four hours, we halted and had some tea and biscuits, and half an hour's rest, during which our carriers (about 600 in number) passed through. They are splendid fellows at carrying the Fantis; men and women stride along at 4 miles an hour with from 50–60 lbs on their heads, and the ladies often have a little baby carried in a fold of their only garment riding on their back. Another hour's march and we arrived at our camp. The sun generally rose about six am, and for an

hour before sunrise and two hours after, there were dense mists; the air was close, about 82 to 84 degrees of heat. On getting into camp the men all stripped and had a good rub down, and changed their shirt etc. Then we went into huts and had breakfast, a sleep and dinner. At 3. 30pm, when the sun had lost some of his power, everyone turned out to wash their clothes, and if possible, bathe. Rum and quinine were served out in the evening.[15]

In contrast to his companions, Prince Henry was provided with a donkey on which he rode, shielding his face from the sun with a small white umbrella.

Despite concerns of strong Asante resistance this was not forthcoming, although the fear of it did result in a few false alarms. On one occasion a rumour that an Asante army was only 2 miles away and heading for the advancing British saw Prince Christian and others hastily organise a barricade of biscuit and meat tins across the path from behind which they crouched for several hours awaiting an imaginary enemy. Violence did erupt between two groups of native irregulars from Sierra Leone and Winneba respectively who came to blows when the former accused the latter of stealing their evening meal. The campaign was not completely bloodless for a private shot his sergeant major in the shoulder over a bitter argument. This action earnt the trooper seven years in military prison.

As the British column neared Kumasi, Prempeh called an urgent meeting of his chiefs at which it was decided that it would be wrong to dishonour the Golden Stool by fighting the British in a war that they realised they could not win. They reluctantly agreed to submit to the 'protection' being demanded by the British and when Scott marched into Kumasi at the head of his troops on 17 January 1896, Prempeh and his chiefs were waiting in solemn, passive dignity. Before this was to happen, tragedy struck the expedition. Both princes had been taken ill with fever and although Prince Christian was able to carry on, Prince Henry was carried back to the coast where his condition worsened. He was taken onboard HMS *Blonde* where he died. Hood wrote of his sadness on learning of the prince's death:

> Shortly after our arrival [in Kumasi] we were met with the very sad news of the death of Prince Henry of Battenburg. He came out on the 'Coromandel' with us, and we all liked him very much indeed. He walked out from Prahsu to meet us on our arrival there, and the next time we saw him was at Kwisa camp, where he was taken with the fever; but we had heard that he was much better on arrival at the coast so it was a great shock to hear of the fatal termination of his illness.[16]

British troops again entered Kumasi. The Hausa band, playing, curiously, 'Home Sweet Home', failed to raise the spirits of men exhausted and weary from the march. Prempeh received the column seated on a raised platform in the square. Beside him sat the queen mother. The troops were then greeted by the thunder of war drums and the tooting of horns which did, mercifully, drown out the efforts of the Hausas. By the evening the troops had laid out a temporary camp and the artillery was positioned to sweep across the square and its approaches if required. Scott and his officers now had a meeting with the king at which he was informed that Governor Maxwell would be arriving the following day, a Saturday and that on the Monday he would talk with the king first thing. Scott bade Prempeh good night and left the people of Kumasi to their thoughts. A strong guard was placed around the palace and centre of the capital, although Hood recorded that their presence did not stop the porters and levies from looting and that Scott made no effort to stop them. The British troops observed compulsory Sunday worship and rested. The ceremonial palaver was announced for 6am the following day and at 7am, with no sign of the king, officers were sent to the palace to hurry along his attendance. Finally, the king and the queen mother sat to face the governor. Maxwell opened the ceremony with a speech that criticised the king for being un-cooperative over the British ultimatum and for allowing envoys to journey to London in an attempt to go above the authority of the local government representatives. The governor accused the Asantes of not fulfilling the 1874 Treaty of Fomena and specifically not paying the indemnity and allowing the practice of human sacrifice to continue. Indeed, it does seem that human sacrifices were still being made, although not on the scale that some, especially missionaries, were claiming. The Reuters correspondent who accompanied the march reported on 18 January that many human skulls had been found in the main square and that there was a smell of death and decay everywhere. Maxwell concluded his initial words by stating that if the king would submit to a British resident and protection and paid the indemnity of 50,000oz of gold, then the British had no desire to depose the king.

It was clear that Prempeh was shocked by Maxwell's hard stance and he took a few moments to compose himself before he and the queen mother slipped off their sandals and walked across to where Maxwell and Scott were sat. The two royals then prostrated themselves and embraced the feet of the two officials in a gesture of submission. Returning to his place, Prempeh drew himself up with an intake of breath and stated that he now claimed the protection of Queen Victoria. Maxwell firmly reminded the king that he still must pay the 50,000oz of gold but Prempeh insisted that he could only afford 680oz and that he would have to pay the rest by instalments.

Maxwell now acted in an obviously pre-planned and orchestrated move, and to the horror and disbelief of the king and all the Asantes present, he announced that the *Asantehene* would be taken into custody, along with his mother, father, brother, two other close relatives and the kings of Mampon, Offinso and Ejisu. At this moment a party of officers drew their swords and surrounded the king and those others specified by Maxwell. All were marched to the Hausa guard-room. Two companies of the West Yorks quickly surrounded the palace, preventing anyone from leaving or entering. The British then destroyed the royal mausoleum at Bantama and blew up the sacred fetish *kumnini* trees in Kumasi. The royal palace was raided, as in 1874, by British troops and valuable gold ornaments were packed for the coast. The Asantes were stunned and it seemed almost in shock for no protests were made and nor was there any attempt to impede the British. Only cries of despair and anguish could be heard. Scott and Maxwell wasted no time and left the next day with their royal prisoners for the coast. It seems that many of the chiefs assumed that the king had been taken as a guarantor for the outstanding gold, but for the British the real aim was to ensure the political weakening of the nation.

The return from Kumasi passed without incident, although the troops of the West Yorks continued to suffer from the climate. Even Hood noted that some of the men of the Special Service Battalion were struggling:

> We left Coomassie on January 22nd, and arrived at Cape Coast Castle on February 6th without adventure. The climate was beginning to tell on all of us. There were about twenty-five sick in the Special Service Corps, but only two or three were bad cases. As a matter of fact, by taking quinine each day, being careful about getting a good rub down at the end of a march, and only drinking boiled water, we found that one could stand the climate pretty-well for the short time we were there.[17]

It is clear that Hood took the risks of 'The White Man's Grave' seriously and he and his companions fared better than some of the other troops. As with many of the men who journeyed to the Gold Coast in 1873–4, the fact that they were only onshore for around six weeks was a definite advantage.

Although there was a degree of criticism of the British action, with some nationalists claiming that Maxwell had tarred the whole Asante nation with the sins of its leaders, generally the governor's stance was supported. *The Times*, in an editorial on the day of the king's arrest, wrote in economic and nationalistic terms of the need for Britain to act:

> Kumasi and some of the adjacent Ashanti districts have long formed a solid block of savagery interposed between the British coast and the Mahomedian interior, which is believed to be capable of supplying

us with a considerable amount of trade. As the French are advancing inland on both sides of us from Ivory Coast and from Dahomy, it is absolutely necessary that we should clear for ourselves a road to the interior, if we are not to be forestalled or headed off from these new markets.

Of course, Maxwell, although resolute and determined to act, was under the firm instruction of the Colonial Secretary. Chamberlain had anticipated the French challenge in the southern part of the hinterland of the Gold Coast. Although Scott's troops and the newspaper correspondents found some skulls and other traces of human sacrifice, this was but a convenient discovery for the official British objective, and public desire, was to end the bloodthirsty reign of a savage king. But the main aim of the expedition was not humanitarian; Chamberlain wanted to confirm British supremacy over Asante and pre-empt French encroachments. This 'bloodless' war was little more than part of the game that was the Scramble for Africa. The French challenge had been answered, and the base secured for future expansion.

The king and his principal chiefs reached the Cape Coast and were led straight onto the beach where a large crowd had gathered to stare and shout abuse at them. To their horror, for none of the captives had ever seen the sea, they were roughly pushed onto small boats and rowed out to the waiting HMS *Racoon*. They were then taken to Elmina where they were held in the castle for a year before being transferred to Sierra Leone, and from there later exiled to the Seychelles.

With the king gone, Maxwell was free to determine Anglo-Asante relations. Before he returned to the coast, he consulted several chiefs and all seemed to want a central government with the authority provided by the Golden Stool, which was hardly a departure from the system that the king had followed. Clearly Maxwell could not countenance this. Instead he appointed the British resident, Captain Donald Stewart, and ordered the construction of a fort as Stewart's residence. Over 1,200 of the porters used in the recent campaign were reemployed to carry several tons of cement and other building materials from the coast and the fort was finally finished three years later and grossly over-budget. Maxwell did define Stewart's position; he was to exercise all ordinary civil and criminal jurisdiction, guided by the principals of English law. Any reports of human slavery or sacrifice were to be investigated and severely dealt with. Yet, Stewart's most important duty was to encourage trade and to improve the net-work of routes to the north so as to gain access to the hinterland. A quarter of Kumasi land was assigned to foreign traders and sites were allocated for mission schools. Mr and Mrs Ramseyer of the Basel Mission returned once more to the capital in June 1896 to establish a mission station. Clearly their experiences of being hostages of Kofi Karikari had not deterred them. Although the union of Asante tribes was now dismantled, Stewart was instructed to interfere as little as possible in the day-to-day running of Asante and that the people should be encouraged to manage their own affairs.

The governor was now pre-occupied by other matters across the protectorate and although he visited Kumasi again in 1897, and could see that resentment was building against the British, he was unable to act upon it, for he died on the voyage back to England at the end of the year. Maxwell's successor, Sir Frederick Hodgson, was far more concerned with dealing with the mining boom, technical issues over British jurisdiction in the protected territories and agitation over the 1897 Lands Bill to focus his attention on Asante. It was not until 1900 that Hodgson looked once more on Asante and his inept handling of relations was to result in the last Anglo-Asante conflict.

The Last Acts of Defiance

In the three years since the exile of King Prempeh Asante had been administered by the British resident and Kumasi itself was placed in the charge of three chiefs, Opoku Mensa, Nenchwi, who was a skilled linguist, and Efirfa of Achuma. The locals viewed these men as little more than British stooges and many drifted away from the capital. The British signed separate treaties with several of the satellite tribes, including Mampon, Kokofu and Ejisu, to reduce further the centralising of power in Kumasi. As time went by resentment grew amongst the Asante people over what was considered to be the treacherous treatment of the king, and there were disturbances in Wam in 1898 and Aguna in 1899. Young Asante men were apparently bitter and resentful that they had not been allowed to defend the *Asantehene* in 1896 and there were numerous rumours as to future British action. One was that the British would bring Achiriboanda from exile on the coast and install him as the new king and that some of the more obstinate chiefs would be ousted. When it was learnt that the new governor would be visiting Kumasi it was reported to Stewart, the resident, that one chief, Kufi Kafia, had been overheard saying that unless the governor brought good news then he could expect a fight. This information was apparently not conveyed to the governor before he journeyed to Kumasi.

The Golden Stool was, and is, the keystone of the Asante political and religious system, because through it the nation is united with its ancestors and its God. According to Wasserman, 'It is revered above all else, including the king, for it contains the sunsum, vitality or life-force of the race, upon which the health (physical) life and well-being of the people depend.'[18] For the British, the stool was seen as a symbol of the power of the king for its presence was required if any new *Asantehene* was to be enstooled; so simply viewed, if the stool was in their possession then the British did not need to fear that the Asante nation would ever have the political power of a king with which to focus their opposition.

First Maxwell and then Hodgson instructed Stewart to seek out the Golden Stool and if found it was to be sent to Cape Coast Castle for safe keeping. In December 1899, on the strength of a story from an Asante youth named Esumi who claimed that he knew the whereabouts of the stool, Hodgson despatched Captain Cecil Hamilton Armitage and a small detachment of Hausas to northern Asante on a wild-goose chase. The initial expedition, although spectacularly unsuccessful, was kept largely secret from the population. It was only after Armitage had returned to the coast that news the British had sought the stool became general knowledge across the Asante nation. Resentment and suspicion of the British was now completely roused and the British designs upon the stool were seen ultimately as an attempt to eradicate the Asante nation. The Asantes would never surrender the stool for they believed their nation would perish if it fell into foreign hands. Thus, if they had to fight for the Golden Stool, they would. The Asantes would not be fighting for a king's throne, as the British saw it, but for the physical survival of their race and nation.

Hodgson decided upon a visit to Kumasi whilst Stewart was home on leave and when the Acting resident, Captain Wilfred Davidson-Houston, learnt of the proposed visit he called a meeting of chiefs to affirm loyalty to the British, whilst at the same time warning missionaries in the area to be ready to shelter in the fort if required. Hodgson was either unaware of the general unrest in Asante or oblivious to it for when he left Accra on 13 March 1900, he did so with only an escort of thirty Hausas which is a sure sign that the governor expected no trouble. He was accompanied by his wife, Lady Mary Alice Hodgson, who was apparently apprehensive. She would later write an account of her experiences in Kumasi from which she emerges as a calm, determined and resolute individual who was very supportive of her husband and his confrontational approach to the Asantes. She seemed aware that the journey would be demanding and uncomfortable, but the fact she would be the first European woman to enter Kumasi seemed to have filled her with enthusiasm. The governor's party included the acting director of public works, for Hodgson was determined to improve the route to Kumasi and bridge the Prah.

After nearly two weeks of being bumped around in hammocks, the governor and his wife approached the outskirts of Kumasi on 25 March. En route the party stopped to rest at houses in various villages and met with local chiefs. At Kwisa, Hodgson had an audience with the king of Adansi and it was here that the governor received the first hint of unrest for the king kept Hodgson waiting and he recorded that he found the king somewhat truculent. The governor's Private Secretary, Captain Armitage, recorded the party's entry into Kumasi as a welcoming one. The Revd and Mrs Ramseyer, as well as local officials, came out to greet the governor and his wife before all passed under a triumphal arch into the capital. On either side of the road the kings and chiefs sat shaded by their large umbrellas and as the governor passed each rose and saluted. The drums thundered out a welcome. On reaching the fort, the governor and his wife went onto the verandah of the residency, in front of which the kings and chiefs passed in procession. It was not until nearly dusk that this parade finally finished, and the governor and his wife were able to retire. Both must have been pleased by their welcome.

The governor used the next three days to work on the speech he would give at a big palaver on the afternoon of 28 March. Once more the kings and chiefs were assembled and placed in a semi-circle, facing the chair on which Sir Frederick Hodgson would address them. Great care was taken that each member of the assembly was placed in strict order of seniority. At 4pm the governor emerged from the fort, dressed in his governor's uniform, which dripped with gold braid. He was accompanied by his military staff and before sitting under an awning he stood to receive a royal salute from the guard of honour of constabulary. Speaking slowly through an interpreter, Hodgson started the palaver.

Sir Frederick immediately took a firm stance. He insisted that the Asante people must understand their responsibilities and obligations. He reminded those gathered that hardly any of the indemnity imposed by the Treaty of Fomena of 1874 had been paid, nor had any of the expenses from the 1896 expedition, which the Asantes had been ordered to make good. Hodgson confirmed that the resident had the right to call upon the Asante people to undertake communal labour in the form of road construction and building of government establishments. He also reiterated that Prempeh would never return from exile and that Asante would be ruled by the government's representative. All this was heard by the Asante chiefs and kings with quiet dignity. Finally, the governor delivered a bombshell when he declared that the Asante nation had displayed an insolent attitude towards him as the representative of Her Majesty's government for he was not happy with the chair he had been given to sit on. Why had he not been allowed to sit on the Golden Stool for he now represented the supreme authority in Asante? Such a statement clearly demonstrated Hodgson's ignorance of the role and importance of the stool. It was a symbol of Asante nationhood and was never sat upon. It was not a symbol of power as Hodgson perceived but the spiritual heart of the Asante nation. As such Sir Frederick's demand was a huge affront to those present and to all the Asante people.

The governor's last statement was first met with a stunned silence and then barely audible muttering. It was of course extremely provocative and has been seen by many historians as the real cause of the rebellion and although it is clear there were a number of grievances that led to the subsequent conflict, Hodgson's ignorant demand was clearly at the heart of Asante anger. In trying to defend her husband, Lady Hodgson in her book denied strenuously that the statement was ever made but the evidence is very much against her. For even in his notes of the meeting which the governor sent to Chamberlain, there appears the sentence, 'Why have you relegated me to this chair? Why did you not take the opportunity of my coming to Kumasi to bring the Golden Stool and give it to me to sit on?'[19]

According to Asante oral tradition, Nana Yaa Asantewaa, queen mother of Edweso and acting chief of Edweso, following the deportation of the chief with Prempeh, was the only Asante woman present. Hodgson asked those assembled if anyone had a question and waiting a moment for any men to speak, which they did not, the queen mother rose and asked if the governor had firstly seen Prempeh, and if he so wanted the Golden Stool he, the governor, should bring the king back to Kumasi so he could show him where the stool was. The governor replied that Prempeh was now exiled in the Seychelles and reconfirmed that he would not be returning to Asante. On hearing that news, Nana Yaa Asantewaa stated: 'Tomorrow, ghost widows would get husbands.'[20] Again, according to tradition these words were understood by those Asantes present to be a declaration of war against the British and in silence those assembled duly dispersed from the meeting.

That evening all the chiefs gathered at a secret meeting led by the queen mother who was outspoken in her demands against the British. The chiefs were split but a majority declared that they would fight to defend the Golden Stool. These included the chiefs of Kumasi, Edweso, Offinso, Atwina, Ahafo, Kokofu, Bekyem, Nkwanta and Adanse. However, the chiefs of Mampon, Nsuta, Dwaben and Aguna were of the view that if they fought now there was a risk that the British would capture the Golden Stool and it would be lost for ever. These four chiefs remained in the fort when it was besieged, although the people of Aguna were split in their loyalty and some fought against the British. Other chiefs, such as those of Bompata, Kumawu, Gyaman and Nkoranza, although opposed to the British, refused to take up arms against them, whilst other chiefs, including those of Wam and Takyiman, decided to remain neutral. Thus, the chiefs were divided but there was sufficient support for armed opposition that the British would soon face another conflict. Some Ghanaian writers, such as Osei Kwadwo, view the split amongst the chiefs as evidence that the British policy of decentralising the king's rule had factionalised the Asante nation. Kwadwo even goes further and states that in his opinion this last conflict cannot be seen as a continuation of the Anglo-Asante wars for the British fought against only one faction within Asante and that the whole nation was not involved. Kwadwo and other Ghanaian historians prefer to view the last hostilities as the Yaa Asantewaa War, named after the queen mother, who was so influential in driving opposition to the British.

The governor remained oblivious to both the anger and hostility his demands had aroused. It seems Sir Frederick sincerely believed that the Asantes were pleased to be under British rule. Given that, in his eyes, the Asantes were an inferior savage people who respected little other than force and authority it seemed completely rational to him to seek to establish the representative of the British queen as the paramount chief in their eyes. Thus, if the Golden Stool was viewed as the paramount chief's source and symbol of power it was perfectly reasonable for him to expect to have it presented to him. With true Victorian arrogance, Hodgson believed that the British mode of government was superior and that the Asantes would be grateful for it. Over the next few days the governor continued his work unaware of the conflict that was brewing. He heard several legal cases relating to lands over which rival chiefs claimed jurisdiction and even planned a visit to the nearby Obuassi mines for the following week. Yet, the governor was still determined to seek out the whereabouts of the Golden Stool.

Yet another rumour reached the governor about the location of the Golden Stool. Once more the boy Esumi claimed that he knew where the stool had been hidden and on the pretext of searching the villages of Nkwanta and Bali, and others en route, for arms and ammunition, he ordered Captain Armitage to command a detachment of forty-five Hausas under Captain Leggett for the search. The party, including Esumi, left Kumasi on the morning of 31 March. Armitage had the presence of mind to send two Hausas, disguised as traders, out ahead of the group to report upon the mood in the countryside. They reported that several large meetings had been held and that the young men seemed aggressive. However, the British were able to search the villages without interference, although Armitage himself noted an air of expectancy amongst the locals.

Leaving most of the detachment at Bali under Leggett's command, Armitage with Esumi leading the way set off through the bush for an exhausting 3-hour hike to a small clearing in which a few dilapidated huts stood. Here, according to Esumi, the Golden Stool could be found hidden under one of them. The soldiers were to put to work with picks and shovels and the floor of each hut was excavated to a depth of several feet, but nothing was found. Much to Armitage's frustration, Esumi exclaimed that he must have been mistaken and the party wearily returned to Bali.

On their arrival, at around 3pm, Armitage and his men found Leggett and the remaining Hausas drawn up in line, weapons ready, facing a very angry crowd of armed Asantes; clearly word of their 'secret' mission to find the stool had reached the locals. Armitage placed his men around the village to reduce the risk of a surprise rush attack and cleared some of the undergrowth that impeded his field of vision. Conscious that any sudden move might trigger a fire-fight, Armitage on hearing that tea had been prepared decided to sit down with Leggett. Just as the tea was being poured a sudden roar of fire hit the village. Armitage described it thus:

> A terrific fire was opened immediately all around the village, the slugs thudding on the walls and falling on the thatched roofs like hail . . . a heavy curtain of smoke hung in front . . . occasionally rent by a spurt of flame as an Ashanti more courageous than his fellows, advanced into the open to fire his Dane gun. Our poor table was bearing the brunt of the enemy's fire . . . As we looked, the tin of condensed milk leapt wildly into the air and disappeared into the bush . . . closely followed by the butter tin, while the enamelled tin cups and saucers kept up a continuous clatter until they, in their turn, dived from the table into the bush.[21]

The scene, if it had not been so serious, would surely have been comical. Armitage ordered all his command to retreat to the relative safety of the huts in which loopholes were made to return the Asante fire. Leggett was hit in both arms and several of the Hausas received flesh wounds. Armitage was more seriously injured when a large iron bullet struck him in the neck, which numbed the back of his head and left a nasty wound. Yet, as dusk approached it didn't stop Armitage leading a charge of Hausas out of the huts to recover the picnic table. Why Armitage thought this a logical move is probably explained by his head wound but the captain was to suffer more as another slug hit him high on his left thigh. He and the battered remains of the table were carried back to the huts. Here Armitage had to endure being butchered by a native orderly who endeavoured to remove the slug. After several painful ineffectual attempts Armitage resolved that the slug should remain, and the wound was bandaged.

The Asantes maintained a storm of incessant fire until around 8pm and throughout the night sharpshooters continued to harass the British. Armitage though seems to have found the Asante war cries more troublesome than their fire. It is clear from the translation of one of the war chants that the warriors were very aware of the British intentions:

> The Governor came up to Kumasi on a peace palaver. He demanded money from us and sent white men to bring him the Golden Stool Instead of money the Governor shall have the white men's heads sent to him to Kumasi The Golden stool shall be well washed in the white man's blood.[22]

Although Armitage was under some pressure from the non-commissioned officers to attempt a night break out from the village, he refused to countenance such a move. He was concerned that in the dark men could become separated and that panic might ensue. Armitage thus ordered preparations for a dawn departure.

Meanwhile, in Kumasi, Captain Houston was receiving worrying reports of Asante dissatisfaction and had learnt that Armitage's column was to be ambushed. Two Hausas were sent to warn of the attack, but these two men evidently fell into Asante hands and were never seen again. Houston had several meetings with the kings and chiefs, and also met Yaa Asantewaa, in an attempt to ascertain their loyalty, but it soon became clear to Houston that the situation was looking increasingly threatening. The governor finally understood the difficulty that the British were facing, and he consulted Houston as to whether a contingent could be sent to Armitage's relief. The acting-resident stated that a force strong enough to aide Armitage would leave Kumasi denuded of its garrison and potentially unable to defend itself. Hodgson realised that Armitage and his detachment would have to save themselves.

Armitage had reached the same conclusion as to the likelihood of rescue, and he resolved to return to Kumasi whatever obstacles the Asantes put in his way. He led his men out of the village in the early morning mist, hoping beyond hope that their flight would go unseen. However, as soon as they had left the environs of the village, they were ambushed by 'Long Dane' fire from either side of the road. In a panic the carriers bolted, knocking Armitage to the ground. The Hausas remained resolute and returned fire and as quickly as possible the detachment headed towards the first natural barrier on the route back to Kumasi, the Ofin River. The party found the river in flood and the Asantes waiting for them. They had no alternative but to attack and Armitage split his command into two lines. Armed with only the single-shot Martini–Enfield rifle, the Hausa lines took turns to fire volleys and then advance under the cover of the others' fire. By this method they were able to lessen the Asante fire and gain ground until the riverbank was reached. This move seems to have sent the Asnates fleeing in panic, but perhaps it was the sight that greeted Armitage's men which had sent the Asantes in retreat for they found an Asante chief, apparently the group's commander, slumped dead in a chair with a British bullet in his chest. The detachment, with the waters lapping above their shoulders, now struggled across the river.

Armitage led his men for the rest of the day along the bush paths, with constant sniping from unseen Asantes. The village of Atchiassi was renowned as a hotbed of fetish and Armitage expected to meet strong resistance there, but yet when he and his men entered they found it to be deserted, although there were signs that a large gathering had recently been held in the centre of the village. Relieved the party carried on, but were only a few hundred metres out of Atchiassi when they were met with a terrific fire and down went many of the Hausas. Although this attack was beaten back, further assaults continued throughout the morning in which both the advance and rear guard of Hausa were repeatedly wounded. It was still only 12.30pm and the party were just an hour's march from the sanctuary of Kumasi, but Armitage realised his situation was desperate. Only four men remained uninjured, and the retiring column's progress had reached a snail's pace for the wounded were so numerous. Provisions had to be abandoned, ammunition was almost spent and the water nearly exhausted. Armitage resolved to cut a clearing in the undergrowth and his party laid down seeking cover. Three rounds were distributed amongst those wounded who could still offer resistance whilst the rest was given to the ten fittest men and under the command of Leggett these troops were ordered to make a dash to Kumasi and seek urgent help. Armitage now settled the remainder of his command down for the night to await their fate in the morning.

Fortune was with Armitage, for overnight the Asantes faded back into the bush and Leggett and his men ran into a small scouting party sent out from Kumasi which escorted them the remaining few miles back to the sanctuary of the fort. Armitage and the rest of his command were likewise returned to safety. Armitage had lost two men killed and one missing whilst the majority of the troops had been wounded by Asante slugs. The Asantes admitted to over 200 dead. Many of the Hausas had distinguished themselves, in particular Sergeant Amadu Fulani who the governor immediately promoted to company sergeant major and who was to later receive the Distinguished Conduct Medal.

The net though was tightening around Kumasi and now thoroughly nervous of his position Hodgson sent telegrams to the coast and the Northern Territories seeking all available units of armed constabulary to be sent at top speed to Kumasi. When news of the rising reached Chamberlain, he ordered urgent troop reinforcements to be sent from Lagos, Northern Nigeria and Sierra Leone. However, as many of these troops where in isolated areas, often in small units, they could only be assembled by marching long distances. It would almost certainly have been quicker to send a detachment from Britain, but the Asantes had chosen the right moment to rebel for the British were locked in a bitter fight with the Boers in South Africa, as well as fighting in China, and no British troops could be spared for a fight in an obscure little outpost of the empire.

Despite Hodgson's hasty telegrams, it was still not clear whether the fighting at Bali would result in a full-scale rebellion. From 5 April onwards the Asantes began to congregate in large camps to the north, east and south of Kumasi and contented themselves with singing and drumming throughout the night. There was a report that Captain Parmeter, an officer of the Gold Coast Constabulary, had been attacked on the Nkoranza road and had had a narrow escape, yet trade continued, and the food markets remained well supplied. Writing the following year, Armitage surmised that if a strong force of Hausas could have been sent from the coast in this 'phoney war' phase then the uprising might have been quelled before it really began. As it was only 100 troops could be sent from Accra. Houston and Hodgson worked together to take precautions against a surprise attack upon the fort and any undergrowth which might allow for a potential enemy to seek cover was removed. The two men also sought reassurances from various chiefs and kings as to their loyalty. The governor, rather than returning to the coast, remained and this was possibly because Lady Hodgson was ill with fever and unable to travel. Houston left Kumasi on 18 April, along with two mining engineers, for he had urgent personal business. These men met with no opposition. The governor now received reports that Yaa Asantewaa had formed a large camp at Abercoom, a small village within 10 minutes' walk of the fort.

On the afternoon of 18 April, a force of Hausas, 107 rank and file, under the command of Captain Middlemist, and accompanied by Captains Marshall and Bishop, arrived at the fort. With this detachment, the governor felt strong enough for a show of force and on 20 and 21 April these troops, along with Captain Leggett, destroyed the Asante camps at Karsi, Aseni and Abercoom. All were found to be deserted. The governor now received reports of a large camp at Kwaman and on 23 April, Captains Bishop and Marshall led a force of 150 men on a reconnaissance. With reports of heavy firing, Armitage left the fort to investigate and at about 10.30am he met the returning column. A wounded Marshall was able to report that the detachment had been ambushed near the Kwaman camp by a large Asante force, which had followed the retreating men back towards Kumasi. Five Hausas had been killed and both Bishop and Marshall, as well as a Dr Hay, were all wounded, along with fifty-five of the troops. That night large numbers of Asantes gathered in the camps now surrounding Kumasi, singing and drumming throughout the night. It seemed clear to all that a rising was imminent.

The Seige of Kumasi
A stalemate ensued on the following day but early on the morning of 25 April, Armitage received a note from Revd Ramseyer of the Basel Mission station stating that one of his Hausas had been killed in the act of obtaining water from a nearby well and that large groups of Asante warriors could be seen moving in the bush just 200m away. Armitage immediately left the fort to see the situation for himself and met the Ramseyers and four other missionaries on the road who, fearing for their lives, had been forced to abandon their mission. All were accommodated in the fort. The governor discovered that the telegraph wire to Accra had been cut. The troops were now placed on full alert, rifles were cleaned and Maxim guns positioned on the corners of the fort.

At 10am the anticipated attack began. The Asantes occupied the Basel Mission building and heavy, but ineffective, 'Long Dane' fire hit the fort and the European buildings close by. Many of the warriors then commenced a wide arching movement between the European cantonment and the fort with the obvious intention of trying to reach the long grass that remained between the fort and the officers' quarters. The sortie was driven back by well-directed volley fire and already the British were demonstrating their technological superiority in weapons, just as in 1874. At noon, with the Asantes still in possession of the Basel Mission, the governor accepted an offer from the king of Aguna, who was in the fort with a number of loyal Asantes, to lead these men in an attack to disperse the rebel warriors. Armitage, despite the wound to his thigh causing him enormous discomfort, accompanied this force. These men with the king and Armitage at the head, slipped through the gates of the fort and charged up the Bantama Road driving the Asante warriors back, but as they neared the Basel Mission building a tremendous fire from within halted their advance. Armitage and the loyal Asantes laid flat and returned fire and this firefight continued for several minutes. From the lofty heights of the fort the governor could see that a large group of warriors was slipping through the bush to outflank Armitage's force on the right. Captain Middlemist was ordered out to warn Armitage to return to the fort.

The retreat to the fort was at first orderly with Maxim fire upon the Basel Mission supporting the men as they slowly returned. However, at this moment a large group of warriors rampaged through the civilian Hausa part of Kumasi forcing the inhabitants to flee for their lives and they stampeded towards the fort, which was their only hope of safety. Three or four rounds from the 7-pounder positioned on the fort ramparts forced back the Asantes, killing several. However, the Hausa dwellings, made as they were in traditional style of wattle and grass, caught fire which added to the sense of panic amongst the fleeing civilians. These individuals, numbering in excess of 3,000, were denied entry to the fort by the governor and to be fair to Hodgson their presence inside the fort at this crucial moment could have led to disaster. These unfortunate Hausas tried to scale the walls and batter down the gates.

Meanwhile, Armitage and Middlemist were rallying their men as the Asante rebels tightened their grip around the fort. All the buildings in the European cantonment were occupied and from within fire was directed at the fort and large groups appeared on both the Bantama and Cape Coast roads. With the light fading the officers decided upon a fighting withdrawal back to the fort where they encountered pandemonium. In trying to gain entry through the gates Middlemist was swept along by the Hausa refugees and crushed against the walls. Only with the intervention of the governor and a few Hausa troops was the officer rescued but he had been badly hurt and he was to die of his injuries on 6 May. As night fell Armitage standing on the fort's balustrades recorded the sights he saw:

The blazing houses in the cantonments and Fanti and Cape Coast lines, some of which the rebels had fired, cast lurid light upon the surging mass of humanity clustering round the Fort walls, from which arose the wailing of women and the pitiful crying of little children . . . Every now and then, amid a whirlwind of sparks, some thatch roof would fall in, converting the four 'swish' walls of the house into a white hot furnace. Away across the swamp glowed the embers of the burned civilian Hausa town, occasionally lighting up the Wesleyan Mission buildings, as yet untouched by the Ashantis. Behind all towered the blank wall of forest which surrounds Kumasi, from which were borne the triumphant shouts of the rebel, who had last caged the white man within the narrow limits of his Fort walls. It was a night never to be forgotten.[23]

The day had certainly been one of success for the attacking Asantes, and the white man had indeed been caged, but what is clear is that whatever leadership Yaa Asantewaa was supplying it did not incorporate a firm strategy on what the rebels could hope to achieve by their action. Certainly, denying the British possession of the Golden Stool was the number one priority and there was undoubtedly a hope that the rebel stand would result in some sort of negotiation to secure the return of Prempeh. Rebel demands submitted in April to the governor were so fanciful that they did not even receive consideration. These included: the return of the king, that slavery should be permitted, that the Asantes should be free of any obligation to construct government buildings or roads, that the fort should be levelled and that all foreigners should leave the nation.

Yet, the rebellion risked the lives of British citizens, and in particular the governor and his wife, and this would have only unleased the most terrible retribution from the British government, confident in knowing that such 'revenge' would be supported by the public. It was also evident from the first day of the siege that the rebels, with the weaponry at their disposal, could never hope to take the fort by force, fighting across open ground against modern Maxim machine guns, although this did not stop them trying and wasting lives in the attempt. The best hope was to take the fort by starvation and to this end stockades were constructed on all the roads approaching Kumasi not only to keep the British in, but also any relieving force out.

The next few days were relatively quiet. Almost unbelievably the rebels failed to stop water parties venturing out the 100m from the fort to a stream and the Hausa civilians were also able to access this source. The Asantes never tried to poison the stream and if they had wanted to see the surrender of the fort's occupants this would have been the easiest and quickest way to achieve it. Although there was a well in the fort, it could never have met the needs of the large numbers inside. Sniping and general harassment continued. The prison, just 200m from the fort, was burnt down; the occupants had been freed on 25 April, some of whom joined the besiegers. For those poor civilians huddled at the base of the fort, the weather was particularly unkind with heavy night-time storms. Shelters soon sprang up, consisting of rough wooden frames covered in skins or salvaged thatch, but despite this the plight of the refugees would be the little-known horror of the subsequent weeks.

Just before the telegraph lines had been cut, news had arrived from Accra that 250 troops had landed from Lagos in answer to the governor's plea for help. The detachment, which included a 7-pounder and two Maxims, was under the command of Captain John Aplin. It was calculated that this force should be expected in Kumasi on about 29 April and with this in mind and to aid the advance of the reinforcements it was decided by Captain Marshall, who was now in overall command for Middlemist was on his deathbed, that the rebels should be kept busy on this day. He ordered his men to snipe at any rebels that showed their heads and this fire seemed to have provoked them. From within the occupied buildings the rebels assembled for a mad rush at the fort. The attack was recorded by Lady Hodgson:

> The advance of the rebels was met by a terrific fire from the maxims in the fort, which I knew was effective for I could see them dropping. But nothing daunted on they came, and now the fire was taken up by the Hausas. The din was very great and so close to the fort was the fighting that the slugs from the rebel's guns fell in the fort yard . . . The rebels were now falling fast and the Hausas were pressing them back. At last a cheer proclaimed that the enemy were retiring. Then it was that our loyal natives, some two hundred who we had managed to arm, came into play and did good service under the Governor's private secretary Captain Armitage, who on this occasion and later controlled and led them. Everywhere were signs of victory.[24]

It was indeed a morale-boosting victory. Later, 130 dead Asantes were gathered from around the fort and buried, and a number must have subsequently died of wounds or have been dragged dead from the field. Armitage managed briefly to dislodge the Asantes from the Basel Mission station which had been plundered and littered by the warriors. In one of the storerooms in a cantonment building Armitage stumbled across the bodies of about thirty to forty Asantes who had taken refugee there. Whether these men were wounded is unknown, but they had been discovered, probably by loyal Asantes, and had met a very bloody end, literally being hacked to pieces. Armitage described the scene as one of carnage and was glad to give the order for the building to be burnt down. The actions of Marshall and Armitage and their troops had done a great service for Aplin and his men who were at that moment struggling to enter Kumasi. Not only had several hundred rebels been killed but many more had been diverted from opposing Aplin and it is quite possible that if these warriors had been available then Aplin's advance might well have been thwarted.

As it was Aplin and his troops had a torrid time in their advance. On the day the Asantes attacked Kumasi, Aplin and his men left Prahsu and for the next three days they continued their advance towards Kumasi. Although no opposition was initially encountered, the villagers they passed were sullen and some warned that they were certain to be attacked soon. At about midday on 28 April they were just 7–8 miles from Kumasi and had halted for a brief rest. Suddenly Aplin's helmet was knocked to the ground as the slug from an Asante sniper penetrated it and then grazed his throat. Within seconds the column was swept with musketry from both sides of the path. Men fell around him and Aplin, quickly regaining his composure, ordered his men forward for he knew they were dead if they tried to defend their position. The rattling of Maxim fire from both the front and rear of the column told the captain that his command was surrounded, and he gave the order to fix bayonets. Pushing the 7-pounder to the front, and ordering rapid fire, Aplin and his men were able to push on to the village of Esiagu. Here the troops formed a defensive perimeter whilst Aplin was able to assess his casualties. In just a few moments he had lost three men dead and twenty-one wounded.

Fortunately, the Asantes did not press home an attack that night and in the morning Aplin and his men were determined to move forward. Expecting an attack at any moment, they were surprised that all was quiet. However, when they were just 3 miles off Kumasi they were again attacked. This time there were many more Asantes, not just hiding in the undergrowth on both sides of the path, but also firing down from the trees. Aplin and his men were incredibly resolute and fired determinedly but after 5 hours of constant battle they had only advanced a mile. Now only 2 miles from their destination they discovered a stockade constructed of fallen trees blocking the path and with scores of Asantes defending it. Aplin called forward both a Maxim gun and the 7-pounder but before either could have any real impact the men serving both were shot down. Aplin now called upon Captain Read, who had been in command of the rear of the column, to bring forward thirty of his men. With fixed bayonets they charged the stockade, but the Asante fire was so intense that they quickly faltered. Read, flourishing his sword at the head of his men, was hit repeatedly and his men were knocked down. Just metres from the defensive position, Read realised that he was alone and managed to drag himself back to Aplin. The brave young officer had received four body wounds and his right arm had been shattered. Aplin was able to pour some whiskey down Read's throat to revive him and he was carried back into the main body.

The situation was now most desperate. The ammunition for the 7-pounder had been expended and the Maxim had over heated and jammed. Aplin ordered that stones were thrust down the barrel of the field piece and these were sprayed at the stockade to keep the heads of the Asantes down. Aplin now called upon another officer, Captain Cochrane, to lead a flanking attack. Although badly wounded in the shoulder, he managed to lead his men to within 20m of the strongpoint and three volleys from his men seem to stun the warriors. Aplin sensed there was at last an opportunity and summoning all his men who were fit enough he led them in a frantic charge at the stockade. To his, and his men's amazement, the Asantes broke and fled and the way to Kumasi was at last open.

Aplin and his command saw the smoke rising in the air from the morning's battle and all must have feared that their Herculean efforts had been in vain. To their horror a large party of Asantes were seen approaching them and, with just a few rounds left per man, each resolved to sell their lives. Yet, as the party of warriors neared Aplin could see a white officer running behind the warriors; it was Armitage with his loyal Asantes! The gates opened to welcome the exhausted column. The price of the advance had been a heavy one. Of the 250 men who had arrived from Lagos, 5 had been killed and 139 wounded. The 7-pounder had been abandoned and the column's supplies and ammunition had been lost or exhausted. Those who would be the rescuers had become the rescued. The governor must have been totally despondent for the hoped-for relief had only brought more wounded and more mouths to feed.

It is worth considering the Asante battlefield tactics. Apart from a couple of mad rushes at the fort which proved costly and ineffective, the rebels can be praised for their general approach. The organisation of the warriors was impressive. Each group had an allocated space or station in the cordon encircling the British, with reserves held at general headquarters. There were also departments of linguists, fetish men and spies. Whilst most of the warriors were armed with the ubiquitous 'Long Dane', the rebels did have a corps of elite shots and these men were armed with captured .303 carbines and .22 carbines. These 'snipers' were placed in vantage points such as trees and in rifle pits and were given instructions to aim for the white men. Indeed, the high casualty figures amongst the British officers reflects how successful these crack shots were.

Knowing how inaccurate the 'Long Danes' were, the Asante chiefs generally placed their men in a fighting formation of three lines, each commanded by individual officers. The aim was to achieve a high concentration of fire; the front line would discharge and then double to the rear to grab a freshly loaded weapon, whilst the second line would run forward, fire and then rush to the rear for a new rifle, whilst the third took its place, and so on. The warriors carried long knives in scabbards held in belts around their waists, but as the British quickly discovered the Asantes were not keen on hand-to-hand combat and a bayonet charge often saw the warriors flee and the position abandoned.

The various camps scattered around Kumasi were readily identified from the fort by rising smoke that curled up from fires that were constantly lit and from the singing, chanting and drumming which was such a feature of camp life at night. During the day the warriors apparently rested and slept, often aided by large amounts of 'trade gin', for which they had a taste. In the early evening Asante women would bring substantial quantities of food to the various camps.

The stockades that surrounded Kumasi were well constructed; they were all of the same basic design, and consisted of two parallel rows of logs, just over a metre apart and braced together using pilfered telegraph wire. The gap between the logs was filled with earth and stones and sometimes loopholed. The ends of the stockades curved backwards in a horseshoe formation which enabled the defenders to bring fire upon anyone trying to flank and enfilade them. In the 1874 conflict 'stockades' were simply made by felling large trees across the jungle paths, so the use of such well-constructed fortifications was a new approach. By placing stockades on each of the roads leading out of Kumasi the town was effectively encircled and paths were cut through the jungle joining each so that reinforcements could quickly move between each one when they were threatened.

Armitage and the governor decided that to maintain morale in light of diminishing food supplies, the occasional foraging or raiding party should be despatched from the fort. Whilst the inhabitants inside the fort were still just about surviving on tinned beef and biscuits the situation for the refugees at the base of the fort was becoming ever more serious. On 2 May Armitage led out his loyal Asantes in a raid in the direction of the Wesleyan mission, which stood a kilometre to the north east of the fort near a stockade. Although the mission and the stockade were apparently undefended, Armitage's men were slow to cross the open ground and the watchful rebels were able to rush to defend the area and within minutes the raiders were pinned down by 'Long Dane' fire. Unwilling to admit defeat, Armitage called up support from one of the 7-pounders but its fire had no effect on the stockade and even this effort was finally abandoned. The men marched empty-handed and dispiritedly back to the fort. The following day the Asantes torched the mission and relocated the stockade to a strongpoint a few hundred metres back. Further sorties on 8, 9 and 10 May were equally unsuccessful. These setbacks, as well as the death of the popular Middlemist on 6 May, really dented morale. Lady Hodgson was particularly distressed by the passing of Middlemist and could not bring herself to attend his poignant funeral.

By the middle of May the lack of food was causing real concern. Whilst rations for those inside the fort were pitiful, the plight of the refugees was desperate. Although Lady Hodgson helped organise a soup service for the children, it consisted of little more than hot water sprinkled with biscuit crumbs. The adults had to make do with stewed weeds or grass and some were so driven by hunger that they ate the 'epi root', which had appeared as one of the few food items to buy. Unfortunately, it was a poisonous root, the consumption of which resulted in the most dreadfully painful death. Several died before the governor was able to ban the sale of the root. By the end of the month these poor Hausas were also visited by smallpox and the mortality rate was around thirty souls a day. Burying parties failed to lessen the stench of death and decay that pervaded the fort.

After the last failed sortie of 10 May the loyal Asante chiefs within the fort asked permission of the governor to open negotiations with the rebels. Visits were made by special envoys to King Bodu's rebel camp on the Mampon road and 'fetish was drunk'. The rebels reiterated their demands of April but on 13 May a truce was agreed, and some food was brought for the refugees, including over 200 loads of plantains. The vigilance at the stockade was also slightly relaxed and this was to be of great benefit to the British for another 'relief' column was now close by.

The commander of the Northern Territories garrison at Gambaga, Major Arthur Morris of the Royal Irish Regiment, had received the governor's plea for assistance on 18 April and immediately began to assemble a force. By 22 April, he had plundered his command and with 3 other officers, 170 soldiers, a 7-pounder and a Maxim he began the torrid march south. Not only was the distance to Kumasi a vast 340 miles, his column had to march through searing heat in a shadeless country and endured torrential rains most nights. Despite these hardships it reached Kintampo, the depot for the Northern Territories in just thirteen days, averaging 18 miles a day. Here Morris was joined by Captain Parmeter who had had a narrow escape as he journeyed south on leave and had to be rescued from the people of Sekodumasi by a force from Kintampo. Parmeter and two other officers, the garrison of sixty troops and over eighty levies now swelled Morris's column and after two days' rest all continued towards Kumasi, now just 102 miles away.

The further south Morris led his detachment the greater the anticipation of attack became but it was not until 14 May when they were just a few miles from Kumasi that they were ambushed. Those levies and troops at the front of the column were hit by a classic Asante ambush in which few of the enemy were even seen. Although casualties were light, and the enemy melted away, Morris and his men must have expected another attack the following day. In the morning the march continued and when just 12 miles from their destination the scouts reported a strong stockade across the path. Morris called forward the 7-pounder which pulverised the stockade and awoke a hornet's nest of Asante warriors who were apparently asleep behind it and unaware of the column's presence. A fierce firefight now ensued for half an hour and Morris realised that more direct offensive action was required. Placing himself at the head of the advance guard, under Captain Maguire, Morris raised his sword and led the men in a rush of the stockade. The attack was met by a hail of slugs, one of which struck Morris in the groin and brought him crashing to the ground. Maguire continued forward and with his men using the bayonet carried the obstacle for the cost of fifteen wounded.

In great pain Morris was placed in a hammock and was carried forward with his command. Two more stockades were passed on the path, but neither were defended, and the column met no further opposition. The truce agreed between the rebels and the loyal chiefs meant that the defenders had been left in camp. When Morris arrived at the fort in the late afternoon the rebels felt betrayed and all further negotiations were abruptly ended in some animosity. The truth was the governor had received no notification of Morris's imminent arrival, so it was just a coincidence that the column had appeared during the truce. As it was the 'relief' column was anything but and, like Aplin's efforts of a couple of weeks before, the extra men placed a further burden on the fort's meagre supplies without providing a force large enough to break the siege. Nearly 800 troops had been added to the garrison and few supplies had accompanied them. In addition, several hundred porters and levies were added to the crowd of starving refugees huddled around the fort.

Despite his wound, Morris assumed command of the fort and after consultation with the governor decided that the situation was now critical. Not only was food quickly running out but there was no definite news of a relief force coming to their aid from the coast. It was thus decided that offensive action should now resume in order to obtain food supplies. Morris resolved to attack the Asante stockade on the Dedesuada road on 20 May. Whilst the stockade was to be attacked by 150 Hausas commanded by Captains Leggett and Bishop and 450 loyal Asantes under Armitage, four 7-pounders, positioned near the prison, were to shell the Mampon road war camp as a diversion. The bombardment began at around 9am and lasted for an hour whilst the attacking forces got into position. Yet, this diversionary fire did not have the desired effect and when the attacks went in, they were beaten back by fierce rebel fire. Captain Leggett was severely wounded, as were a further twenty-five troops. Morris now tried an early morning attack with 220 troops under Captains Marshall and Maguire, supported by a 7-pounder and a Maxim. Whether Asante spies were aware of the plan or not the Asante defenders were certainly ready for the assault which was again beaten back. On this occasion losses were high; Marshall was severely wounded in the chest and Maguire killed. Finally, a night attack led by Armitage and Bishop upon the Mampon stockade on the night of 26 May turned to farce when bells attached to tripwires alerted the rebel sentries of the presence of the attacking force and the Hausas refused to advance.

Not only were the British unable to break through the rebel encirclement, but food was now nearly exhausted, and the rains had arrived in force adding to the discomfort and disease in and around the fort. The mortality rate was running at 10 per cent a week amongst the wretched Hausas refugees huddled outside. Troops were too weak from lack of food to function against a determined foe. Morris and Hodgson knew that the fort could not hold out much longer and that a different approach would have to be adopted.

On 10 May, several hundreds of miles away from Kumasi, a journey was to begin that would transform the fate of the fort and of the whole protectorate. Colonel James Willcocks CMG, DSO, the Second-in-Command of Northern Nigeria's West African Frontier Force, was three days' march north of Jebba. Willcocks was en route to Zaria where he was ordered to lead an operation against the hostile emir. These plans were rapidly altered when he received a message from his superior, Brigadier General Frederick Lugard, which included a telegram from Chamberlain stating that Willcocks was to assume command of the forces assembling for the relief of Kumasi.

Willcocks knew of the Asante uprising and that units had already been sent to the Gold Coast, but his appointment came as something of a surprise to him and others. He set off for Lagos the following day and despite delays caused by food poisoning, a lame pony and discomfort from an old leg wound, he reached his destination on 24 May. Within two days he was struggling through the surf at the Cape Coast.

Willcocks was an inspired choice to lead the relief force. He was 41 years old and he had been a soldier since 1878 when he commissioned into the 100th Regiment, The Leinsters. He had served in India and had fought in the Second Afghan War of 1878–9, Waziristan in 1881 and again in 1897, the Sudan in 1885 and in Burma in 1886–7. With such experience nothing seemed to daunt him which was just as well for when he arrived at the Cape Coast he was inundated with demands, panic and misinformation. Just before the telegraph line had been cut Hodgson had managed to get a message out stating that the fort could not hold out beyond 26 May and Willcocks was able to deduce that both Aplin and Morris had reached Kumasi. The actual situation though was open to conjecture, but Willcocks was able to slice through the 'fog of war' and he realised that his immediate task was not the relief of Kumasi but the replenishment of food and ammunitions to the besieged. Knowing that he could not expect British battalions, for the demands of China and South Africa had placed too high a burden, he knew he would have to rely on native forces. Yet, his biggest concern was not obtaining troops and supplies but, as in 1873–4, it was the need to 'recruit' thousands of porters to travel the 150 miles from the coast to

Kumasi. 'Volunteer' porters were not readily available, and the local constabulary was used to 'recruit' natives, as Colley had done in 1873. The net had to be spread wide and porters were brought in from Sierra Leone and even from as far away as Zanzibar, such was the desperate need.

The gathering of the porters took weeks but once done Willcocks could look to assemble the 'Ashanti Field Force', as it became known, as it was soon clear that it would have to be composed of a number of very small, diverse units drawn from across West Africa, with the bulk coming from the Hausas of the Gold Coast Constabulary. Troops came from the West African Frontier Force (WAFF) of Northern Nigeria, consisting of two battalions of infantry, mainly Hausas and Yorubas, and three batteries of artillery, including one equipped with new powerful 75mm guns. The Lagos Constabulary were also drafted across. Sierra Leone provided the West African Regiment, a War Office, rather than Colonial Corps, of high professional standards, with British officers. Fifty Frontier Policemen also journeyed from Sierra Leone. Finally, troops of the Yao, Atonga and Angoni tribes of Nyasaland who made up the Central African Regiment, led by British officers and Sikh NCOs, completed the force. Obviously to collect such a diverse force would take time and time was one thing that the inhabitants of the fort did not have.

The situation continued to worsen for those in and around Kumasi fort. The sorties out to try to secure food had been completely unsuccessful and had served only to expend both ammunition and the remaining energies of the troops engaged. Hunger gripped all and nearly every day false hopes were raised when someone announced that he could hear the sound of gun fire coming from the Cape Coast road, only for that hope to be dashed. Rumours abounded that a relief force was nearby, and signal rockets were fired high into the air from the fort's bastions, but each time there was no response. Several of Armitage's men volunteered as runners to take messages to the coast to inform the relief column that food and ammunition were desperately needed but none returned so those in the fort had no idea whether their pleas had been received. On the night of 19 June Morris ordered one of the fort's 7-pounders to fire a number of timed fused shells high into the air. When this attempt failed to attract a response Morris and Hodgson called a meeting of the officers for clearly the time had finally come to try and break out of the fort.

Plans had been discussed for the past weeks, but to risk a break-out, especially when previous attempts to storm the stockades had all ended in failure, was always seen as the last option. Yet, the time had now come. A rumour was spread around the fort, with the hope it would reach the rebels, that any break-out would be via the Cape Coast road, but rather than heading south Morris and Hodgson had devised a plan to take the Patasi road west in the hope of breaking through the cordon. The logistics were as daunting as the risks involved.

Around 600 troops, the governor and Lady Hodgson, the missionaries, and a further 1,000 non-combatants, porters and carriers (for the ladies would be carried in hammocks), and the remaining refugees and loyal Asantes made up the column. All food for the march would have to be carried as well as ammunition for the men's rifles, two 7-pounders and three Maxims. Captain Armitage and a recovered Leggett would lead the column with 114 troops. In the rear was Captain Aplin, with fifty Lagos Hausas, a Maxim and one of the field pieces.

At the fort 115 troops were to remain, with 90 too sick or wounded to travel. The medical officer detailed to look after them was himself too incapacitated to stand up and the Hausa NCO who remained was nearly 70 years old and had served with Wolseley's expedition. The two white officers ordered to continue the defence, Captain Bishop and Lieutenant Ralph, smiled weakly at the governor's suggestion that their chances of surviving were better than his as the two men looked around at their command. For although they were well supplied with munitions for the five 7-pounders and five Maxims that remained, they must have thought how could this group of starving invalids offer any resistance to a determined attack? Indeed, three soldiers died of starvation the following day and hardly a day passed when the death toll didn't rise. The survivors were too weak to dig graves and the bodies of the unfortunates were simply rolled into a shallow trench outside of the fort and covered with earth.

The gates of the fort swung silently open at 5am on the morning of 23 June and everyone was greeted with a thick, clinging white mist that fortunately deadened some of the sounds as the Hausa refugees gathered their loads upon their heads. It took 15 minutes for the column to assemble and enter the thick undergrowth which almost concealed a muddy track. Not a rebel was seen, and the column pushed silently on. After half an hour the path brought them to the Patasi stockade, and it seemed that the ruse had worked for the defence was light as presumably many of the defenders had been transferred to the Cape Coast road. Only twenty-five warriors had been left at Patasi and although these men offered a stout defence, Armitage led a rush. Captain Leggett was hit by a slug in the stomach and several Hausas were wounded, but Armitage ordered most of his command to lay a hot fire onto the defenders whilst he led twenty Hausas in a right flanking movement which took the stockade. Interestingly some of the rebels were, at the same time, attempting a flanking attack of their own but took the left flank so Armitage's men avoided a potential costly encounter in the bush.

The Patasi stockade was a massive construction, 3m high and nearly as thick, built of immense tree trunks, with loopholes for the defenders to fire through. The column was delayed for some time whilst the stockade was dismantled to allow for the bulk of the column to pass. The short sharp battle had cost the column four dead and ten wounded. Leggett's injury was severe, and he had to be passed to the rear before the advance guard continued and Captain Marshall was sent forward to replace the unlucky officer. It can only be imagined how high the casualties would have been if the stockade had been manned with a larger force. As it was, all feared that the sounds of gun fire would have aroused the defenders of the other stockades and that these warriors would be rushing to attack. Indeed, when the Asantes had realised that the column had broken through the cordon by the Patasi road, Akwesi Bodu, representative of Yaa Asantewaa, ordered another rebel chief, Antoa Mensa, who was in charge of the force responsible for rushing to any stockade that was under British attack, to follow in pursuit with a large force of 1,500 warriors.

The column pushed on with as much as haste as possible. Yet, their fears were met for every metre of path now seemed to have a hidden warrior defending it. Fire from the right flank was especially severe; a number of Hausas were hit, and Marshall was mortally wounded in the head, although he would bravely struggle on for several more days. The village of Patasi was reached after much fighting and here Morris called a halt for the column to reform and for everyone to grab some food. Plantains and green corn were found and greedily consumed, and it was with some difficulty that Armitage managed to 'persuade' the advance guard to push on. By 1.30pm Armitage had moved through the village of Tekiman and just outside he and his men met stiff opposition from the rebels and the whole afternoon was spent in firefights against an invisible foe. The village of Terrabum was reached and here the villagers had loopholed many of the huts and the advance guard had to go house-to-house with the bayonet to evict the inhabitants. Morris and the main column joined Armitage here and it was decided to fortify the village as much as possible and stay the night. Aplin brought the rear guard in just before dusk and reported that he had been leading a fighting withdrawal all afternoon and that many of the refugees and porters had been lost and their loads abandoned.

The column spent a miserable night. Torrential rain turned the ground to a sea of mud, fires were hard if not impossible to light. The many wounded were placed in two huts, the sides of which collapsed from the pressure against their flimsy walls and food was non-existent. Morning brought continued rain and a heavy fire from the Asantes who had surrounded the position, leaving only the road south free. Naturally, Morris thought this was a trap but with no alternative Armitage and the advance guard were ordered to push on. Fortunately, the undergrowth thinned the further south the column marched and the chance of ambush from unseen enemy was thereby lessened. A good pace was maintained, although Aplin's command was heavily engaged all day holding back the rebel warriors.

The retreating column was again lucky in that nearly all the porters abandoned their loads which were discarded by the side of the path. The Asante attacks against the rear guard were not as well coordinated or determined as they should have been for many of the warriors, including their commander Antoa Mensa, stopped to pillage the loads. Modern Ghanaian writers, such as Kofi Tieku, are very critical of Antoa Mensa and his men for these acts for they believe the slow pursuit of the column allowed the governor to escape and that if Hodgson had been captured the rebels would have been in a strong negotiating position. Osei Kwadwo even goes as far to state that it was the chief's love of money and wealth, his greed, that allowed the governor to flee and this ultimately resulted in the defeat of Yaa Asantewaa.

That night was even worse than the previous one. The rains returned, there was little shelter and all provisions had been lost or discarded. The following morning the column pushed on to the Nkwanta, where the chief, Kwachi Nketia. had professed his loyalty to the British. Hodgson and his surviving companions could only hope that the loyalty remained. As the bedraggled column wearily trodden into the village, they, much to everyone's relief, were greeted with smiles and parcels of food. Hodgson managed to drag himself across the palaver square at Nkwanta to receive the salute of the exhausted troops. Once this act was completed, he promptly collapsed with exhaustion. On hearing that the column had reached the safety offered by chief Kwachi Nketia, Antoa Mensa turned his men around and marched back to Kumasi where he was received in disgrace. Although the column did not now fear attack, the march continued to be arduous and hazardous as well as filled with tragedy; both Leggett and Marshall succumbed to their wounds en route, and the governor and his wife almost drowned whilst crossing the swollen Ofin River. The sheer fatigue and exhaustion of those returning saw the column split into three, each moving at a different pace and it was not until 10 July that the governor and his wife finally reached the sanctuary of Cape Coast Castle.

Beside the two officers, twenty-three troops had been killed and a further sixteen were to die of their wounds. A further thirty-seven were wounded and thirty-nine missing. This was a casualty rate in excess of 20 per cent amongst the troops. For the Hausa refugees and porters no records were kept but losses in excess of 50 per cent seem to be a realistic estimate. The Hodgsons, both sick with fever, were transported by warship to Accra where they were finally able to change their clothes. The governor was recalled to London the following month, in some disgrace. He was later found a position as governor of Barbados and after that British Guinea where his involvement with the Masonic Lodge there caused some controversy with the Roman Catholic Church. His retirement could not have come soon enough for the Colonial Office.

Willcocks was of course delighted that the governor was safe, but Kumasi still had to be relieved and the rebels would have to be beaten and stern lessons taught. Immediate relief was in the hands of Captain Hall who had arrived in advance of Willcocks and by 20 May had reached Fomena. Having made a feint attack towards Edjumun, on 24 May Hall moved towards Kokufu, which he aimed to destroy and then switch north to reach Kumasi. Outside of Kokufu Hall's detachment met a large body of Asantes and for several hours both forces fired into each other. Despite the presence of a 75mm field gun, which clearly unsettled the rebels, they refused to withdraw, and Hall realised that his only offensive option was a bayonet charge across open ground against an enemy at least ten times larger than his own. In these circumstances, Hall decided to retreat towards Esumeja where he thought the presence of his troops would at least weaken the force besieging Kumasi and would be well placed to impede any Asante attack from the east.

Willcocks had now had time to organise enough porters for at least a small force to rush to Kumasi from the coast. Lieutenant Colonel Carter led 200 men of the Southern Nigeria Battalion north to Kwisa to join forces with Colonel Wilkinson, Inspector General of the Gold Coast Constabulary. Willcocks himself left the coast with 11 officers and 280 men on 5 June for Prahsu. Carter should have joined Wilkinson advancing towards Kumasi but was heavily defeated at the Dompoasi stockade by native Adansi warriors and was forced to retire back to Kwisa. Here he had to hand over his command to Wilkinson and return to the coast due to illness. Willcocks, now knowing of the governor's escape but also of the terrible state of those remaining in Kumasi, ordered Wilkinson to Bekwai where he joined a detachment led by Colonel Burroughs. The combined force rushed the Dompoasi position in a surprise night attack and by 1 July had reached Bekwai. From here, against Willcocks's orders, Burroughs had the column push on to Kokofu but there they met stiff resistance and after 3 hours of heavy fighting they were forced to retire to Esumeja. Burroughs had received a severe wound and there were a further eighty casualties. Willcocks was decidedly unimpressed, and later Hall had to fight off a determined Asante attack on his Esumeja position.

These early reversals must have disappointed Willcocks, but they certainly did not lessen his determination. On 1 July he had left Prahsu with all available forces and crossed the Prah. By 9 July he had reached Bekwai, having encountered no resistance. Willcocks now sent a column in a diversionary attack upon Kokofu and on 13 July he personally led a force out of Bekwai which consisted of 60 British officers, 1,000 troops, 2 75mm guns, 4 7-pounders and 6 Maxims. The fact that Willcocks had been able to assemble this detachment in such a short period of time in the face of a resilient enemy speaks volumes for his organisational skills, persuasive nature and tenacity.

The skies emptied all day and it took nearly 24 hours for the force to cover the 15 miles to Peki, where they collapsed for the night. Captain Leland of the Gold Coast Constabulary wrote to his sister of his experience, 'I was Rear Guard the first day and got into camp at 2am having been on the go since 4 am with no food. All I got was half a biscuit, a little piece of yam, and some whisky I had in my flask.'[25] Such tough conditions, with little food and rest and constant downpours, began to take a toll on the officers. The following day Willcocks encountered strong resistance at the village of Trede, which was rushed and destroyed. The column halted at Nkwanta, just 5 miles from Kumasi for the night. Willcocks knew that by the end of the following day, 15 July, either Kumasi would be relieved, or his men would have died trying.

For Bishop and Ralph and their dwindling command in the fort each day was much like the next. The collecting of bodies of yet more men who had succumbed to disease or hunger became a morning ritual. Rumours of setbacks to the relief column or other rebel successes were frequently reported by local women who would occasionally bring scraps of yam to the fort to sell at outrageous prices. Otherwise the daily ration was a small square of meat and a shared biscuit. Bishop later admitted to a Reuters reporter that neither he or Ralph thought they would survive but, 'we kept up an appearance of cheerfulness for the sake of the men, who bore their sufferings with the greatest fortitude . . . they maintained perfect discipline and never complained'.[26] When smallpox struck the fort the cases had to be moved to a hut outside the walls, which Dr Hay visited regularly but when he himself contracted the disease Bishop felt that he must at least try and get news to any potential relief column. He promised £100 to any man who could get through with news of the fort's desperate state. Two Lagos men tried, but both returned without breaking through the rebel cordon. A second attempt was made by a coastal Hausa and one of the Lagos men. The latter was killed in the attempt, but the Hausa did finally make it through to Willcocks, who promoted him to sergeant on the spot and he eventually received the promised £100.

Yet, the fact that Willcocks had been reached was not known to Bishop and his command. With two-thirds of the men now buried in shallow graves, Bishop, Ralph and Hay resolved, once the very last morsel of food had been eaten, to destroy the 7-pounders and Maxims and cut their way out of the fort under cover of darkness. Dr Hay supplied poison to anyone who preferred death rather than capture and probable torture. Yet, the evening of 14 July brought some hope as the remaining men thought they had distinctly heard the report of 7-pounders. Shells were fired from the fort as a signal, but as usual no response was forthcoming, and the men settled back into despair and lethargy.

By the following morning, Bishop distinctly heard the sound of volley fire, but still he and the garrison refused to believe that after all this time help really was at hand. Finally, at 4.30pm, Bishop was convinced that relief was close, and he opened a surviving bottle of champagne to celebrate. By 5pm British cheers could be heard and the sound of shells whistling through the air became more distinct. By 6pm those in the garrison who were sufficiently strong enough managed to drag themselves to the balustrades to witness the first troops of the relief force emerge out of the bush. On the verandah of Kumasi Fort two buglers had just enough strength to sound 'Welcome!' as the survivors erupted in hysteria, of both joy and relief.

Willcocks and his men had endured a dreadful day as they attempted to reach Kumasi. On the move by dawn they soon encountered Asante sniping which continued to intensify as the march wore on and it took the best part of the day for the column to cover the few remaining miles. It was not until the late afternoon that the advance guard reached the final stockade guarding the route to Kumasi. With the daylight rapidly fading, Willcocks realised that he had no time to waste and the whole column marched on, including the bewildered porters who would have expected to be shielded from any direct fight.

As it was the Asantes concentrated their harassment on the porters so as to split the column. Many fled in panic, but the rear guard came up, beat back the Asantes and restored the line, thus avoiding a potential catastrophe at the last moment. The advanced guard now came under sustained attack from the stockade and Wilkinson brought up the field pieces and soon shells were crashing into the defences. Yet, still the Asantes maintained a heavy fire. Willcocks realised that the bayonet would have to be used and under the cover of shell fire he arranged his troops into a line of infantry, 600–700m long. Willcocks ordered a final minute of concentrated artillery and Maxim fire upon the stockade before giving the order to charge. He was to later record this as the greatest moment of his life:

> I looked along our lines, and then in the direction of the enemy's stockades, from which rose volumes of smoke, and then ordered the massed buglers to sound the 'Cease Fire'. With one accord each company took it up immediately, and it evidently re-acted on the enemy, for with us he ceased fire also. The drums and bugles then took up the 'Charge', the finest music my ears shall ever hear; like a wave up rose the ranks, and there was no doubt now. No Ashanti ever born would stand before that line of steel.[27]

Willcocks was right. In a moment hundreds of officers and troops had stormed the barricades, screaming, shooting, stabbing and those Asantes who survived the initial onslaught broke and fled. It was now that the damage inflicted by the 75mm guns could be assessed. Massive gaps had been torn in the huge timbers and dozens of Asantes were either blown to pieces or mutilated by flying shell and timber splinters. They lay in heaps and the back area of the stockade was covered in blood, body parts and entrails. The British officers were in awe of how the Asantes could have endured such a punishment for so long. Most officers and troops now rushed on to the fort as all opposition melted away. Willcocks had to have the assembly sounded to bring back some order so that the column could now march with dignity towards their goal. One officer, so exhausted by the march and the day's fighting, was found sound asleep amongst the chaos, his sword still held firmly.

In a true Victorian understatement, Captain Harold Bliss, of the West African Frontier Force and part of the relief force, wrote on entering the fort, 'Upon our arrival at the fort about 6p.m., we found the garrison well, only one officer being down with fever . . .'.[28] With a death rate amongst the garrison in excess of 60 per cent and the survivors little more than walking skeletons it is hard to comprehend Bliss's comments. Willcocks himself was horrified by the state of the garrison and thought that they would have been incapable of fighting off a determined Asante attack. His views would later cause some controversy and angst between him, Morris and Hodgson for the latter both took Willcocks's views as a personal slight. The relief force made the survivors as comfortable as possible and all were eventually returned to the coast. The area in and around the fort was cleared of bodies in varying degrees of decomposition and fires burnt for days. A force of 200 fit men was left behind in the fort whilst the remainder returned to Bekwai and from here Willcocks coordinated his forces to bring his total strength to bear upon the remaining rebels.

The Last Campaign

With Kumasi relieved many considered that the Asante rebels might yield to negotiations. The British were only getting stronger and the rebels could not realistically expect to defeat them in battle. Yet, Yaa Asantewaa was as resolute as ever that the fight should continue, and her determination ensured that the rebel chiefs would carry on fighting. This illustrates just how angry the rebels still were over the British desire to seize the Golden Stool, as well as the complete lack of trust that they now had for the British. Willcocks and his men were determined to exact revenge upon the rebels whilst they remained defiant.

Willcocks's initial strategy was to defeat the rebels who remained south of Kumasi. This made sense in terms of operational logistics and to lessen the threat upon the new garrison. Kokofu, which had become such a thorn in the side of the British, was attacked on 22 July, by a force led by Lieutenant Colonel Thomas Morland, consisting of 800 troops, 3 75mm guns and 2 7-pounders. Based on the two previous attempts to take Kokofu, Morland was expecting a hard fight. Major Melliss was in command of the advance guard, with Captain Bliss and his company of Hausas given the honour of leading the first assault. As the Kokofu stockade was approached through the cover of the bush, Morland joined Melliss in a short council of war. According to Bliss, Morland was considering cutting a fresh path to outflank the Asante position, but Melliss persuaded him that as they had apparently secured the element of surprise a sudden rush with the bayonet might carry the stockade. Luck was with the British; Melliss, Bliss and the Hausas achieved complete success for as they clambered over the stockade, they discovered it was empty. It appears that the defenders had left to have breakfast in the nearby village. Shouting and firing alerted the British that their presence had been detected but by this point the advance had poured over and around the position and as the Asantes ran to meet the threat they received a mass bayonet charge and fled. Kokofu was thus taken in a somewhat anti-climactic attack. The British could not believe that the attack had been so complete and so sudden.

Morland's force then moved on to Kwisa to take the strong Adansi position at Dompoasi. Major Beddoes was given command of a flying column of 400 troops and after a 3-day march, during which they met no opposition, they arrived in the vicinity of the stockade. Now they were heavily engaged, and a Maxim had to be brought up to lessen the enemy fire. Rather than their usual tactics of remaining behind the stockade, the rebels ventured out several times to attack the West African Field Force and on one occasion almost captured one of the 7-pounders. It was not until late in the afternoon that the Lagos Hausa Force under Captain Neal were able to outflank the stockade, but even then, the Adansis did not flee in panic but the bulk of the warriors retired in a fighting withdrawal. The fighting had been intense, and success came at a price; Beddoes had been severally wounded in the thigh and Lieutenants Philips, Monck-Mason and Swabey also received serious injuries. At this time Willcocks's headquarters at Bekwai received a constant stream of sick who had to be invalided home, casualties of the dreaded climate as well as battle. Special Service officers arrived in dribs and drabs to fill the many vacancies.

The next weeks saw the West African Field Force tackle the remaining rebel positions south of Kumasi in a methodical fashion. The stockade outside Bantama was captured by Major Melliss and his men on 6 August and Major Cobbe carried the stockade on the Kintampo road on the same day. The fight at Bantama was particularly tough and although both the 75mm field gun and Maxims were deployed against the stockade, many casualties were inflicted upon the gun crews by Asante snipers. The fire of these weapons apparently had little effect on the position so Melliss again called for a bayonet charge. As the bugler, a young boy named Moma, sounded the charge he was hit in the head by a slug. As the blood ran down his face he continued with his duty. Bliss left an account of the charge:

> Once again the familiar notes of the 'Charge' pierced the din; and in
> an instant every man scented blood . . . Like panthers, the Hausas
> made one wild spring forward; and down the slope they rushed,

jostling each other in their eagerness. Major Melliss, with his usual recklessness for his own safety was already yards ahead of all. Over went the officers, one dropped the eight feet on the other side, landing on the ground, and almost instantaneously running his sword through one of the enemy. By this time bayonets began to bristle over . . . A short hand-to-hand fight took place, fierce while it lasted; and cold steel did its work. At last the rout began.[29]

At the Kintampo stockade the fighting was similarly severe and Major Cobbe and Colour Sergeant Foster were severely wounded, and both had to be invalided home. A force of fifty Sikhs had fought and seventeen had been killed and wounded. In these two engagements there had been seventy casualties which reflected the rebels' desire to fight on.

The stockade on the Accra road outside of Kumasi was the next to be taken by a force led by Colonel Burroughs. Here a night attack was completely successful and the Asantes lost heavily, although Lieutenant Greer was killed in the initial charge. He was hit by several slugs and as he lay dying in a pool of his own blood he was seen still waving his sword defiantly in the air and crying 'charge' to encourage his men forward. There was a further reversal for the British for Captain Benson, leading a command of Akim levies, was marching on Kumasi from the south east. At Boankra Benson's detachment was repulsed by a strong rebel force. The Akim now deserted Benson and in despair at what he took to be his own personal failings, the tortured officer killed himself.

With the rebels now largely pacified or defeated south of Kumasi, Willcocks moved his headquarters to Kumasi on 31 August and from here he planned the last campaign to defeat the remaining rebellion in the north. The rebel forces now either scattered or began to surrender under flags of truce. By 16 September, Willcocks was able review 1,750 troops of the West African Field Force and this was such a sight that more rebels were encouraged to put down their weapons, now realising that continued opposition would be fruitless and a number of the northern chiefs, including Enchwi, the Offinso leader, capitulated. Yet, there were still battles to fight.

Reports were received that 3 chiefs had concentrated a force of around 5,000 warriors just 10 miles north of Kumasi. On 29 September Willcocks himself led a force 1,200-strong to engage them. The next morning a battle ensued at Aboasu and only after repeated charges and fierce hand-to hand fighting did the stubborn rebels give way. Two charges stalled under fierce Asante fire. Those troops manning the Maxims and field guns were targets for Asante snipers and many fell wounded. Willcocks arrived at the front line with a detachment of Sikhs and his staff officers. He ordered a third attempt which was seen and recorded by Lieutenant Colonel Arthur Montanaro of the Royal Artillery: 'Major Melliss, of course, led this final charge, and he and Captain Godfrey raced down the road, followed by the Sikhs and several staff officers, who, carried away by the excitement of the moment, joined in the charge.'[30] The Asante retreated in good order to the village of Isnsu and it was only when Willcocks's men threatened to outflank this position did the Asantes finally give way. Willcocks had lost three killed and forty-two wounded, including six officers. Montanaro estimated that up to 150 rebels had been killed and several hundred wounded and he declared that at no other engagement in the uprising had the Asantes been given such a hard lesson.

Captain Donald Stewart, the Kumasi Resident and Political Officer, recently returned from England, had accompanied Willcocks's column. His presence was fortuitous for he had a good relationship with many of the remaining rebel chiefs and at his urging Willcocks announced on 3 October that only those Asantes found guilty of murder would be punished and those that now surrendered would be treated as belligerents and not as rebels. This induced many more to surrender. However, there was still resistance in the north west and many rebel chiefs, notably Kobina Cheri of Odumase, had fled there. In early November columns under Montanaro and Major Browne set out. In an operation which lasted just over 3 weeks, the British swept the region and captured 900 'Long Dane' guns and 31 rebel chiefs, including Kobina Cheri.

Justice was swift against Kobina Cheri and just two days after he had been led into Kumasi he was tried by a military commission and sentenced to death. He was hung in the marketplace in the presence of the whole garrison and populace, maintaining his dignity and defiance until the end. Over the next weeks all the principal leaders of the rebellion were captured including Yaa Asantewaa, Nana Koki Fofie, Nana Osei Kwadwo Krome and Nana Kwadwo Antwi. Akwesi Bodu manged to escape to French territory. All were held in prison in Kumasi Fort for many months whilst the British determined what to do with them. Whilst the queen mother had a small dark cell to herself, conditions were poor, if not harsh for the elderly woman. There was an element of revenge and racism in how the British dealt with the captured rebel chiefs. Asante oral history claims that they were forced in large groups into windowless cells in which they were unable to sit down, for the conditions were so cramped. Whilst there is no documented proof that this was the case, the author himself has viewed the few tiny cells within Kumasi Fort and if there is any element of truth in the Asante claims then the chiefs were indeed imprisoned in the most barbaric conditions.

Later in the year, fifteen leaders and originators of the rebellion, including Yaa Asantewaa, were deported to the Seychelles where they joined Prempeh. A further thirty-one chiefs were imprisoned in Elmina Castle. The old war indemnity was re-imposed, but dropped a few years later. The ownership of rifles was strictly regulated so that only a few licensed hunters were allowed to own such weapons.

Stewart was now returned as resident and by the new year of 1901 he was able to report that all was quiet and that the process of reconstruction, both physically and politically, was underway. With so many rebel chiefs in custody the British used the opportunity to appoint loyal Asantes, such as Yao Awua of Ejisu and Kwamin Tua of Kumasi, to the vacant stools of the various chiefdoms. Thus, towns and tribal areas such as Kokofu, Bechim and Adansis, to name just three, received new chiefs and this process certainly aided the British in imposing further political changes on the Asante nation going forward.

The rebellion, the last conflict between Britain and members of the Asante nation, was over. The Asantes had fought resolutely to maintain their independence and their identity which was of courses central to their beliefs surrounding the Golden Stool. It is easy to see why many of the British troops involved came to admire their courage and tenacity, and even Willcocks himself wrote: 'Notwithstanding their cruel nature [they were] gentlemen once the "Commence Fire" was sounded, and remained so until the "Cease Fire" . . . They never asked for mercy and never showed any; but after all, it was a square deal.'[31] Whilst it will be never known how many Asantes died in the conflict, the rebel chiefs themselves admitted to in excess of a thousand warriors. This is likely to be an underestimate and of course on top of this there were many more wounded.

For the British the 'butcher's bill' was equally as depressing. There were 9 British officers killed and a further 43 wounded. A further 6 died of disease. Of the British NCOs 9 were wounded and 1 died of disease. The native troops lost 114 killed and 683 wounded and 41 missing. A further 102 died of disease again showing the dangers of 'The White Man's Grave'. Of the injured 19 officers and 7 NCOs were invalided home as a result of wounds and 23 officers and 14 NCOs were sent home due to disease. The only figures known for the porters were that 400 died of disease but this figure was undoubtedly higher and of course no records were kept of the over 3,000 refugees who initially sheltered under the walls of the fort but it is highly probable that over 2,000 of these individuals died of starvation, disease and at the hands of the Asantes as they tried to flee Kumasi. Of course, the campaign was fought during the rainy season, unlike Wolseley's earlier expedition, and the high sickness rate clearly reflects the dangers of the climate at this time of year.

This brief, but brutal war had been avoidable, but perhaps too it was inevitable in the Scramble for Africa, and in the general European attempts to move Africans away from slavery and human sacrifice. Of course, the numbers of casualties would indicate that the British were militarily triumphant, and the eventual political settlement suggests that there was only one winner in this conflict. Yet, many modern Ghanaian writers do not view the war's outcome in these terms. It was chiefly fought to stop the British claiming the Golden Stool and in that the British were unsuccessful. In this regard alone, the war is not viewed as a defeat by many Ghanaians.

In 1921 another war nearly occurred as a result of a false rumour that the British were again attempting to seize the Golden Stool. It was averted as a result of the British governor's renunciation of any desire for the Golden Stool on the advice of Rattray, the Government Anthropologist. Writing at the time, Rattray stated: 'I believe it will be found that all the obedience, respect and great loyalty we have been given by the Ashanti is given through and by reason of the Golden Stool. I believe that far from benefiting had we ever taken this stool . . . its power would have worked against us.'[32] At least it seemed by 1921 the British had learnt something from history.

Conclusion

Almost as soon as Hodgson had reached the safety of the coast in July 1900, Chamberlain, the Colonial Secretary, was drawing up plans for the future of the Asante nation. The general consensus was that it should become part of the empire, yet the new Governor of the Gold Coast, Major Matthew Nathan, was no 'yes' man and he refused to agree without formulating his own views on the ground. His visit to Kumasi in March 1901 was part of that process. The mining lobby were also keen to influence Nathan's view and they also petioned Chamberlain. It was felt that a railway planned from the coast to Kumasi would substantially increase trade.

After his visit Nathan concurred with most of Chamberlain's views with one important caveat. Asante was to be annexed by the Crown, and the peoples become British subjects, but Nathan proposed that it should not form part of the Gold Coast Colony but should be administered separately. Nathan had the sense to realise that the independent nature of the Asante nation would never be totally lost and that this must be respected. He was backed in his decision by the Chief Justice, William Brandford Griffith, who felt that the railway line and the economic boom that it would unleash would then naturally gravitate power away from the Kumasi to the coast without the need for total political assimilation.

The Colonial Office accepted Nathan's views and Asante was annexed on 26 September 1901 as a separate protected territory, and the governor, not the legislative council, was empowered to legislate in this territory, and the court system was also kept separate. The governor's powers were exercised by a locally based chief commissioner. This order was enforced by the 'Ashanti Administration Ordinance' of 1 January 1902, which divided Asante into four provinces.

The railway did indeed lead to something of an economic boom in and around Kumasi, although wealth did not always trickle down to all. Mining and rubber and cocoa production increased considerably, and Kumasi was rapidly transformed into a prosperous town. Indeed, when Prempeh was allowed to return from exile in 1925 he found his city composed of tidy parks where swamps were once found and European shops and residential homes where thatched huts had been. The British had only allowed Prempeh his freedom as a private citizen, but the following year he was recognised as *Kumasihene*, implying that his sphere of influence was confined to Kumasi. He wore European suits and drove around in an official car. Where once there had been human sacrifice was a missionary building, which now as a Christian convert Prempeh visited. When he died in 1935, his successor, Prempeh II, was restored as the *Asantehene* and all kings since have been allowed this title.

One of the legacies of the 1900 rebellion was a military one. The West African Field Force distinguished itself in that conflict and would continue to do so. By the outbreak of the First World War, Kumasi Fort was the headquarters of the Gold Coast Regiment. In August 1914 the regiment under the command of Major Bryant invaded and captured German Togoland. It then took part in the Cameroon and East Africa campaigns in which, under the command of Lieutenant Colonel Rose, it gained a fearsome reputation as a fighting unit. It returned to Kumasi in 1918 to a hearty welcome from the locals. Although only 1,000 Asantes joined the Gold Coast Regiment during the First World War, the people generously contributed to the government war funds and despite the fact that local forces were naturally depleted to supply troops for the war, there was no agitation amongst the Asante people. In the Second World War the Gold Coast Regiment, now with significantly more soldiers from Kumasi, fought again with distinction in Burma and Abyssinia. The citizen soldiers of Kumasi, along with recruits from other tribes, fought and died together and the regimental flag on display in Kumasi Fort today is a testament to their courage and bravery.

Today Kumasi is a busy, dusty vibrant place, if not sometimes chaotic. The city and its people are proud to be Ghanaian, but even prouder to be Asante. They maintain a level of independence and dignity. The Ghanaian flag is, of course, respected but so is the Asante flag that flies alongside. The king is revered and the Golden Stool, which still appears every five years from its secret location, remains the epicentre, the life of the people. Asante is still a proud region, if not now a separate nation, that maintains an independent feel, which it should, for its people still hold the Golden Stool.

Appendix
Victoria Cross Winners of the
Anglo-Asante Wars

Taken from the *Register of the Victoria Cross* and *The Victoria Cross 1856–1920*.

The 1873–4 Campaign
Lieutenant Mark Sever Bell (Later Colonel), Corps of Royal Engineers
Place/Date of Birth: Sydney, NSW, Australia, 15 May 1843.
Place/Date of Death: Windlesham, Surrey, 26 June, 1906.
Account of Deed: On 4 February 1874 at the Battle of Ordashu Sir John McLeod
   was an eye-witness of his gallant and distinguished conduct and considers
   that this officer's fearless and resolute bearing, being always in the front, urging on and encouraging an unarmed work party of Fante labourers, who were
   exposed not only to the fire of the enemy, but also to the wild and irregular
   fire of the native troops in the rear, contributed very materially to the success
   of the day. By his example he made these men do what no European party
   was ever required to do in warfare, namely, to work under fire in the face of
   the enemy without a covering party.

Gifford, The Lord Edric Frederick, Lieutenant (Later Major) 2nd Bn,
   24th Regiment
Place/Date of Birth: Ropley, Hampshire, 5 July 1849.
Place/Date of Death: Chichester, Sussex, 5 June 1911.
Memorials: Bosham Church, Sussex, Harrow School, Harare Cathedral,
   Zimbabwe.
Account of Deed: During the 1873–4 Asante Campaign, Lieutenant Lord
   Gifford was in the command of scouts after the army had crossed the Prah
   River and he daily took his life in his hands, performing this dangerous duty.
   His courage was particularly conspicuous at the taking of Bekwai, into which
   he penetrated and held for some time before the main army joined in support.
   Wolseley wrote that Lord Gifford displayed gallantry and courage that was
   'most conspicuous'.

Lance Sergeant Samuel McGaw (Later Sergeant), 42nd Regiment, the
   Black Watch
Place/Date of Birth: Kirkmicheal, Ayrshire, Scotland, 1838.

Place/Date of Death: Larnaca, Cyprus, 22 July 1878, died of sunstroke.
Memorials: English Cemetery, Kyrenia, Cyprus.
Account of Deed: 31 January 1874 at the Battle of Amoaful. He led his section through the bush in the most excellent manner, continuing to do so throughout the whole day, although badly wounded early in the engagement.

Major Reginald William Sartorius (Later Major General), 6th Bengal Cavalry, Indian Army
Place/Date of Birth: Portugal, 8 May 1841.
Place/Date of Death: Cowes, Isle of Wight, 8 August 1907.
Memorials: Baddesley, Hampshire.
Account of Deed: On 17 January 1874 during the attack on Abogu, Asante, Major Sartorius removed, under heavy fire, a Hausa non-commissioned officer who was mortally wounded, and placed him under cover.

It is generally accepted that both Lord Gifford and Major Sartorius won their VCs for not one specific incident but for constant bravery in situations where death was highly likely. In the case of Gifford, it was when he frequently led from the front during scouting operations and with Sartorius it was during his epic journey through Asante-held territory to locate Wolseley's headquarters.

The 1900 Campaign
Sergeant John Mackenzie (Later Major), 2nd Bn, the Seaforth Highlanders, employed West African Field Force
Place/Date of Birth: Contin, Ross-shire, Scotland, 22 November 1870.
Place/Date of Death: Near Cuinchy, France, 17 May 1915.
Memorials: Guards Cemetery, Windy Corner, Cuinchy, France.
Account of Deed: On 6 June 1900 at Dompoasi, Sergeant Mackenzie, after working two Maxim guns under heavy fire and being wounded whilst doing so, volunteered to clear the stockade of the enemy. This he did, most gallantly, leading the charge himself and driving the enemy headlong into the bush. He was later promoted to Second Lieutenant. A man of dauntless courage, he is said to have been absolutely fearless under fire, and inspired everyone round him with the fighting spirit which never left him.

Captain Charles John Melliss (Later Major General and Sir Charles), Indian Staff Corps and West African Force
Place/Date of Birth: Mhow, India, 12 September 1862.
Place/Date of Death: Camberley, Surrey, 6 June 1936.
Memorials: St Peter's Churchyard, Frimley, Surrey, Sanctum Crypt, St Luke's Church, Chelsea, London.

Account of Deed: On 30 September 1900 at Obassa, Captain Melliss gathered together a party of men and charged into the bush at the head of them, into the thick of the enemy. Although wounded in a hand-to-hand encounter, his bold rush caused panic amongst the enemy. In the fight one Asante fired at Melliss who ran at him with his sword, which Melliss managed to parry and they rolled over together. At this point another Asante shot Melliss in the foot, paralysing his leg. He was rescued by a fellow officer, Captain Godfrey, who shot the grappling Asante dead. Melliss had already behaved courageously on three other occasions in the campaign.

Notes

Introduction
1. R. Gocking, *The History of Ghana* (Greenwood Press, Westport, Connecticut, 2005), p. 29.
2. Ibid., p. 32.
3. H. Brackenbury, *The Ashanti War – A Narrative – Prepared from the Official Documents*, 2 vols (William Blackwood, Edinburgh, 1874), Vol. 2, p. 63.

Part I
1. M. Dodds (ed.), *History of Ghana* (American Women's Association in Ghana, Accra, 1974), p. 25.
2. Ibid., p. 26.
3. Gocking, p. 26.
4. O. Kwadwo, *An Outline of Asante History*, 2 vols (O. Kwadwo, Kumasi, 2000), Vol. 2, p. 1.
5. See D. Kimble, *A Political History of Ghana – The Rise of Gold Coast Nationalism 1850–1928* (Oxford University Press, New York, 1963), p. 265.
6. B. Vandervort, *Wars of Imperial Conquest in Africa 1830–1914* (University College London Press, London, 1998), p. 15.
7. Taken from A. Lloyd, *The Drums of Kumasi – The Story of the Ashanti Wars* (Panther, London, 1965), pp. 25–6.
8. Taken from B. Bond (ed.), *Victorian Military Campaigns* (Tom Donovan Publishing, London, 1994), p. 169.
9. Ibid.
10. Lloyd, p. 37.
11. F. Fuller, *A Vanished Dynasty – Ashanti* (2nd edn, Frank Cass, London, 1968), pp. 67–8.
12. Lloyd, p. 45.
13. Fuller, pp. 73–4.
14. Kwadwo, p. 24.
15. Fuller, p. 81.
16. Gocking, p. 32.
17. Brackenbury, Vol. 1, p. 22.
18. Fuller, p. 97.

Part II
1. Bond (ed.), p. 173.
2. Ibid.
3. W.D. McIntyre, 'British Policy in West Africa: The Ashanti Expedition of 1873–4', *The Historical Journal*, Vol. 5, No. 1 (1962), p. 20.
4. Bond (ed.), p. 175.
5. Brackenbury, Vol. 1, p. 31.
6. Bond (ed.), pp. 175–6.
7. Fuller, p. 114.
8. Lloyd, p. 70.
9. Letter Keate to Lord Kimberley, Colonial Secretary, 1 March 1873, C.O. 96/96.
10. D. Coombs, *The Gold Coast, Britain and the Netherlands 1850–1874* (Oxford University Press, Oxford, 1963), p. 127.

11. McIntyre, p. 27.
12. Ibid., p. 28.
13. Minute by Kimberley, 28 May 1873, C.O. 96/107.
14. McIntyre, p. 29.
15. Kimberley to Cardwell, 26 July 1873, Cardwell Papers, Public Record Office Gifts and Deposits: PRO 30/48/5/33, pp. 48–51.
16. S. Manning, *Evelyn Wood VC, Pillar of Empire* (Pen & Sword, Barnsley, 2007), p. 69.
17. McIntyre, p. 32.
18. Vandervort, p. 89.
19. Lloyd, p. 87.
20. Letter Cardwell to Kimberley, 1 August 1873, Cardwell Papers, PRO 30/48/5/33, p. 60.
21. McIntyre, p. 33.
22. B. Farwell, *Queen Victoria's Little Wars* (Allen Lane, London, 1973), p. 192.
23. Manning, p. 69.
24. Letter Cardwell to Gladstone, 20 September 1873, Gladstone Papers, 44120/140.
25. Lloyd, p. 81.
26. Brackenbury, Vol. 1, p. 141.
27. Fuller, p. 123.
28. Ibid., p. 124.
29. Brackenbury, Vol. 1, p. 141.
30. Ibid., p. 144.
31. Wolseley to Lady Wolseley, 27 September 1873. Taken from G. Arthur, *The Letters of Lord and Lady Wolseley, 1870–1911* (William Heinemann, London, 1923), p. 10.
32. Brackenbury, Vol. 1 pp. 157–8.
33. Bond (ed.), p. 180.
34. See McIntyre, p. 38 for the exact breakdown of timings.
35. Manning, p. 71.
36. L. Maxwell, *The Ashanti Ring – Sir Garnet Wolseley's Campaigns, 1870–1882* (Leo Cooper, London, 1985), p. 28.
37. Ibid., p. 30.
38. E. Wood (ed.), *British Battles on Land and Sea*, 2 vols (Cassell, London, 1915), Vol. 2, p. 693.
39. W.W. Claridge, *A History of the Gold Coast and Ashanti*, 2 vols (John Murray, London, 1915), Vol. 2, pp. 92–3.
40. J.H. Thomas, *A Full and Authentic Diary of the Ashanti Expedition* (printed by William Emelow of the *Pembroke Advertiser*, Pembroke, 1875), p. 6.
41. Lloyd, p. 102.
42. Letter Captain Buller to Lieutnenant Gordon, NAM 1988-08-90.
43. Wolseley Journal, 10 December 1873, TNA, WO 147/3.
44. Thomas, p. 7.
45. J.H. Lehmann, *All Sir Garnet: A Life of Field Marshall Lord Wolseley* (Jonathan Cape, London, 1964), p. 186.
46. I. Beckett (ed.), *Wolseley and Ashanti* (The History Press for the Army Records Society, Stroud, 2009), p. 266.
47. Ibid., p. 287. TNA, WO 147/3.
48. Ibid., p. 297. CUL, RCMS 131/6, Glover MSS.
49. Lloyd, p. 153.
50. Ibid., p. 123.
51. Beckett (ed.), p. 307.
52. Wood (1915), p. 696.
53. Major General C.W. Robinson, 'The European Brigade Under Sir Archibald Alison in the Ashanti War, 1873–4', *Royal United Services Institution Journal*, Vol. 63 (1918), p. 17.
54. Beckett (ed.), p. 309.
55. Manning, p. 80.

56. R. Brooks, *The Long Arm of Empire – Naval Brigades from the Crimea to the Boxer Rebellion* (Constable, London, 1999), p. 125.
57. Robinson, p. 19.
58. Lehmann, p. 197.
59. Lloyd, p. 169.
60. I. Heron, *Britain's Forgotten Wars – Colonial Campaigns of the Nineteenth Century* (Sutton Publishing, Stroud, 2003), p. 190.
61. M.D. McLeod, *The Asante* (British Museum Publications, London, 1981), p. 46.
62. Lloyd, p. 179.
63. Cambridge MSS, RA VIC/ADD E/I/7327.
64. Thomas, p. 19.
65. Ibid.
66. Ibid., p. 23.
67. Cost of Principal British Wars 1857–1899 – compiled by the War Office, NAM 8008-70.
68. G. Wolseley, *A Soldier's Life*, 2 vols (Methuen, London, 1904), Vol. 1 p. 370.

Part III

1. Brackenbury, Vol. 2, pp. 345–8.
2. *The Times*, 28 April 1874.
3. CO/96/114.
4. Kimble, p. 273.
5. Ibid., p. 277.
6. *Gold Coast Times*, 20 May 1882.
7. Kimble, p. 279.
8. R. Robinson and J. Gallagher, *Africa and the Victorians – The Official Mind of Imperialism* (Macmillan, London, 1961), p. 385.
9. Letter of 7 May 1991, from King of Ashanti to Brandford Griffith, enclosed in his Despatch of 3 June 1891, to Knutsford; C.7917.
10. *Gold Coast Chronicle*, 30 November 1894.
11. NAM 9406-1-90 Diary of Lieutenant Hood.
12. Ibid.
13. Unknown author, 'The Coming Ashanti War', *British Medical Journal*, Vol. 2, No. 1820 (16 November 1895), p. 1250.
14. NAM 2005-06-737. Postcard from Lieutenant Llewelyn W. Atcherley, Army Service Corps, to his Aunt Lucy Atcherley, dated 17 December 1895.
15. NAM 8009-46.
16. Ibid.
17. NAM 8009-46.
18. B. Wasserman, 'The Ashanti War of 1900: A Study in Cultural Conflict', *Journal of the International African Institute*, Vol. 31, No. 2 (1961), p. 176.
19. F. Myatt, *The Golden Stool – Ashanti 1900* (William Kimber, London, 1966), p. 33.
20. Kwadwo, p. 49.
21. C.H. Armitage and A.F. Montanaro, *The Ashanti Campaign of 1900* (Sands & Co., London, 1901), p. 9.
22. Ibid., p. 10.
23. Ibid., pp. 32–3.
24. Myatt, pp. 48–9.
25. Ibid., p. 122.
26. Lloyd, p. 237.
27. Myatt, p. 124.
28. H. Bliss, *The Relief of Kumasi* (Methuen, London, 1901), p. 239.
29. Ibid., pp. 244–5.
30. Armitage and Montanaro, p. 192.
31. Myatt, p. 173.
32. Wasserman, p. 177.

Bibliography

Armitage, C.H. and A.F. Montanaro. *The Ashanti Campaign of 1900* (Sands & Co., London, 1901).

Arthur, G. (ed.). *The Letters of Lord and Lady Wolseley, 1870–1911* (William Heinemann, London, 1923).

Beckett, I. *Victoria's Wars* (Shire, Princes Risborough, 1998).

Beckett, I. (ed.). *Wolseley and Ashanti* (The History Press for the Army Records Society, Stroud, 2009).

Black, J. *War in the Nineteenth Century* (Polity, Cambridge, 2009).

Bliss, H. *The Relief of Kumasi* (Methuen, London, 1901).

Bond, B. (ed.). *Victorian Military Campaigns* (Tom Donovan Publishing, London, 1994).

Boyle, F. *Fanteland to Coomassie* (Chapman & Hall, London, 1874).

Brackenbury, H. *The Ashanti War – A Narrative – Prepared from the Official Documents*, 2 vols (William Blackwood, Edinburgh, 1874).

Brice, C. *The Thinking Man's Soldier – The Life and Career of General Sir Henry Brackenbury, 1837–1914* (Helion, Solihull, 2012).

Brooks, R. *The Long Arm of Empire – Naval Brigades from the Crimea to the Boxer Rebellion* (Constable, London, 1999).

Butler, W. *Akim-Foo (Ashantee 1874) – The History of a Failure* (Sampson Low, Marston, & Searle, London, 1874).

Claridge, W.W. *A History of the Gold Coast and Ashanti*, 2 vols (John Murray, London, 1915).

Coombs, D. *The Gold Coast, Britain and the Netherlands 1850–1874* (Oxford University Press, 1963).

Cope, W. *The History of the Rifle Brigade, Vol. 2: 1816–1876* (Leonaur, Driffield, 2010).

Corvi, S. and I. Beckett (eds). *Victoria's Generals* (Pen & Sword, Barnsley, 2009).

Dodds, M. (ed.). *History of Ghana* (American Women's Association in Ghana, Accra, 1974).

Edgerton, R. *The Fall of the Asante Empire – The Hundred-Year War for Africa's Gold Coast* (The Free Press, New York, 1995).

Farwell, B. *Queen Victoria's Little Wars* (Allen Lane, London, 1973).

Fuller, F. *A Vanished Dynasty – Ashanti* (2nd edn, Frank Cass, London, 1968).

Gocking. R. *The History of Ghana* (Greenwood Press, Westport, Connecticut, 2005).

Harding, M. (ed.). *The Victorian Soldier – Studies in the History of the British Army, 1816–1914* (National Army Museum Publication, London, 1993).

Haythornthwaite, P. *The Colonial Wars Source Book* (Arms & Armour Press, London, 1995).

Hernon, I. *Britain's Forgotten Wars – Colonial Campaigns of the Nineteenth Century* (Sutton Publishing, Stroud, 2003).

Hernon, I. *The Sword and the Sketch Book – A Pictorial History of Queen Victoria's Wars* (Spellmount, Stroud, 2012).

Hodgson, Lady. *The Siege of Kumasi* (Pearson, London, 1901).

Kimble, D. *A Political History of Ghana – The Rise of Gold Coast Nationalism 1850–1928* (Oxford University Press, New York, 1963).

Knight, I. *Queen Victoria Enemies, Vol. 2, Northern Africa* (Osprey, Oxford, 2005).

Kochanski, H. *Sir Garnet Wolseley – Victorian Hero* (Hambledon Press, London, 1999).

Kofi Tieku, A. *History and Facts About Ashante Kingdom and Ghana* (Schrodinger's Publications, Accra, 2016), Vol. 1.

Kwadwo, O. *An Outline of Asante History* (O. Kwadwo, Kumasi, 1994).

Kwadwo, O. *An Outline of Asante History*, 2 vols (O. Kwadwo, Kumasi, 2000).

Kwadwo, O. *A Handbook on Asante Culture* (O. Kwadwo, Kumasi, 2002).

Lehmann, J. *All Sir Garnet: A Life of Field Marshal Lord Wolseley* (Jonathan Cape, London, 1964).

Lloyd, A. *The Drums of Kumasi – The Story of the Ashanti Wars* (Panther, London, 1965).

McLeod, M.D. *The Asante* (British Museum Publications, London, 1981).

Manning, S. *Evelyn Wood VC, Pillar of Empire* (Pen & Sword, Barnsley, 2007).

Manning, S. *Soldiers of the Queen* (Spellmount, Stroud, 2009).

Manning, S. *The Martini-Henry Rifle* (Osprey, Oxford, 2013).

Manning, S. *Bayonet to Barrage, Weaponry on the Victorian Battlefield* (Pen & Sword, Barnsley, 2020).

Maxwell, L. *The Ashanti Ring – Sir Garnet Wolseley's Campaigns, 1870–1882* (Leo Cooper, London, 1985).

Metcalfe, G. *Maclean of the Gold Coast – The Life and Times of George Maclean, 1801–1847* (Oxford University Press, London, 1962).

Myatt, F. *The Golden Stool – Ashanti 1900* (William Kimber, London, 1966).

Nkansa Kyeremateng, K. *The Akans of Ghana – Their History & Culture* (Sebewie Publishing, Accra, 1996).

O'Moore Creagh, Sir. *The Victoria Cross 1856–1920* (The Standard Art Book Company, London, 1920).

Pakenham, T. *The Scramble for Africa* (Weidenfeld & Nicolson, London, 1991).

Register of the Victoria Cross (3rd edn, This England, Cheltenham, 1997).

Robinson, R. and J. Gallagher. *Africa and the Victorians – The Official Mind of Imperialism* (Macmillan, London, 1961).

Spiers, E. *The Late Victorian Army 1868–1902* (Manchester University Press, Manchester, 1992).

Spiers, E. *The Scottish Soldier and Empire, 1854–1902* (Edinburgh University Press, Edinburgh, 2006).

Stanley, H. *Coomassie & Magala* (Sampson Low, Marston & Co., London,1874).

Thomas, J.H. *A Full and Authentic Diary of the Ashanti Expedition* (printed by William Emelow of the *Pembroke Advertiser*, Pembroke, 1875).

Vandervort, B. *Wars of Imperial Conquest in Africa 18301914* (University College London Press, London, 1998).

Williams, C. *The Life of Lieut-General Sir Henry Evelyn Wood*, Vol. 1 (Sampson Low, Marston, 1892).

Wolseley, G. *A Soldier's Life*, 2 vols (Methuen, London, 1904).

Wood, E. *From Midshipman to Field Marshal*, 2 vols (Methuen, London, 1906).

Wood, E. (ed.). *British Battles on Land and Sea*, 2 vols (Cassell, London, 1915).

Wood, E. *Winnowed Memories* (Cassell, London, 1917).

Journal Articles

McIntyre, W. 'British Policy in West Africa: The Ashanti Expedition of 1873–4', *The Historical Journal*, Vol. 5, No. 1 (1962), pp. 19–46.

Manning, S. 'Learning the Trade: Use and Misuse of Intelligence during the British Colonial Campaigns of the 1870s', *Intelligence*, Vol. 22, No. 5 (Oct, 2007), pp. 664–60.

Meyers, J. '"Cyclops" and the Ashanti War', *James Joyce Quarterly*, Vol. 29, No. 2 (Winter, 1992), pp. 408–10.

Patterson, R. '"To Form a Correct Estimate of Their Nothingness when Compared with it": British Exhibitions of Military Technology in the Abyssinian and Ashanti Expeditions', *Journal of Imperial & Commonwealth History*, Vol. 44, No. 4 (August 2016), pp. 551–72.

Robinson, Major General C.W. 'The European Brigade under Sir Archibald Alison in the Ashanti War, 1873–4', *Royal United Services Institution Journal*, Vol. 63 (1918), pp. 15–38.

Ukpabi, S. 'The British Colonial Office Approach to the Ashanti War of 1900', *African Studies Review*, Vol. 13, No. 3 (December 1970), pp. 363–80.

Ukpabi, S.C. 'West Indian Troops and the Defence of British West Africa in the Nineteenth Century', *African Studies Review*, Vol. 17, No. I (1974), pp. 133–50.

Unknown author. 'The Coming Ashanti War', *British Medical Journal*, Vol. 2, No. 1820 (16 November 1895), p. 1250.

Ward, W. 'Britain and Ashanti, 1874–1896', *Transactions of the Historical Society of Ghana*, Vol. 15, No. 2 (December 1974), pp. 131–64.

Wasserman, B. 'The Ashanti War of 1900: A Study in Cultural Conflict', *Journal of the International African Institute*, Vol. 31, No. 2 (1961), pp. 167–79.

Wood, E., 'The Ashanti Expedition of 1873–4', *Journal of the United Services Institution*, Vol. XVIII (1875).

Index